CW00539290

DARTMOUTH

AND ITS NEIGHBOURS

A HISTORY OF THE PORT
AND ITS PEOPLE

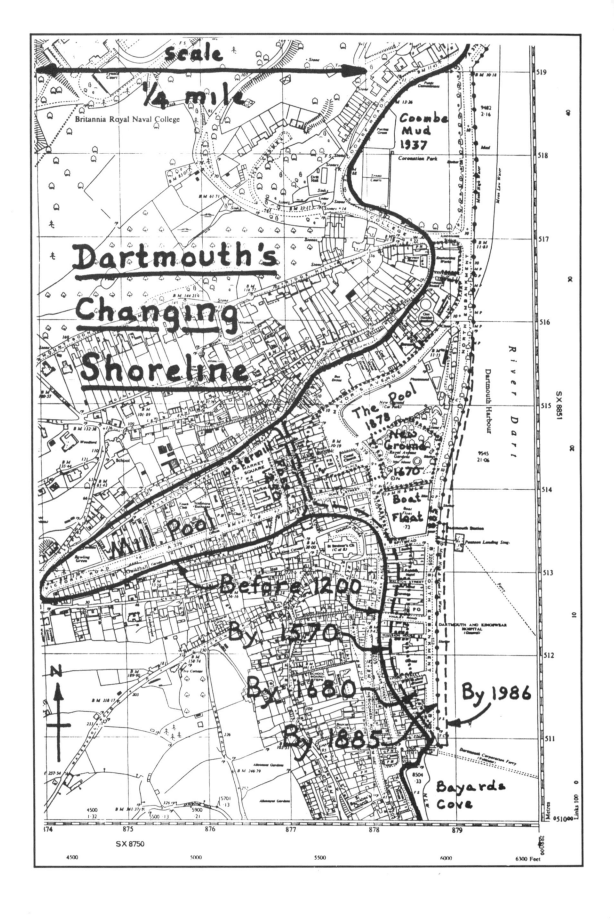

Scale
¼ mile

Britannia Royal Naval College

Coombe
Mud
1937

Coronation Park

Dartmouth's
Changing
Shoreline

The Pool
1878

New
Ground
1670

River Dart

Dartmouth Harbour

Boat-
Float

Mill Pool

Before 1200

By 1570

By 1680

By 1986

By 1885

Bayards
Cove

N

SX 8851

SX 8750

DARTMOUTH

AND ITS NEIGHBOURS

A HISTORY OF THE PORT AND ITS PEOPLE

RAY FREEMAN

Richard Webb

Text copyright ©1990 Ray Freeman
Chapter 18 Text copyright ©2007 Ray Freeman

The right to Ray Freeman to be identified as the Author of the work has been asserted by her in accordance with the Copyright, Designs and Patents Act 1988

Some original material published in 1983 in *Dartmouth: A New History*
by Harbour Books, Dartmouth
First published in 1990 by Phillimore & Co Ltd, Chichester
Reissued in 1997 by Dart Books, Dartmouth
Republished in 2007 with additional material by Richard Webb, Dartmouth

All rights reserved. No part of this publication may be reproduced, stored in a retrieval system, or transmitted, in any form of binding or cover other than that in which it is published and without a similar condition being imposed on the subsequent purchasers.

A CIP catalogue record for this book is available from the British Library

ISBN 978-0-9536361-6-7

Printed and bound in the United Kingdom by Short Run Press, Exeter

Additional material design and artwork Anonymous Design Company, Christchurch, Dorset

RW.UK Ltd trading as Richard Webb, Publisher

Richard Webb, Publisher
Dartmouth, England

www.dartmouthbooks.co.uk

Contents

List of Illustrations and Maps (map pages designated in **bold** type)

Acknowledgments

I would like to thank the many people without whose help this book could never have been produced. I am particularly grateful to Karen Bailey for her fine line drawings of details of carvings, plasterwork and stained glass and for her series of maps.

I must also especially thank Ivor Smart, who has generously allowed me to make use of material about the history of Dartmouth which he has amassed over 30 years. He has enabled me to look at many copies of the *Dartmouth Chronicle*, some the only ones in existence, and others which I had not seen before. He has also shared much of his information, collected in the Public Record Office and elsewhere, which has filled in many gaps in my own knowledge.

The following organisations and people have helped in many vital ways, by supplying or giving permission to use information, photographs, pictures, old prints, maps, records or memories: Dartington Rural Archive, Dart Harbour Navigation Authority, Dartmouth Town Council, the Henley Museum, Dartmouth Museum, Devon Record Office, Devon County Council Sites and Monuments Register, Duchy of Cornwall Office, Elmhirst Library Dartington, Exeter City Reference Library, University of Exeter Library, Royal Albert Museum Exeter, Public Record Office, Torquay Library Local History Collection, South Hams Newspapers, West Country Studies Library; John Allen, Roy Barnes, Mr. S. Bell, Mrs. E. Bishop, Francis Bennett, Tom Blamey, Eric Bovey, Peter Clare, George Collings, Don Collinson, Sam Cox, Mr. and Mrs. F. Hannaford, David Hannaford, Mrs. H. Hoare, Nicholas Horne, Miss E. Huddy, Tom Jaine, Roy Jones, Mr. and Mrs. E. Kain, Mr. Key, Miss M. Leslie, John Lichfield-Smith, Miss Lidstone, Mrs. E. Lidstone, Capt. C. Morre, Lady Ann Newman, Mr. W. Parr-Ferris, Philip Pensabene, Harry and Maurice Pillar, Mrs. G. Plowright, Kevin Pyne, Mr. and Mrs. Scardifield, Miss I. Scawn, Sir John Seale, Roy Skinner, Miss Smith, Reg Snell, Mr. and Mrs. M. Sutton-Scott-Tucker, Rev. Alan Teage, Rev. Paul Trenchard, Mrs. I. Tozer, Mrs. Uphill, Arthur Waite, Eric Wingate, Harold White, John White, Rev. Ronald White, Mrs. M. Williams, Dr. T. N. P. Wilton, Denis Woods.

For photographic help, the author wishes to thank Roy Jones, Steve Baker, R. Carr, G. Weatherley, Reg Green and Cal Bailey.

The author is grateful to Karen Bailey for maps 2, 6, 7, 8, 13, 36, 38, 49, 50, 54, 76, and for drawings 1, 3, 4, 16, 17, 18, 20, 34, 37, 45, 47, 51, 52, 67, 68, 72, and 102; David Freeman for the endpaper map and map 53; Sally Hill for maps 40, 41, 43, 44, and drawing 39; Bill Leedham for maps 21, 22, and 27. Also to N. Horne for Plate 56, Ski Harrison for Plate 97, and Alan Wilson for Plates 9, 10, 11, 15, 19, 70, 74, 78, 81, 82, 86, 91, 105, and 116.

She is also grateful to the following for permission to use illustrations: Ashmolean Museum, Oxford, 71; Rev. J. Butler, 25, and for allowing illustrations to be made of St Saviour's; F. G. Collings, 59, 60; Dartmouth Museum, 11, 26, 48, 83, 88, 89, 91, 113, 114, 115; Dartington Rural Archives, 55, 57, 58, 62, 63, 64, 79, 80, 85, 90, 93, 95, 98, 99, 100, 101, 106, 107, 109, 110, 111, 112, 117, 119; D. Gerrard, 104; Henley Museum, 28, 61, 65; H. Hutchings, 108; Lady Ann Newman, 78, 105; Ordnance Survey, the endpaper map; Royal Albert Museum, Exeter, 5; Science Museum, London, 66; Sir John Seale, 74, 81, 82, 84, 103; G. Weatherley, 118; E. Wingate, 96; Rev. R. White, 24.

Ray Freeman

Ray Freeman, a history graduate from Durham University, came to Devon in 1964 to become head of history in a grammar school where she introduced the study of local history documents into the courses at all levels.

After retiring Ray Freeman has spent her time on her own researches from which *Dartmouth: A New History* was published in 1983 and then the more comprehensive *Dartmouth and Its Neighbours* in 1990 with this new 2007 updated version being the third edition. She has spent many hours consulting documents in the Devon Record Office in Exeter, the Public Record Office, parish registers and family documents still in the possession of private families. She has actively helped the Dartington Rural Archive which collects and indexes old photographs, as well as taping the memories of old people, both providing valuable material for use in her books. She was for many years a trustee of Dartmouth Museum, helping to set up exhibitions and make publicity material. She has written articles for local newspapers and the *Devon Historian*, and has given slide talks to local societies.

Since completing her last book Ray Freeman founded the Dartmouth History Research Group which has published over 30 short booklets written by people with special knowledge of small topics in local history. The Group has placed copies of the parish registers in the local libraries, and transcribed the Census Returns for the town for 1861 and 1891, also located in the libraries. The Group has also set up a website www.dartmouth-history.org.uk on which copies of Dartmouth historical records are being placed, including many hundreds of family letters, enabling far-flung descendants whose forebears once lived here to access their family history from all over the world. Copies of many useful documents are available on computer in the new Library in the Flavel Centre, Dartmouth where members of the Group are sometimes available to help with enquiries.

Outside her historical interests Ray Freeman enjoys her family and grand-children, while relaxing at her home beside the river Dart, a place which has provided her with so many years of enjoyment.

Foreword

This, the third edition of *Dartmouth and its Neighbours*, has been brought up to date with the addition of a revised final chapter and new photograph covering the years up to 2007. The opportunity has been taken to improve the cover and endpapers with colour illustrations, to enhance digitally some of the earlier illustrations used and correct earlier minor errors. Otherwise, the text of this edition remains the same. It covers the history of Dartmouth, one of the most interesting towns in Devon, with the adjoining villages which like it depended for their existence on the use of the river Dart, from prehistoric times to the present day.

The sources used for this book start with the most recent archaeological discoveries, and continue with contemporary written records through all periods, ending with oral history. These include the extensive manor and borough archives now in the Devon Record Office, naval and commercial records, as well as the church documents. Included in the latter are churchwardens' and Poor Law accounts which light up the lives of ordinary people often forgotten in earlier times. In the Public Record Office the 17th and 18th century Port Books have provided valuable information about ship owners and cargoes, while the Duchy of Cornwall Archives deal with the relations with the Borough Council over the Water of Dart. The papers of major local families including the Seales, Newmans, Teages and Haynes have provided most valuable information about how the gentry lived. The census returns along with local newspapers especially the *Dartmouth Chronicle* give more information from the 19th century onwards as do Philip & Son's shipping records. Leases of old property give names of owners and those next door over a long period. Old maps and pictures illuminate the story of the growth of the area, while the development of photography enables us to compare 'now' with 'then'.

By the latter 20th century the memories of old people are available, often recorded on tape, which has enormously increased our understanding of how things were. Once history books only told us about the upper and ruling classes. However the aim of this book has been to show how everyone lived and worked in both town and village. It is a history of the port and its people.

Ray Freeman,
Dartmouth 2007

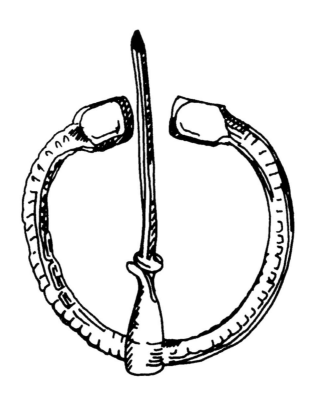

A silver brooch,
probably Celtic,
found at Capton.

Chapter One

The Lower Dart Valley before the Norman Conquest

The Prehistoric Period

The earliest peoples to inhabit south Devon in the Palaeolithic times (roughly 40,000 to 10,000 years ago) used large flint axes and other tools which have been found in caves in Torbay, such as Kent's Cavern and Brixham Cavern. At this time the sea level was lower than it is today, as can be seen at very low tides when tree stumps from submerged forests are visible at Blackpool Sands and in Torbay. These people were hunter-gatherers, who moved about following the animals on which they relied for food, bone tools, and skins for warmth, and used caves only in winter.

Mesolithic People by the Dart

By the Mesolithic period which followed (*c.*12,000-6,000 years ago) they had learnt to make much smaller tools, such as delicate barbed arrow heads which could be fixed on to wooden shafts. In 1974 a small collection of flakes from worked flints of this type was found after a storm washed away several feet of beach in Southtown.[1] As the sea level was still much lower, what is now beach would then have been on the bank of a river running in the deepest channel of today's Dart. Excavation at a settlement of a similar period at Westward Ho in North Devon, also below the modern high tide level, has revealed how these people might have lived. They spent the summer on Dartmoor, where many of their flints have been found, hunting for deer, wild boar, wolf and goat. In the winter they moved beside the sea, presumably for a somewhat milder climate, and fish and wildfowl were plentiful. Some still used the caves, like palaeolithic men. They were able to fell trees and sharpen the points of branches and trunks to form palisades and shelters. By the end of the period, some were beginning to tame sheep and goats to supplement their hunter-gatherer diet. The size of the group was small, probably not more than ten families, and, having few pos-

1. Mesolithic flint chippings found on the beach in Southtown, 1974.

sessions, they moved about freely in a thinly-populated land where there would have been little need to establish clearly-marked territories.[2]

The Neolithic, Bronze and Iron Age Peoples

The next peoples who inhabited Devon were the Neolithic farmers, who brought their skills from Europe and were able to cross the sea by boat, Britain by now having been cut off from the rest of Europe by a rise in sea level. They knew about growing crops, taming animals for milk and wool, spinning and weaving, and making pottery. They buried their dead in chambered tombs, covered by long barrows, to which successive members of the family could be added when they died. Their beautifully shaped and polished tools have been widely found all over the South-West peninsula. For their way of life, boundaries had

1

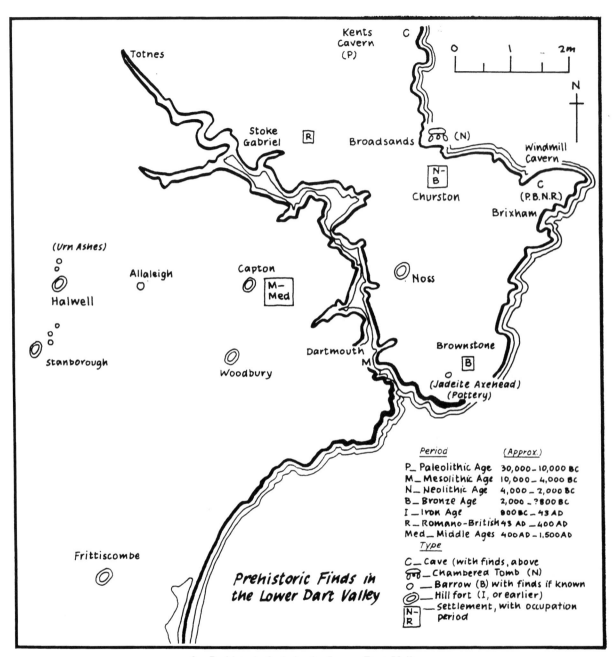

2. Prehistoric finds in the Lower Dart Valley.

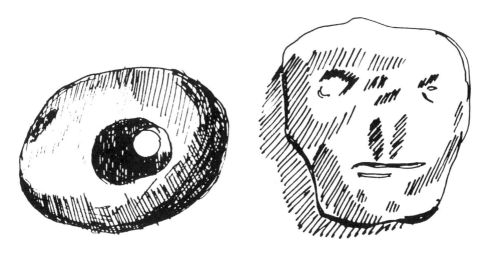

3. Finds at Capton: (a) loom weight, (b) carving of a human face.

to be made to show who had planted which field, and walls built to keep animals safe for their owners. In fact, they were the first people to own anything which could not be carried on their backs.

For such invaders, the Dart estuary has from the earliest times provided easy access on a rising tide from the coast upriver to Totnes. There are plenty of creeks and hards on which small boats can be beached, and which give access to the valleys on either side.

The recent discovery at Capton Fruit Farm of large numbers of flint tools shows an occupation of the site spanning a period of over six thousand years from the Mesolithic period to about A.D. 1500. As flint is not naturally found here, it must have been brought from elsewhere, possibly by trading, for working by the farmers. Traces of hearths and huts have been found, and the many tools include weights for looms with which they would have woven woollen cloth from their flocks of sheep. There is also what appears to be a small carving of a human face: our first known sculpture?

On the east side of the Dart, at Churston, Neolithic tools have recently been found, with others which show that here too occupation continued over a long period.[3] There seems little doubt that much more remains to be discovered by archaeological methods in the Dart valley.

Somewhere about 2,000 to 1,500 B.C. there arrived a new people from Europe with knowledge of metals, especially of bronze. At what date it was discovered that Dartmoor and Cornwall contained tin, one of the two main constituents of bronze, is not known, but by the middle of the second millennium B.C. the so-called Wessex culture was flourishing and traders were coming to the South West from the Mediterranean for tin. Traces of their settlements can be seen all over Dartmoor: hut circles, stone rows, reaves marking land boundaries, ritual circles, and large round barrows. All this indicates a considerable social organisation, which must have existed in south Devon as well though few traces remain there.

Only 33 Bronze Age barrows, which were burial mounds for important people, are known in the whole South Hams, many of which can no longer be seen as they have been ploughed out. There are small clusters around the hill forts at Stanborough and Halwell, both

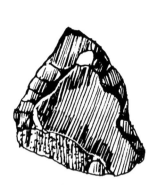

4. Neolithic flint tools found at Capton.

excavated in the 19th century, and the only record is that an urn was found in one and some ashes in another.[4] On the east side of the Dart, however, a round barrow at Brownstone near Kingswear was excavated in the 1930s and found to contain in the centre a cremation of the bones of a child of ten. In a stone cist placed 8 ft. away from the centre of the mound was a green jadeite polished axehead of great beauty. This must have been imported from either Switzerland or Brittany, the nearest sources, and illustrates both the trade goods coming to the area and the prestige of the dead child's father that such an object was buried with him. There were also some pottery sherds.

The next group of invaders were the Celts, who between 800 and 500 B.C. came from Spain and Portugal, bringing a knowledge of iron. This was so much superior for both weapons of war and making tools such as ploughshares that the use of flint and bronze died out. They too farmed the land, making square-shaped fields, and cut down some of the forest in the lowland part of Devon with their sharp iron axes if they needed more arable land.

They were living during the period of the Roman Empire in Gaul, and during the last two centuries B.C. built for themselves a series of hill forts for defence. Stanborough, Halwell and Woodbury are examples of such forts which can be seen on the west side of the Dart, and Noss on the east side, each perhaps to defend Iron Age estates. However, since Bronze Age barrows have been found near to the first two, it is possible that they were originally built by the earlier peoples and re-used in the Iron Age. Excavation at Hembury fort near Honiton has shown that it dates from the Neolithic age, and was then defended by the Celts against the Romans in A.D. 47.

During the Roman occupation of Britain, Exeter grew up as the most westerly major Roman town and the Celtic Dumnonii recognised Rome's supremacy. The Romans built a road west of the Exe running to the north of Dartmoor on the way to Cornwall, with at least three, and possibly five, forts along the route. Extensive search by archaeologists since the Second World War has failed to find any evidence of actual Roman occupation in the area covered by this book. In Stoke Gabriel parish is the site of a farm occupied from the first to the fourth century A.D. when the Romans were in Exeter. Excavation has shown that the way of life continued much as before, except that they traded with the conquerors. They also enjoyed freedom from external attack while Roman power lasted.

Saxons and Danes
Their dependence on Roman protection is clear from what happened when the Roman legions were withdrawn from Britain in A.D. 410. Attacks from Saxons and others were so fierce that many fled to Armorica, modern Brittany, so named because of the large number of British living there. The Saxons invaded from the east, and reached Exeter by about 670 when, having become Christian, they set up a monastery there. They reached the Dart from the east side by 705, and the Tamar by 712. All of Devon now formed part of the Kingdom of Wessex.

5. Green jadeite polished axehead found at Brownstone in a stone cist near a round barrow.

A hundred years later, when we have the first surviving charters of land grants, nearly all the place names are Saxon. The Derentune Homm charter of 833, in which King Egbert granted land formerly owned by their father to three sisters, is thought to include the Dart — 'Derentune' — as its eastern boundary. The eldest of the three sisters, Beornwyn, had already retired to take up her dower in Dumnonia in a house suitable for a noble Saxon lady. The grant to her father must have been made in the first decade of the ninth century. Two other charters, the Om Homme of 846 and the Hiwisce of 962, give boundary place names which identify them as lying immediately to the west of the 833 charter in the South Hams, around the Kingsbridge area and extending from the coast to Dartmoor. It is interesting that these Saxon charters refer to boundaries formed by earthworks — such as hedge banks — which must have been there from Celtic times, and probably took over whole estates rather than carving out new boundaries for themselves.[5]

Some isolated Celts may have struggled on in remote farmsteads, others may have fled to Cornwall or Brittany, while many undoubtedly became slaves to the Saxons. Three hundred years later, in Domesday Book, the proportion of slaves in Devon is about twenty per cent, much higher than in any other part of England — an indication that the Celts had nowhere left to run.

While no Anglo-Saxon buildings survive in this area, their legacy lay in their place names, language, laws, taxes, measurements, and system of local government, which lasted for a thousand years. They divided their state into shires, subdivided into 'hundreds'. The land to the west of the Dart was in the hundred of Cadelinton (Chillington), later changed to Coleridge, by which it was known up to the 19th century. The whole of Torbay was in Haytor hundred. The Hundred Court administered justice, and collected taxes (geld) from the villages or estates in the area. The tax system depended on assessing the number of 'hides' and the number of plough-teams in each estate. The hide was a unit of land measurement, once said to be 120 acres, and based on the amount that one plough could plough in a year, which in practice varied with the fertility of the soil. The crown had the means to assess every shire and hundred in hides and ploughs for payment of geld.

While some of the Dumnonians had been converted to Christianity before the Saxons came, there is no evidence of any continuity from the Celtic church in the area covered by this book. It has been suggested that St Petrox church at the mouth of the Dart is on the site of a monastic cell founded by followers of this sixth-century saint, whose body was buried at Bodmin. However, the first reference to a monastery there was not until 1192, when it was referred to as that of St Peter.

When the Saxons came to Devon they brought with them their own church organisation, of bishops, monasteries and parishes. Crediton was at first the centre of the Bishopric, before being replaced by Exeter in 1050. In the early days of their conquest, 'Minsters' were set up in the more important centres whose clergy acted as missionaries to the surrounding area. Churchstowe, near Kingsbridge, and Totnes have been suggested as possible sites for these, though unlike Axminster in East Devon they have not retained the name.

A late 10th-century ordinance of King Edgar shows that under the minster there had developed two smaller kinds of churches: parish churches with a graveyard, and in some places just a field church without a graveyard. No one knows when the parish boundaries were first determined, but it seems reasonable to suppose that the Saxon thegns, being Christian, would set up churches to serve their newly-won estates, whose boundaries, at least at first, would also be the parish boundaries. They usually follow streams, ancient trackways, landmarks and old hedge banks. The expenses of these churches had to be met by the laymen. There was a tax called 'plough alms' — a penny on every plough to be paid around Easter. The payment of tithe was enforced by the law of the land by the 10th century. However, at least part of this went to the minster church, not to the parish or field church. It is probable that these simple cob or wooden churches were set up in most of the estates in this area, but no traces of them now remain.

The Saxons did not long enjoy their conquest uncontested. The Danes (or Vikings), like themselves, first attacked the East coast of England, but seaborne raids on South Devon began in the mid-ninth century. In 851 the Danes landed in Torbay, but were defeated by the Saxon defences. In 876 a Danish army spent the winter in Exeter. To deal with the nationwide threat they posed, the Saxons at least as early as Alfred the Great (871-899) organised a series of burhs or fortified centres across Wessex, which were to be manned and supplied from the countryside around. The old Iron Age earthwork at Halwell was named in the 'Burghal Hidage', probably drawn up between 880-890, as one of this chain of forts, and as having 300 hides to support it. This meant that it needed 300 men to defend it, one from each hide. The rest of the community would have to provide each man with his weapons and food from their holding. Later, in the reign of Athelstan, 925-939, the burh was moved from Halwell to Totnes.

The tax system was now used to meet the enormous cost of the Danish wars. Villagers had not only to grow enough food to feed themselves, but to support an army. Recent research in other parts of England suggests that the wars led to the introduction of the open field system of semi-communal farming, in which villagers grew a rotation of crops in strips in large common fields, leaving one fallow every third year. This system produced more food and, so it is suggested, was imposed by the government on earlier Saxon villages based on individual plots which have been found to lie below them. This would have involved a major upheaval of country life, comparable with that of the agricultural revolution of the 18th century.

Asser, the chronicler of the reign of Alfred, relates how only fear of the Danes forced people to agree to these heavy burdens. By the time of the Grately Code, A.D. 930, when the king went to war he could demand from his thegns (nobles) two mounted men for every

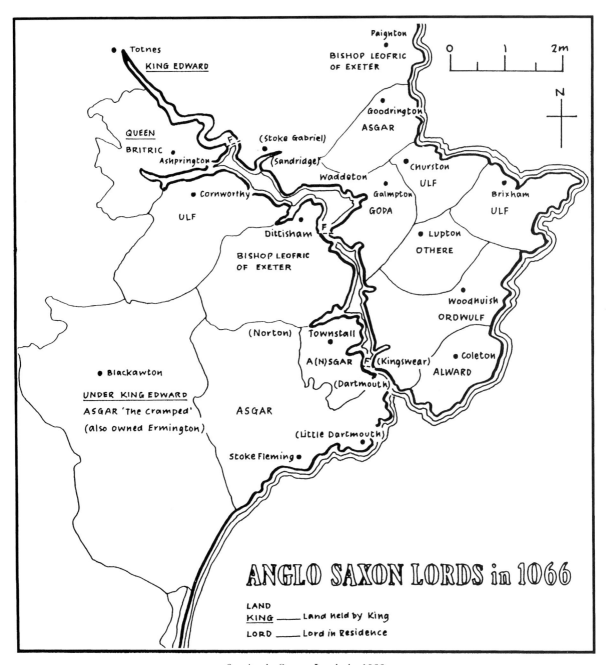

6. Anglo-Saxon Lords in 1066.

plough, who formed a well-armed cavalry, the officer class. Lesser thegns fought under the great nobles: by Anglo-Saxon law a man might choose his lord, a right which was taken away by the Norman Conquest. The villagers were allotted taxes to pay according to the number of hides for which they were assessed, and had to fight as the equivalent of the 'poor bloody infantry', on foot and ill armed. Already their services to their lord were laid down in detail: so many days' ploughing, making hay, cutting wood, payments in kind of crops, animals, and so on. They also had to pay one tenth of their produce to the Church. What was left was, however, theirs to enjoy — at least they were better off than the slaves.

By the beginning of the 11th century Ethelred the Unready had begun the disastrous practice of trying to bribe the Danes to stay away by raising a new tax, 'Danegeld'. The sums collected began as £10,000 in 991, increased yearly and reached the enormous sum of £48,000 by 1012. Despite this, Danish attacks increased. Tavistock was sacked in the 990s and Exeter once more in 1003. After years of conflict in 1016 Canute the Dane became king of all England when Ethelred died. He still collected Danegeld, however, which reached £72,000 in 1018. It had become, in effect, a war tax. He later became ruler of Denmark and Norway. When Canute's own sons died, Ethelred's son Edward became king in 1042, but, as his nickname 'the Confessor' indicated, he was more suited to the religious life than to that of king in conflict-torn England.

For most of the middle of the century there was a power struggle between the Danish royal family, the Saxon Edward, and the Saxon Godwin family, Earls of Mercia and ambitious to rule themselves. Godwin married Gytha, a Danish relative of Canute, and by her had six sons all of whom became powerful men. He forced King Edward, against his will, to marry his daughter Edith, to which Edward reacted by living as a monk. The family dominated Edward, who came to hate them. The eldest son, Swegn, among many other atrocities such as the rape of nuns, murdered his Danish cousin Beorn after inviting him apparently in friendship aboard a ship in Bosham harbour in 1049. He then took the body and buried it at Dartmouth — the first mention of that place in the Anglo-Saxon Chronicle. Swegn's brother Harold removed the body for honourable burial at Winchester. Swegn died in 1052, and Harold, the second son, became the chief minister to King Edward for the last 12 years of his reign.

The effect of these struggles on the lives of the ordinary people was to make them wary of living by the sea, where sudden attacks could be made by the Danes or other pirates. Villages and farms were sited a little inland. A watch could be kept on the coast, so that the inhabitants could flee if raiders were seen. Even walled towns, such as Totnes and Exeter, were a few miles up estuaries to give time for warnings of attack.

We have a record in Domesday Book of who were the lords of all the lands of England just before the Norman conquest. Plate 8 shows their names in the estates on either side of the lower Dart valley. Several later towns and villages including Dartmouth, Kingswear and Stoke Gabriel were not mentioned by name, but were included in larger units. The boundaries of these estates were not altered by William, who simply parcelled them out whole among his followers. The Saxon thegns whose names are recorded here vanish without trace after 1066 — killed or reduced to lower status as the conquerors took over, leaving their common people to be ruled by new masters. The landscape of the England which fell under the Norman rulers had been shaped by its previous owners, perhaps reflecting boundaries going back over 3,000 years.

Chapter Two

The Arrival of the Normans

On the death of King Edward in 1065, the Saxon Witan chose Harold Godwinson as the next king, ignoring Edward's own choice of William of Normandy. A third claimant was Harold Hardrada of Denmark, claiming to be heir to Canute. In this three-cornered contest William emerged the winner after landing an army in East Sussex, defeating and killing Harold Godwinson at Hastings in 1066.

Gytha, mother of Harold, was living in Exeter, a royal possession, and the city refused to surrender to William until he came in person in 1068 and besieged it. Gytha and her daughter were allowed to leave unharmed but William was determined to have no more risk of rebellion in the South West. He ordered the building of a castle inside the walls of Exeter, and of another inside Totnes. Their purpose was to crush revolt from within, as well as to defend against attack from outside.

The Normans began to take over the Saxon lands soon afterwards. According to the feudal system, in Saxon as in Norman times, the king was the owner of all the land, and could either keep it himself or let it out to others. William himself took all the lands of the Saxon royal family. The lands formerly held by the Saxon Bishop Leofric of Exeter passed to his Norman successor Bishop Osbern. These two groups included the most valuable estates. After that, the leading Norman barons had their share, though William was careful not to give any of them so much land in one place that they could become a threat to himself. Lastly, the lesser French (or Breton or Flemish) followers were rewarded. Any tenant-in-chief, that is, holding direct from the king, could sublet to someone else, and some were themselves subtenants either to the king or to another great baron.

William's reign was filled with wars, and he made full use of the Saxon geld system to extract money from the English. However, in 1086 he decided to have a survey made of the value of the possessions of all his barons, great and small. He may have believed that they were not paying him enough in feudal dues, and he determined to find out just what they were worth.

Domesday Book, 1086

In Domesday Book, produced in the year 1086, we have a survey unmatched not only in 11th-century Europe but for many centuries after.[1] For the south-west counties there is also the Exeter Domesday, commonly known as Exon and now in Exeter Cathedral, an earlier and more detailed version of the information which was put into the final version at Winchester. It even records how many animals there were on every estate on the day on which the figures were drawn up. Its information was compressed into standard abbreviations by the exchequer scribe, thus reducing its length by at least half. Animals were omitted presumably because their value would be included in the annual revenue from the estate, but the records are of interest to us in filling in the picture of animal husbandry in the 11th century. Also included in Exon but omitted in the final book was the division between the hides in the lord's own estate known as the demesne, on which geld was not paid, and those of the villagers on which it was.

We can see now not only who were the lords, but how many people were on their estates, and how they were divided into categories. First comes the Norman tenant in chief, followed by the former Saxon owner. Then is the entry: 'It paid geld for (x) hides', followed by 'there is land for (y) ploughs', and the number which were actually there. This meant plough teams, including the usual number of eight oxen to pull them. It was in fact a better clue to the value of the estate than the number of hides, since it showed how much land was cultivated. Then follows the number of plough teams in the lord's land, with, in Exon only, the number of hides he had.

Next the people are listed: first the slaves, then the villagers who shared in the common fields, then the smallholders who had a few acres in isolated farms, and, rarely in this part of Devon, cottagers who had a house but no land at all. These were only the workers, not children or women who did not work on the land, so to arrive at an estimate of the total population one must multiply by four or five. The order of Domesday usually lists the slaves immediately after the lord's ploughs, and before the number of villagers, which looks as if all the slaves worked on the lord's demesne. However, Exon lists the slaves after the villagers and smallholders, leaving their position uncertain.

After the various people come their hides, plough teams and the meadow, pasture and woodland in which they had rights of grazing, collecting wood and so on. Any source of wealth such as mills or fisheries was noted, and, in Exon only, the number of animals. The annual value was usually recorded both as it was before the Normans came and at the time of the survey. Comparisons between the two are often revealing. In no case where both figures are given in this area has the value gone down, and in some cases the increase is considerable.

The information was collected by sworn evidence given before the hundred court by representatives from each village, answering a set list of questions. Within each hundred they were sorted to put one lord's holdings together, while the final version grouped together all the possessions of each lord in one county, in a set order of hundreds, with an index in the front for easy reference. It was as logical, in its day, as a modern telephone directory. A summary of extracts from Domesday, including those from the Exeter version, is given in Plates 7 and 8.

Some lords held many estates, and could not possibly live in all of them. They employed reeves, or agents, to look after them, direct the labour of the slaves and villagers and collect the dues owed to the lord. The lord could visit most of his estates within a day's ride on horseback, but if he wished to stay overnight the reeve would provide accommodation. It would be wrong, however, to imagine that there was a 'manor house' on every lord's estate at this period, more likely a simple cob or timber and thatched farmhouse. These reeves are not mentioned in Domesday, but the system would not have worked without them.

Totnes, a royal borough, was held from the king by Judhael, a Breton, who built its castle and made it the centre of his barony. It was an important borough, with 95 families inside its walls and 15 more outside it — about 500 people, assuming an average family of five. Formerly the inhabitants paid £3, but now in 1086 they paid £8. Judhael, with 107 estates, was the largest landholder in Devon after Baldwin the Sheriff and was clearly trusted by William to hold this vital river crossing. He was also given Brixham, Churston, Lupton and Coleton which together controlled the whole peninsula of Brixham — a key area for defence against outside attack.

The king also sublet to Judhael Ashprington, a small but valuable riverside estate. The lord's private demesne had one hide, and two plough teams. There were four slaves, seven villagers and eight smallholders with two hides, and three plough teams. They had one carthorse, two cattle (cows or bulls) and 100 sheep. There were also two fisheries, most likely for salmon though this is not specified, and one salt house — for making salt by evaporating sea water. Salt was used to preserve many vegetables and meat as well as fish for the winter. There were 40 acres of pasture, and woodland one league long by half a league wide. The annual value was £4, both before and after the conquest. Before 1087,

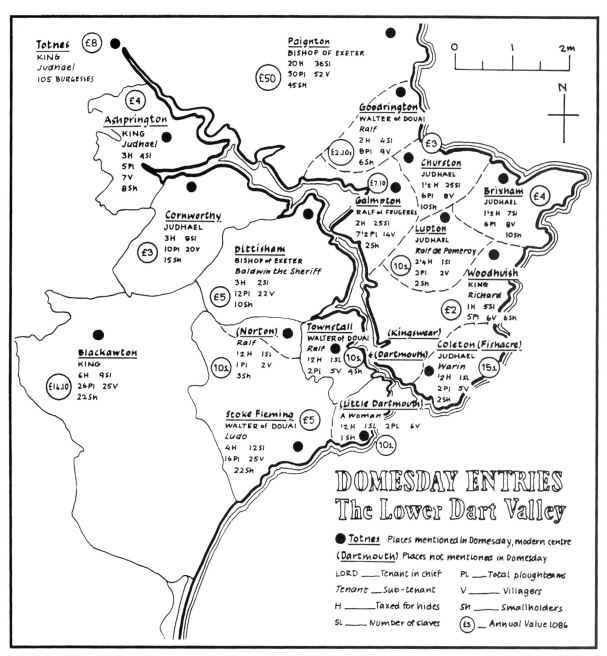

Totnes £8
KING
Judhael
105 BURGESSES

£4

Ashprington
KING
Judhael
3H 4Sl
5Pl
7V
8Sh

Paignton £50
BISHOP OF EXETER
20H 36Sl
50Pl 52V
45Sh

Goodrington
WALTER of DOUAI
Ralf
2H 4Sl £2.10s
8Pl 9V
6Sh

Churston £3
JUDHAEL
1½H 25Sl
6Pl 8V
10Sh

Brixham £4
JUDHAEL
1½H 7Sl
6Pl 8V
10Sh

£7.10

Galmpton
RALF of FOUGERES
2H 25Sl
7½Pl 14V
2Sh

Lupton
JUDHAEL
Ralf de Pomeroy
2½H 1Sl 10s.
2Pl 2V
2Sh

Cornworthy £3
JUDHAEL
3H 9Sl
10Pl 20V
15Sh

Pittisham £5
BISHOP of EXETER
Baldwin the Sheriff
3H 2Sl
12Pl 22V
10Sh

Woodhuish
KING
Richard £2
1H 5Sl
5Pl 6V 6Sh

(Norton)
Ralf
½H 1Sl 10s.
1Pl 2V
3Sh

Townstall
WALTER of DOUAI
Ralf
½H 1Sl 10s.
2Pl 5V 4Sh

(Kingswear)
(Dartmouth)

Coleton (Fishacre)
JUDHAEL
Warin 15s.
½H 1Sl
2Pl 5V
2Sh

Blackawton £14.10
KING
6H 9Sl
26Pl 25V
22Sh

Stoke Fleming £5
WALTER of DOUAI
Ludo
4H 12Sl
16Pl 25V
22Sh

(Little Dartmouth)
A Woman
½H 1Sl 2Pl 6V
1Sh 10s.

DOMESDAY ENTRIES
The Lower Dart Valley

● **Totnes** Places mentioned in Domesday, modern centre
(Dartmouth) Places not mentioned in Domesday
LORD ____ Tenant in chief   PL ____ Total ploughteams
Tenant ____ Sub-tenant   V ____ Villagers
H ____ Taxed for hides   Sh ____ Smallholders
SL ____ Number of slaves   (£s) ____ Annual Value 1086

7. Domesday entries in the Lower Dart Valley: I.

Judhael gave Ashprington to the Priory of St Mary's, Totnes, which he had recently founded, and it continued to be owned by the Priory until the dissolution in 1539.

The king held for himself the larger and more valuable estate of Blackawton, then extending to the sea near modern Strete, with an annual income of £14 10s. This too had a salt house, but its chief value lay in its fertile land. The lord had two and a half hides, and two ploughs. There were nine slaves, 25 villagers and 22 smallholders with 24 ploughs and three and a half hides. With 30 acres of pasture, and the same of woodland, it supported 120 sheep and 20 goats.

Judhael himself held Cornworthy, valued formerly and now at £3 yearly. The lord had in his demesne two ploughs and one hide. There were eight slaves, 20 villagers, and 15 smallholders who had eight ploughs and two hides. There was a fishery 'paying 30 salmon' to the lord, and a mill. There were 100 acres of pasture, 30 acres of woodland, and 70 acres of underwood. Animals listed included one carthorse, five cattle, 11 pigs and 140 sheep.

Brixham, held with much of the Berry Head peninsula for defensive reasons by Judhael, was formerly worth £3, now £4, and had two and a half hides. The Lord had half a hide, with two plough teams. There were two slaves, 15 villagers, and 12 smallholders who had eight plough teams and two hides. Four acres of meadow, 12 acres of pasture and 12 acres of woodland supported two horses, four cattle, 10 pigs, and 180 sheep.

Judhael held Churston himself, valued formerly and now at £3. It was taxed on one and a half hides, of which the lord kept half, with two plough teams. There were seven slaves, and three cottagers as well as eight villagers and seven smallholders, who had four plough teams and one hide. With 15 acres of woodland and 12 acres of pasture there were six cattle, one horse, eight pigs and 120 sheep.

Inland, was the tiny estate of Lupton, assessed at only a quarter of a hide. It was held from Judhael by Ralph of Pomeroy — himself an important tenant-in-chief in his own right. Valued formerly at five shillings, it was now worth double. There were two plough teams there, with one slave, two villagers and two smallholders who had four acres of woodland, two cattle, 13 pigs and 57 sheep.

In between Judhael's estates of Lupton and Coleton, the king sublet Woodhuish to Richard, son of Thorolf. It had also doubled in value since 1066 to £2. It was taxed for one hide, and had in the demesne two plough teams. There were five slaves, six villagers, and six smallholders with two and a half plough teams. There were two acres of meadow and six acres of woodland but no animals are mentioned. The nearby place names of Kingston and Kingswear suggest that this estate extended to include them, possibly farmed by one of the smallholders.

Warin held Coleton (Fishacre) from Judhael, formerly worth five and now 15 shillings. It paid tax on half a hide. There were two plough teams, one slave, five villagers and two smallholders who had four acres of pasture, six cattle, 14 pigs, 70 sheep and six goats. This tiny estate overlooked the entrance to the River Dart from Brownstone, and with the four estates above completed the ownership of the Brixham peninsula.

The Bishop of Exeter held the most valuable estate of all at Paignton, whose annual income had increased dramatically since the Norman arrival from £13 to £50. This had 20 hides, six in the demesne with eight plough teams. There were 36 slaves, 52 villagers, 40 smallholders and five pigmen who may be regarded as specialist farmers who paid a 'rent' of 50 pigs. Between them, they had 42 plough teams and 14 hides. There was a salt house, which paid 10 pence, 18 acres of meadow, 40 acres of pasture and 41 acres of woodland. Animals mentioned include four cart horses, 20 cattle, and 350 sheep. The area covered by this vast estate included Stoke Gabriel on the bank of the Dart, and extended to St Marychurch in the north.

On the opposite bank of the river, at Dittisham, the Bishop sublet to Baldwin the Sheriff

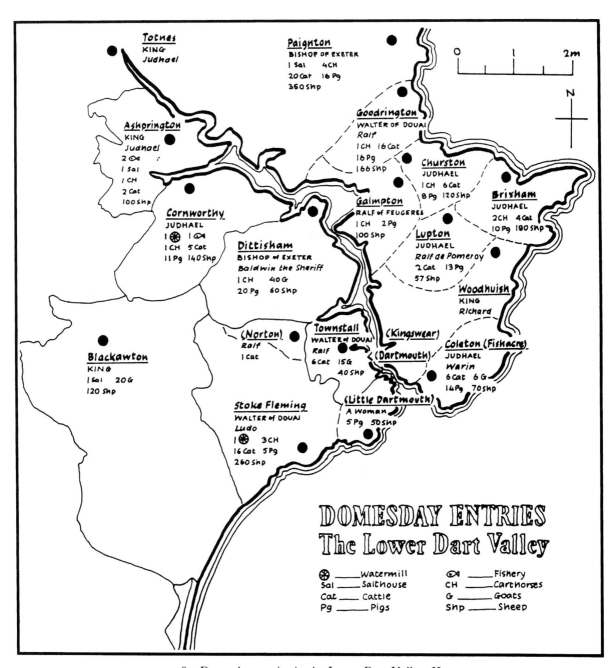

Totnes
KING
Judhael

Paignton
BISHOP OF EXETER
1 Sal   4 CH
20 Cat   16 Pg
350 Shp

Goodrington
WALTER OF DOUAI
Ralf
1 CH 16 Cat
16 Pg
166 Shp

Churston
JUDHAEL
1 CH   6 Cat
8 Pg 120 Shp

Brixham
JUDHAEL
2 CH   4 Cat
10 Pg 190 Shp

Ashprington
KING
Judhael
2 ◁
1 Sal
1 CH
2 Cat
100 Shp

Cornworthy
JUDHAEL
1 ⊛ 1 ◁
1 CH   5 Cat
11 Pg 140 Shp

Dittisham
BISHOP of EXETER
Baldwin the Sheriff
1 CH   40 G
20 Pg   60 Shp

Galmpton
RALF of FEUGERES
1 CH   2 Pg
100 Shp

Lupton
JUDHAEL
Ralf de Pomeroy
2 Cat 13 Pg
57 Shp

Woodhuish
KING
Richard

Blackawton
KING
1 Sal   20 G
120 Shp

(Norton)
Ralf
1 Cat

Townstall
WALTER of DOUAI
Ralf
6 Cat   15 G
40 Shp

(Kingswear)

(Dartmouth)

Coleton (Fishacre)
JUDHAEL
Warin
6 Cat   6 G
14 Pg   70 Shp

Stoke Fleming
WALTER of DOUAI
Ludo
1 ⊛   3 CH
16 Cat 5 Pg
260 Shp

(Little Dartmouth)
A Woman
5 Pg   50 Shp

DOMESDAY ENTRIES
The Lower Dart Valley

⊛ ——— Watermill	◁ ——— Fishery
Sal ——— Salthouse	CH ——— Carthorses
Cat ——— Cattle	G ——— Goats
Pg ——— Pigs	Shp ——— Sheep

8. Domesday entries in the Lower Dart Valley: II.

the estate of Dittisham, with an income which had increased from £3 to £5 since Saxon times. Here the lord had in demesne one hide, and two plough teams. There were two slaves, 22 villagers and 10 smallholders with 10 plough teams and two hides. The pasture extended to 60 acres, with 40 acres of underwood. Their animals consisted of one cart horse, 20 pigs, 60 sheep and 40 goats.

Galmpton estate was held by Ralph of Feugeres, who only held two manors in Devon, the other being Ipplepen, and the value of the two together is given as £30. As Ipplepen was much larger, most of this must have been for that estate, but if Galmpton was even a quarter of it, £7 10s., it seems a lot for only two hides. The lord had in demesne one hide, and two plough teams. There were two slaves, 14 villagers, and two smallholders, who had five and a half plough teams for another hide. There were four acres of pasture, one acre of meadow, and underwood one league long and 12 perches wide, with one horse, two pigs and 100 sheep.

Stoke Fleming and Townstal, two estates at the mouth of the Dart, forming roughly a rectangle bordered by the river on the east and the sea on the south, were held by Walter of Douai. He, like Judhael, must have been trusted by William to defend this important river entrance. He married a Saxon lady, Eddiva, widow of Heming, who had been in 1066 the owner of Uffculme which Walter now held himself presumably through his marriage to her. Stoke took its second name 'Fleming' from Walter, Douai being in Flanders. It seems likely that Townstal was once part of Stoke Fleming before it was divided off and became an estate of its own. In Saxon times both were held by Asgar along with Goodrington and 10 houses in Exeter, all of which passed to Walter after the conquest.

Walter sublet Stoke to Ludo, its annual value unchanged since 1066 at £5. It had a mill — perhaps in the Blackpool valley — but only for the use of the lord. In demesne the lord had one hide and four plough teams. There were 12 slaves, 27 villagers and 16 smallholders with three hides, and 12 plough teams. Four acres of meadow and 30 acres of underwood supported three cart horses, 16 cattle and 260 sheep.

Two small outlying parts of Stoke Fleming are listed separately. One was sublet by Walter to 'a woman' — Exon adds that he 'gave it to her in alms'. She had half a hide, one plough team and one slave. Six villagers and one smallholder had another plough team. Seven cattle, five pigs, and 50 sheep complete the picture of this small estate, worth ten shillings. This may be the present Little Dartmouth, and possibly extended down the Week valley to Warfleet and the river mouth. The other was held from Walter by Ralph, who also sublet Townstal from him. It is likely that this was the adjacent Norton, which later descended in the same ownership as Townstal. It was also small, valued at 10 shillings before and after the conquest. It had half a hide, the demesne with one plough team and one slave, and the two villagers and three smallholders with another plough team. There were four acres of woodland, only one animal (cow or bull) and 30 sheep.

Townstal, its value also unchanged at 10 shillings, paid tax on half a hide, and had two plough teams, two slaves, five villagers and four smallholders. They had six cattle, 40 sheep, and 15 goats. No separate area for the demesne and villagers' land is given in Exon which suggests it was all held by Ralph. Clearly these two estates had much land which was too steep to plough, and was only fit for keeping a few goats and sheep, hence their low value. It was on this tiny estate that the future Dartmouth was to grow — there is no mention of it in Domesday Book as a separate village, and its possiblities as a port were entirely unexploited.

Goodrington, which Ralph also held from Walter, had doubled in value from £1 5s. to £2 10s. The lord's land had two ploughs, with half a hide. There were four slaves, nine villagers and six smallholders with six ploughs and one and a half hides. There were 20 acres of woodland. They had one horse, 16 cattle and 166 sheep.

9. Townstal Farmhouse, possibly the lord's demesne farm.

10. Townstal church, centre of the pre-Norman manor.

What then does Domesday tell us about this whole area? The Normans had increased its annual value in almost every case. This value was mostly dependent on the number of ploughs in use in the estates, though, from their large numbers, sheep must also have provided a good income. While villagers are mentioned in every estate, some are in such small numbers, for example two at Lupton, five at Townstal, that it is hard to see how they could have run a proper open field system. Even in the larger estates, such as Stoke Fleming, they probably only farmed one village in this way. The most conspicuous feature in every estate is the large number of small holders, who may well represent the continuation of independent farmers from very ancient times. In many cases, their successors are still there today on the same sites.

Nowhere in the Domesday entries for these manors are churches or priests mentioned — indeed in the whole of Devon only nine churches and seven priests are listed, and then only when they owned some land. It seems therefore that they were not listed if they were not liable for paying tax, but would actually have existed on most estates.

On the west side of the Dart, boundaries have been assumed to be the same as those of parishes. On the east side, where there are many more estates than parishes, the boundaries are diagramatic, not based on any geographical consideration.

After the Norman Conquest

The Growth of Dartmouth
It was the Normans who first appreciated the fine natural harbour of Dartmouth, placed so conveniently opposite William's lands in the Channel Islands and Normandy, and it seems likely that they brought over Frenchmen to build houses and port facilities. The names of the tenants in the earliest deeds of the town were French, not English.[2] Either side of the creek, now the market area of the modern town, two small communities grew up known as Clifton and Hardness. On the opposite side of the river, people from Woodhuish and Kingston seem to have moved down to the waterside to form Kingswear, probably so called from the watercourses or wears for the mill which once stood at the head of Waterhead creek, and were involved in all the activities of the growing port.

By 1147 Dartmouth was well enough known in Europe to be chosen as an assembly place for an international force of 164 ships which were about to set off on the Second Crusade.[3] This implies that besides the naturally sheltered harbour there were skilled craftsmen ready to supply and repair this huge fleet. In 1190 a fleet of 37 ships left the Dart to join Richard I on the Third Crusade.[4] Indeed, in every war from then onwards, whether against Welsh under Edward I, the Scots under Edward II, or the French in the Hundred Years' War, Dartmouth played a leading part.

When Henry II gained Bordeaux by marriage in 1154 this opened up the wine trade on which Dartmouth flourished for the next 300 years, exporting wool, wheat and fish in exchange. The Norman conquest of Ireland led to trade in Irish hides and timber. One way and another, the town prospered.

By the 14th century the ships used for these voyages were called 'cogs', an improvement on earlier vessels in having a rudder attached to a stern post. They had one large square sail, and were built up at bow and stern into 'castles' in which, in the frequent sea fights, sailors took shelter to shoot their arrows. They could carry troops, cargo or horses, their size averaging about 140 tons burden. It was the wealth made from these cogs which enabled the port to flourish, and it is hardly surprising that the earliest seal of the town, dated 1281, shows one such high-prowed ship.

11. Model of a 14th-century cog, of the type used in the Bordeaux wine trade.

New Lords After Domesday

The landholding recorded in Domesday Book did not last long. On William the Conqueror's death in 1087 many barons rebelled against his son William Rufus, and both Judhael of Totnes and Walter of Douai lost their lands for treason. Judhael was restored to favour by Henry I, who before 1100 gave him the barony of Barnstaple. He lived there until 1130 as an important landowner in North Devon, but he ceased to have influence around the Dart valley.

Judhael's Totnes barony passed to the de Nonants, then to the de Braiose family, and by the late 13th century to an heiress, Eva, who married William de Cantiloupe. Their heiress, Milisent, married first Ivo de la Zouche and then John de Monthalt.[5] They claimed to have the lordship of the river Dart from Totnes down to the mouth of the river, and the right to dues on all shipping using it. They also claimed the right to dues from the market in Dartmouth in 1244.

Walter of Douai's lands in Stoke Fleming, Townstal and Goodrington were given to the honour of Marshwood[6] in Dorset, held from the time of Henry I by Geoffrey de Mandeville and passed down in that family for 200 years. The subtenants did not however change.

Stoke Fleming passed from Ludo to his heirs, all of whom were known as 'the Fleming', confirming the second name of the manor. In 1236 Stoke Fleming was sold to Reginald de Mohun, and after three generations in that family passed by 1303 to John de Carew through his marriage to the heiress Eleanor de Mohun.[7] There is a statue in Stoke Fleming church which is believed to be of Eleanor. The Carews were lords until 1575, playing an important part in the story of Dartmouth as they owned the land by the mouth of the river on which the castles were later built.

Townstal and Norton were soon acquired, under Geoffrey de Mandeville, by William Fitz (son of) Stephen, who presided over Dartmouth for 150 years, during which period it grew from a tiny village to a port of international importance.

The FitzStephens of Townstal and the Flemings of Stoke Fleming must have worked closely together, as they shared the sea shore stretching from modern Dartmouth out to the river mouth on the west side. In 1192, apparently after acting as guardian during the minority of Richard the Fleming, William FitzStephen restored to Richard 'all the land of Dartmouth which is next the township, between the monastery of St Peter and the land of Stoke'.[8] This is the first mention of what is today the church of St Petrox. It was probably the cell of a monk, perhaps acting to provide a light at the entrance to the harbour. Certainly no traces or mention of a monastery for a group of monks has ever been found.

In the same year, Richard of Flanders was granted the land of Strete — in Domesday, part of Blackawton. From 1201-1202, he was made sheriff of Cornwall, and took over the castle of Launceston with the stamps of the stannary for the tin industry there.[9] Clearly Richard was one of the leading lords in the South West to merit being entrusted with this post.

The Church as Landowner

As has been seen, the Bishop of Exeter was a major landowner at the time of Domesday Book, with his huge manor of Paignton including Stoke Gabriel, as well as Dittisham on the west bank of the Dart. Stoke Gabriel remained as before under the Bishop. The earliest documentary reference to its church was in 1148, though it may have existed much earlier. In 1283 Bishop Peter Quivil gave the benefice to the Chancellorship of Exeter Cathedral, then held by Clement de Langford. In 1300 there was an enquiry into the 'dilapidations' of the church, suggesting that it had been there for a very long time. Sandridge, in the parish of Stoke Gabriel, was held from the bishop as a separate manor by Martin of Sandridge in 1272, passing down in his family through four ownerships until 1428.[10]

Many of the other manors in the lower Dart valley were soon under the control of the church, as the Norman lords began to endow new monastic orders, often cells of those already established in Normandy.

Totnes Priory Judhael of Totnes before 1086 gave the church of St Mary at Totnes with the chapel of St Peter to the church of St Sergius and St Bacchus at Angers, in France.[11] He endowed them with the manor of Follaton, just outside Totnes, as recorded in Domesday Book. This became the Priory of Totnes, the church being used by the townspeople as a parish church. Before 1087, when he was deprived of his barony, he also gave the Priory his estate of Ashprington, and later it was given Brixham.[12] In 1316, the Prior of Totnes was given as the Lord of Dittisham, although this may only have been the advowson of the church. Hugh de Courtenay and his successors later held the manor from the bishop, subletting in turn to others.

The object of these gifts was that the monks should pray for the soul of the founder. It meant that the monastic order became the feudal lord over the people living in these estates, collecting their rents and dues, and in turn the order owed services and dues to the overlord above them in the system, ultimately to the king. They also had the advowson, or right to appoint the priest to the local church.

Popular monasteries sometimes became very wealthy indeed, and the need to run their estates in a businesslike way must sometimes have conflicted with their religious aim of cutting themselves off from the cares and temptations of the world. When the king demanded a 'knight's fee' — that is, a tax to pay for equipping a knight in his army based on the value of each manor --the monasteries had to be responsible for their share, too.

Cornworthy Priory Not all, however, became wealthy. Cornworthy, one of Judhael's estates in 1086, had passed along with his Honour of Totnes to the de Braiose family by 1219. After the death of William de Braiose in 1229, it seems his heiress Eva, wife of William de Cantiloupe, founded a priory there for 13 Augustinian canonesses, and gave them the estate and advowson to the church.[13]

The prioress thus became the Lady of the Manor, under the Honour of Totnes. She in turn held it from the king. In 1238 the Priory was given Allaleigh, and in 1366 Tideford, both originally part of Cornworthy but previously let out separately. The O.S. map shows, near the present day remains of the gatehouse of the priory, a house called 'Court Prior' — once the courthouse where the prioress collected rents and dues, and arranged for new tenants when old ones died. Every feudal holding had such a courthouse to deal with these important matters. However, the

12. The Gatehouse, Cornworthy Priory.

number of canonesses had fallen to nine in 1377, and by the time of the dissolution in 1539 there were only seven.[14]

Torre Abbey It was a very different story with Torre Abbey, to which in about 1198 William FitzStephen granted the church of Townstal for the souls of himself and his wife. This abbey was newly founded in 1196 by the Premonstratensian order, which originated early in the 11th century in northern France. They trained canons to serve as priests in the churches they were given, and wore white cassocks with a loose skull cap on their heads. Among the witnesses to this deed of gift were Richard the Fleming and William Bacon.[15]

For nearly 300 years the Abbots of Torre appointed the Vicars of Townstal, and came to play an important part in the life of the growing town of Dartmouth, as well as in the whole area. Soon after 1198 the canons must have begun to build the stone church dedicated to St Clement at Townstal which we see today, replacing the wooden building presumed to

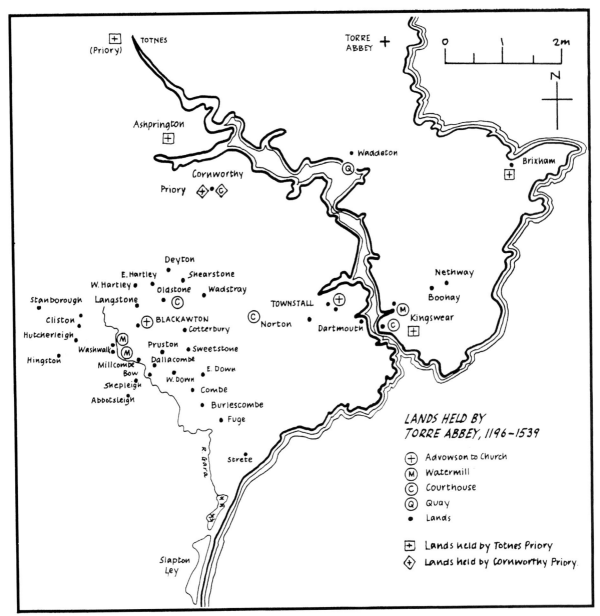

13. Lands held by Torre Abbey, Totnes Priory and Cornworthy Priory.

have existed before. In the south transept lies the tomb of William's wife, Isabella de Languire.

The FitzStephen family lived on their estate of Norton, where many charters were signed. Although they had a church at Townstal, like many other lords of the time they also had a private chapel in their own house for the use of the family. In 1250 one of the charters of Torre records an agreement made with the canons by Gilbert FitzStephen whereby he could keep the offerings made in the chantry chapel at Norton by himself, his wife and the young men of his family, but all others given by freemen or servants were to go to the church of Townstal.[16]

Mr. D. Seymour, in his book *Torre Abbey*, suggests that the medieval manor house was at the old entrance to Norton Park from the B3207, where a group of houses form a rectangular enclosure. On the west side is a house with very thick walls which may date back to that period. A quadrangular building projecting eastwards from it is shown on the tithe map of 1841, which would be the right place for the chapel, but only the foundations are now visible under the lawn at the front of the house. Over the next century more land at Townstal, Norton, Dartmouth and at many other places was given to the canons of Torre.

Kingswear was in the parish of Brixham, the advowson and tithes of which were given by Judhael of Totnes to the priory he had founded there. When a chapel of ease dedicated to St Thomas was built at Kingswear, at least as early as 1170, it too belonged to Totnes Priory. In about 1200, however, Walter De Vasci, who by then was lord of Kingston and Kingswear, gave all his lands to the Canons of Torre except those which belonged to the Prior of Totnes. Later gifts were made of Nethway, Woodhuish, Bowhay including the mill at Kingswear, and Kittery, where the Canons had their court house. Here tenants of Torre Abbey would come to pay their dues, and changes of tenancies would be recorded.[17]

At Waddeton, on the north side of Galmpton Creek, the canons were given 36 acres by Isabella de Waddeton, a widow, in 1260-70. Here the meadow still keeps the name 'Tors', and the wood 'Tors

14. Burlescombe in the 19th century, once held by Torre Abbey.

Wood'. It included a quarry, with a quay nearby which can still be seen on the banks of the Dart, from which stone was exported in a profitable industry.[18]

The largest holding of the canons of Torre in this area was at Blackawton, where they had not only the advowson to the church but eventually held 99½ ferlings — a variable unit of area which averaged 33 acres in these parts. The two main donors of these lands were Peter Fitz Matthew and William le Spek, who appear to have been successive sub-tenants from the king in the middle of the 13th century. Through gifts the abbey came to hold most of the farms of this large and wealthy manor, as well as both a fulling mill and a corn mill, which the tenants were obliged to use. They held their court at Oldstone, later converted into a farmhouse.

Some of the farms they owned have remained simple cottages, no doubt rebuilt on older foundations, while others have become grand houses, but the location of almost all of them can still be traced. When Henry VIII took over the lands of Torre Abbey at the dissolution of the monasteries in 1539, Blackawton manor was valued at £54 14s. 8d. annually — the highest of any of their properties — and it was sold to Lord John Russell and his wife Ann.[19]

Monasteries and churches were slotted into the feudal system in exactly the same way as laymen, holding lands from the king or higher lords, and subletting to tenants. The only difference was that, unlike laymen whose heirs often died out so that the manor was sold to someone else, the church held on to its land for ever. In alarm at the prospect of so much land ending up in the 'dead hand' of the Church, in 1276 Edward I passed the Statute of Mortmain forbidding any more land to be given to it without the King's express permission.

Chapter Three

From Manor to Borough

The Rule of the FitzStephens

The FitzStephen family ruled Dartmouth from their small manor house at Norton, where a court was held by their bailiff or Provost in which changes in tenancies of their houses were recorded. When any property changed hands, the new owner had to pay an entry fine to the lord as well as the annual rent from then on. He also paid the previous tenant or vendor, often in gifts such as a pair of white gloves, cummin, wax, or wine. Deeds survive from 1220 recording such transactions.[1]

Tenants were also obliged to pay suit of court, that is to be present at the lord's court at which these land conveyances were signed, and rents and acknowledgements paid. This was an irksome duty which many tried to avoid by paying a fine instead.

The names of occupations also appear: Oliver the Taverner, Richard the Tailor, Martin the Coggar (maker of cogs?) as well as a Korker (one who caulked ships?), a goldsmith, a glover, a skinner and a baker. At Hardness, mention is made of a house with a 'yard' adjoining — this was a piece of firm beach used for shipbuilding right up until the 19th century.

The Foss

In 1243 comes the first mention of a Fosse, when William Fitz Stephen granted Adam Cade a messuage on the western side of his 'foss of Hardness'.[2] This was a dam made across the tidal creek, to provide power for a mill. Water came in on the rising tide through the mill gullet, and was trapped in the creek by lowering a sluice gate at high tide. When the tide fell, water was channelled through the mill race to turn the wheel. Millers had to be prepared to work night and day as the tide dictated.

There were tidal mills in Normandy, where some still exist, and the knowledge of how to build them was probably brought from there. One survived on the creek at Stoke Gabriel until the 1860s (see plate 59). In 1296 Philip Rurde paid the then enormous sum of £200 for the grant of the mill, an indication of how much money he could expect to make from it.[3] Such was the demand that by 1344 a second wheel was built opposite the first.[4] They are shown clearly on a map dated 1619 (see plates 43 and 44) and remained in use until about 1815. During all this time what is now the centre of Dartmouth, from the Market Square to Ford, was under water as part of the Mill Pool.

A Market and a Fair

Richard FitzStephen was given the right to hold a weekly market in 1231, as well as an annual fair.[5] William of Canteloupe, Lord of Totnes, successfully claimed that he had the right to dues on all goods sold there, and the right to settle disputes in his court.[6] Providing justice was one of the services rendered by feudal lords, but it was certainly not free.

The Water of Dart

With the growth of trade, William also began to charge dues on all cargoes on ships using the river. The townsmen disputed his right to do this in court in 1281, claiming that before his time the water had been free of such tolls.[7] It was decided that the Lord of Totnes did have this right between Totnes Bridge and the Blackstone outside Dartmouth Harbour. These rights were soon after to pass to the Duchy of Cornwall.

The First Borough
From about 1250 Gilbert FitzStephen began to refer to the people of Dartmouth as 'my burgesses', and they paid suit to a court in the town, not at Norton, though the latter continued to deal with the affairs of Townstal.[8] This was an important step towards self-government. Henry III in 1270 recognised the burgesses as an organised body, and by 1281 they had their own seal for legal .documents, a picture of a high-prowed ship with single mast and sail.

Edward I, for whom Dartmouth had provided ships for his wars in Wales and Scotland, came to visit the town in 1286. He gave the burgesses permission to build a church down in the town, to save them the long walk up to Townstal.[9] In 1298, two burgesses from Dartmouth were summoned to a Parliament at York. These two, first of a line lasting until 1868, were John the Baker and William at the Foss, a smith.[10]

Nicholas of Tewkesbury
From 1293 onwards Gilbert FitzStephen was often short of money, and resorted to borrowing from Nicholas of Tewkesbury, a clerk to the king, on the security of Norton, Townstal and Dartmouth, although he still remained their lord.[11] Nicholas grew in power and wealth, until in 1306 he bought from the Lord of Totnes the ownership of the Water of Dart, with its right to dues.[12]

Gilbert FitzStephen faced other problems. In 1308, a commission was set up to enquire into the alleged adultery of his wife Ysolta with Nicholas of Tewkesbury. Nicholas was absolved for adultery, which implied the charge was true.[13]

Dartmouth becomes a Royal Borough, 1327

Gilbert was unable to redeem his mortgages on his lands, and by 1316 Nicholas was listed in the Parliament of that year as lord of the borough of Dartmouth.[14] In 1327, he conveyed both the town and the port to the new king, Edward III, and was rewarded for his services by being given a pension for life. Dartmouth now became a royal borough.[15]

On the occasion of this last transfer, a survey of Dartmouth was made, taking evidence from 12 'honest and law-worthy men' to find out the customs of the town and what it was worth. This gives some illuminating detail about life at the time, and how the borough court business was carried out.[16]

Nicholas had been paid an annual rent from the tenants of '115s. 9d., 1 pound of pepper, 1 pound of wax, and 1 pound of cummin'. Spices were often used as currency in those days, being valuable, long lasting, and light. At Michaelmas, the survey continues:

> The tenants must choose a reeve called a 'portreeve', also a beadle called a 'catchpol' to serve the Lord, to make arrests and levy rents, tolls and customs . . . and other profits due to the Lord . . . and deliver them to the Lord by the hands of the Reeve, taking nothing for his labour.

These elections would be one of the many duties laid on the townsmen when they paid suit of court, and no doubt they all had to take turns in the task of collecting rents and dues from their fellows. They also had to elect an ale taster, 'to take from each brewing a pottle of ale'. Any complaints about the quality would be dealt with at the 'Assize of Bread and Ale', a court which enforced by fines strict standards on bakers and brewers. In this way small communities dealt with their own petty offenders.

The Lord was entitled to heriot, a death duty by which, when a tenant died, his heirs had to pay double the rent for the right to continue the tenancy. The survey concludes that the profits from the courts, tolls and dues were worth £15, while customs from the port were worth £5.

A similar survey in 1332 showed that there were 80 'free' tenants in the town, who were obliged to attend the court of the Lord.[17] If their families, servants, and labourers are included, this suggests a population of six or seven hundred.

The Prince of Wales and the Water of Dart

Edward, however, did not long keep the union over both the water and the borough in his own hands. First, he granted the Water of Dart to his brother John, Duke of Cornwall, in 1333.[18] When John died, in 1338 he granted it to his son, the Prince of Wales — the Black Prince — who was also made Duke of Cornwall. Since then it has been held by successive Princes of Wales.[19] It was known as the Waterbaileywick, and the official appointed to look after its interests locally was referred to as the Waterbailiff. Over the years its rights were defined to include all the land covered by the water at high tide within its area, with the right to charge dues on anything that floated, moored, was beached, or anchored, as well as tolls on cargoes imported or exported. It also claimed a right to a share in any 'wreck of the sea' and prize ships taken in war.

In 1335, Edward granted Dartmouth to Joan de Carew, for services to the King and Queen Philippa.[20] Perhaps Joan, whose husband John was Lord of Stoke Fleming, was being rewarded for her services as a lady in waiting to the queen.

1341 — The Royal Charter and a new Lord, Guy de Bryan

However, after the Hundred Years War with France had started, Edward seems to have decided that such an important port of embarkation across the channel should be held by one of his leading ministers, Guy de Bryan. Joan obediently granted her rights to Guy.[21]

In 1341 Edward granted a charter, signed at the Tower of London, to the Mayor and Community of Dartmouth. In recognition of the loyalty of the burgesses, and the fact that they undertook to provide two ships of war of 120 tons burden with double the usual equipment for 40 days a year, he granted them a range of privileges. They could from amongst themselves elect their own mayor, who had to swear loyalty to the king, and preside over the borough court, which the townsmen were obliged to attend.[22]

They were to be free for ever from a range of tolls: keyage, strandage, anchorage and a dozen more obscure terms which were the dues payable to the Waterbaileywick. This was interpreted as applying only to the Freemen of the borough, from whom the mayor and bailiffs (the name given to the 12 leading burgesses) were chosen.

There was soon a dispute between the burgesses and Guy de Bryan as to their respective rights, since Guy claimed that these liberties infringed his lordship. In 1343 Guy was in Dartmouth and met the leading burgesses, John Gordon the mayor 'and William Bacon among them. A compromise was reached: Guy had the right to profits from rents, services, and breaches of the Assize of Bread and Ale, and could appoint a seneschal or steward to hear such cases. The mayor and bailiffs had the right to determine pleas about land transfers and disputes about possession in the borough. They agreed that the steward and the mayor together should hear all pleas. This agreement was ratified two months later in London by Guy, the mayor and 11 leading citizens who proved the seriousness of the matter by making this lengthy journey to defend the interests of the town.[23]

Sir Guy de Bryan was the son of a minor baron who owned land in Pembrokeshire and Devon.[24] He was the Lord of TorBryan, which still bears his name, and Slapton, where in 1373 he founded the chantry whose ruined tower can still be seen beside the *Tower Inn*. He lived from 1307-1390, and became a close friend of and devoted minister to Edward III, who was just a little younger than himself. He distinguished himself as a soldier fighting against the Scots and the French, and also at sea where he acted as admiral. He was used as an ambassador to the Pope, the French, the Count of Flanders, and to Genoa, among others. He was out of England for 20 out of the 40 years between 1340 and 1380. Even when in England, he was sent by the king to deal with the king's affairs wherever needed. He was made a Knight of the Garter in 1370, a rare honour, and became a very rich man. Bearing in mind that all journeys were on horseback, or by boat, the extent of his travels is astonishing, but he can seldom have had time to be in Dartmouth.

Sir Guy left no male heirs at his death in 1390, and John Holand, Earl of Huntingdon and builder of Dartington Hall, who was made guardian of his two grand-daughters, became the lord of Dartmouth until they came of age. However, 10 years later Holand was beheaded by Henry IV, his estates forfeit to the crown for treason. No more is heard of payments to a lord or his steward in the town. Nearly 200 years later in 1579 Sir Thomas Kitson tried to claim the right to collect dues and appoint a steward as the heir of the de Bryans. The Corporation resisted strongly and, after a long legal wrangle, in 1620 they bought from Kitson a formal conveyance of the lordship of the town. In effect, then, the borough was independent of any lord from 1400 onwards.[25]

The borough made two important gains during the next 150 years. A charter of 1393 from Richard II allowed them the right to choose a coroner, and one of 1463 from Edward IV allowed them to join Southtown to the borough. This was so that they could keep watch at Gallants Bower to guard against enemies.[26] The part they owned consisted only of a narrow strip east of Above Town to enable them to reach the mouth of the river where the castles were built. The manorial rights to the land still belonged to the Lord of Stoke Fleming, and it remained in that parish.

The lordship of Dartmouth had now been separated from that of Norton, which by 1346 passed to the Courtenay family, the Earls of Devon, who kept deer there but seldom lived in the manor as they had much land all over Devon.[27] In the 14th century, Edward Courtenay married Emmeline Dawnay, whose family held land in Goodrington and Brownstone, and the manor was afterwards known as Norton Dawnay down to the 19th century.

New Chapels for the Borough: St Clare's and St Saviour's

St Clare's Chapel

Already, by about 1230, the people of Dartmouth found the journey up to Townstal church arduous, and in 1235 there is the first of many references in a deed to 'the chapel of St Clarus' in Hardness.[28] Its name survives in the modern St Clair's Terrace, at the top of Browns Hill. It was dedicated to a Breton saint, called in the original Latin St Clarus, a masculine ending mistakenly written in later versions Clare or Clair. It was a small chapel with a cemetery attached, both being mentioned in numerous deeds. Its site has been established in the triangle of land formed where Browns Hill joins Clarence Hill. Many people must have preferred to bury their dead there rather than carry the bodies up the hill to Townstal church, and the chaplains would have offered prayers for the dead. Regular services such as mass, however, could only be held at Townstal.

From 1233 two chaplains are referred to in land grants, Thomas Ivon and Peter the Chaplain. Neither of these was the priest at Townstal, since he is always referred to as the 'vicar', not the chaplain. Priests were supposed to be celibate, but Thomas was described as the father of two daughters, Sabina and Ricarda, in deeds of 1290 which convey property received from him.[29]

The Story of St Saviour's

In 1286, when Edward I visited Dartmouth, the burgesses took the chance to petition the king for permission to build a church down by the waterside in Clifton, because of the 'very great fatigue of their bodies' in going up to the one at Townstal. William Bacon offered a site of an acre for the purpose. The Bacon family are first mentioned in documents of 1166, when Roger Bacon held two-thirds of a fee given him by the Lord of Townstal 'with my child'.[30] This suggests he married the lord's daughter, and would account for the fact that the Bacon family owned such a large area in a very small town. The family had remained prominent ever since, under the FitzStephens.

Edward granted their wish in a charter of 16 February 1286, in which Bacon was given a licence under the Statute of Mortmain (which prohibited gifts to religious houses) that he '*may* assign to the Convent of Torre' an acre of land in Clifton.[31] The charter gave the Abbot and Convent permission to 'build anew the parish church', but they were most reluctant to do so. The Canons did not want Townstal church to be replaced by another, which would drain money away from it. Consequently, since neither the Abbot of Torre nor the Bishop of Exeter would consent to the new church, the acre of land remained in Bacon's possession, and the people had to continue to climb up to Townstal.

By 1329 matters became desperate for the people of Dartmouth when the Vicar of Townstal was alleged to have committed suicide by drowning — a crime which the Bishop punished by placing the church and cemetery under an interdict for two years.[32] No services,

15. St Saviour's, Dartmouth, as it is today. Once the cemetery extended over the present road.

whether marriages, burials, christenings or masses could be held in the church. William Bacon, probably the son of the owner of the site in 1286, was given permission to have an oratory within his house in Dartmouth where a chaplain could celebrate secretly, behind closed doors, without the ringing of bells. This, however, did not help the rest of the people.

In June 1331, the Bishop of Exeter gave a licence to Torre Abbey to celebrate mass in the chapel of St Clare 'for aged and infirm parishioners'.[33] Clearly Torre Abbey which owned both St Clare's Chapel and St Clement's insisted that all young and fit parishioners should journey up to the mother church at Townstal.

The Augustinian Friars Build a Chapel

William Bacon was not satisfied with this. In 1331 he obtained a licence to give one acre of land in Clifton, Dartmouth, to two Friars of the Hermits of St Augustine on which to build an 'oratory and dwelling houses'.[34] Since Clifton was very small, it is unlikely that this was a different acre from the one already offered by his father in 1286 for the building of the church, which had not been started.

The Austin friars, as they were popularly called, must have immediately started to build on it as, later in the year, the bishop ordered proceedings to be taken against two men 'posing as priests' in a certain oratory or chapel at Dartmouth. Bacon was excommunicated for his pains, and only restored in 1334. In 1335, the bishop who had previously forbidden the friars to use the chapel 'newly built by them', relented and allowed them to do so. However, they were forbidden to hear confession or celebrate mass. Friars by tradition were preachers, but they were not supposed to compete with the usual parish clergy in saying mass.

The next obstacle to the chapel was that in 1340 Elena Cove, a widow, accused William Bacon, several other leading burgesses and the friars of unjustly depriving her of a house and half an acre of land in Clifton, Dartmouth. She won her case at the Exeter assizes, and her half acre was returned to her. The site of the chapel was thus reduced by half.

By 1344 the Austin friars were ordered by the Bishop of Exeter and the Court of Canterbury to demolish their chapel, which they had built on a site 'belonging to the Abbot and Convent of Torre'. They appealed to the Pope's court in Rome against this, but that too eventually declared their oratory illegal and imposed 'perpetual silence' on them. News of this decision, however, took some time to reach Devon: Rome was a long way away.

Brother Hugo Intervenes

The prayers of the burgesses seemed to be answered by the arrival in the town in March 1344 of a certain Brother Hugo, dressed as a layman, wearing a sword and buckler and at first saying he was an envoy of the king. When he was inside the Friars' chapel he dressed himself as a brother of their order. He took a staff in his hands, placed a mitre on his head, and caused all the parishioners to be summoned. He then told them he was the Bishop of Damascus sent to the very place of the Brethren by the Pope to consecrate their oratory, and that they had been successful in their appeal to Rome against the Convent of Torre. If Rome was a long way from Dartmouth, Damascus was even further. No one could dispute his claim, nor did anyone apparently want to.

After that he walked around the oratory and sprinkled water in a very convincing manner. He granted many indulgences, confirmed girls and boys, heard confessions, and absolved several who had been excommunicated for acts of violence in the town. He ended the day being invited to drink with William Smale, the Mayor, and William Bacon in their hall.

At a later enquiry into his actions, it was revealed that Hugo had in fact come from Cambridge and had never been near Damascus. He claimed that when a local bishop refused to consecrate the churches of their order, the Brethren had the privilege from the Pope to have them consecrated by any Catholic bishop. Hugo said he wore lay clothes on arrival because he was told that he would be attacked by the supporters of the Convent of Torre if they thought he was coming to consecrate the cemetery of the oratory. When he put on his priest's attire he was mistaken by a sailor for the Abbot of Torre who had come to expel the Brethren. The sailor struck him, and threatened to come with his friends and kill everyone in the town if Hugo did not at once grant him absolution, so in fear he did so.

Hugo was granted absolution after the enquiry, but his consecration of the chapel was never considered legal by Bishop Grandisson of Exeter, who continued at intervals to denounce the Austin friars. In 1352 he licensed the two Brothers John de Clyve and John of Bradford of the Hermits of St Augustine to celebrate mass and hear confessions 'anywhere in his diocese except in the parish of Townstal'. We hear no more of them in the town, and they may have been silenced.

The chapel, however, was not pulled down. It is referred to in deeds of 1351, and in 1356 a grant of land in Clifton was made to two men described as 'chaplains'.[35] John Clerk in 1363 bequeathed a silver mark 'to the fabric of the new church of Dartmouth'.[36] There seems little doubt that the church went on being used.

It was not until Bishop Brantyngham succeeded Grandisson that in 1370 a licence was given to the Mayor and Community of Dartmouth to celebrate in a chapel 'newly built to the honour of the Holy Trinity', on condition that the rights of the mother church at Townstal were respected.

The Charter of 1372

This was followed on 5 October 1372 by a formal charter between the Bishop, Abbot of Torre, Vicar of Townstal, and the Mayor and Corporation.[37] This said that 12 named members of the Corporation, described as 'parishioners', had presumed to build a certain chapel in Dartmouth without the licence of the Abbot or Vicar. They were now allowed to erect a chapel, with baptistry and cemetery, and to provide a chaplain, all at their own expense, but were to be under the control of the church at Townstal. The Vicar of Townstal could take the services if he wished, and all the parishioners were to honour the mother church once a year by attendance on the feast of St Mary Magdalene. On 13 October 1372 the bishop himself dedicated the chapel in honour of the Holy Trinity.

The named parishioners undertook for themselves and their successors to fulfil the obligations in the charter. It was not until the 19th century that the interests of the Corporation were seen not to be identical with those of the parishioners, and the seeds of much later conflict were sown.

The small chapel already existing is probably represented by the two pairs of columns at the west end of the nave with their pointed arches, which appear earlier in style. The two pairs of columns with arches to the east of them have clearly been joined on later, probably soon after 1372. In 1396, the Mayor and Corporation undertook to pay £5 a year towards the cost of the chaplain 'in order that the chapel might be enlarged'. This enlargement was the building of the chancel, and in 1400 another bishop, Stafford, licensed 'the chapel of St Mary, newly built at Dartmouth'.[38]

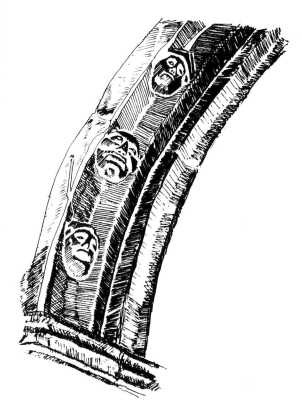

16. Carved heads, one wearing the cap of a canon of Torre.

The new chapel was known at first by the names of Holy Trinity and St Mary. By 1416 it was called St Saviour's, when Walter Thoreslegh and Agatha his wife asked in their will to be buried there,[39] but the name Holy Trinity was still used occasionally. The church of the Canons at Torre was also dedicated to St Saviour, and eventually this name became the one by which it is known today.

John Hawley, who was the most powerful man in Dartmouth during the 40 years when the church was being completed, was buried in the chancel in 1408, where his brass with his two wives on either hand is a fitting memorial (*see* plate 25). On the south side of the chancel is a stone sedilia, with seats for three priests and a stone piscina where they would have washed their hands.

There was already a bell tower and clock by 1430, when both are mentioned in the earliest churchwardens' accounts which survive. The clock did not have a face, but chimed the hours on a bell. It worked by a large stone weight hung by ropes from the clockwork mechanism. 'Organs' (in the plural) worked by bellows are referred to as being mended in 1433.[40] They were then in the west end of the chapel, near the bell tower. The transepts were built early in the 15th century. A chantry to St John the Baptist was founded in 1437 in the south transept, with an altar to St Anne in 1469.[41] A similar gild to St Nicholas lay in the north transept.

17. Piscina in the chancel.

The beautiful wooden screen dates from the last part of the 15th century, its patterns of ropes entwined with grapes, once painted, reflecting the importance of the seaborne wine trade to the merchants of the town (*see* plate 18). The unusual painted stone pulpit may date from the same period, and shows the head of a canon of Torre wearing his distinctive cap. Another carving of the head of a canon is on one of the arches in the nave (*see* Plates 16 and 86).

The font, which is very plain, is first mentioned in the churchwardens' accounts in 1434, but is probably as old as the earliest part of the church. The old wooden door, with its massive ironwork, looks to the writer to be the original one despite its date of 1631. The leopards and tree of life have a medieval style, and the leopard was the symbol of the Plantagenets in whose reigns the chapel was built. The date seems more likely to be that of the repair to the ironwork when the church was rebuilt in the 1630s. A smith was paid £3 6s. 2d. for his ironwork on the door, but there was no sum allocated for the substantial timber of the door itself.

Recently discovered near the pulpit during church restoration was the stone carving of a 15th-century priest in full vestments, sadly with his head broken off in a later act of vandalism. There were usually two assistant priests to the chaplain at this time, perhaps in training to succeed when a vacancy occurred, as happened in several cases in St Saviour's. Priests were given the title 'Sir', the equivalent of 'Reverend' today.

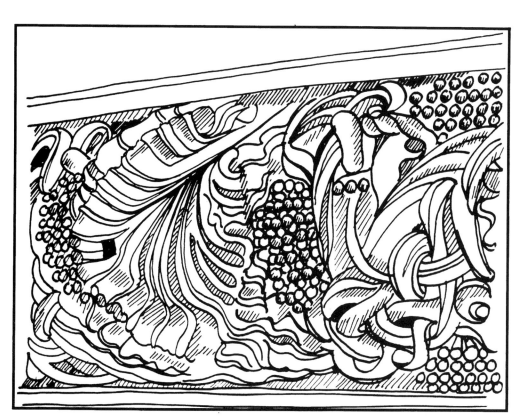

18. Grapes, ropes and shells
decorate the wooden screen.

19. Old door, St Saviour's.

Several documents tell us that the priests' house lay just to the north of the chapel of St Saviour, in the lane outside the cemetery.[42] They were next to the first Guildhall, which was in modern Anzac Street, on the site later to be known as the Palladium when it became one of the early cinemas. At one time there was a small first-floor room over the south porch which was referred to as the 'priest's chamber', and on one occasion was used as a place to isolate a sick person. The space seems too small to have been a dwelling house, but perhaps was used by the priest who was on duty for early or night services in the chapel.

During the 15th and early 16th centuries the people of Dartmouth showed their pride in the chapel by leaving it much money and property in their wills — to pay for prayers for their souls, for repairs to the building, for the priests' stipends or to give to the poor. Soon it possessed valuable church jewels, such as silver gilt crosses and chalices, and a silver ship.[43] Churchwardens were appointed to look after the church property, collect rents, and pay for repairs to houses and the chapel. Their accounts, which exist from 1430 onwards, cast great light on the way of life of the town.

The chapel down by the river must have drained wealth away from St Clement's, which became rather neglected. However, Townstal was regarded as one of the most important of Torre Abbey's possessions, and no less than three vicars of Townstal in the 14th and 15th centuries went on to be Abbots of Torre. The last abbot in 1531 prudently chose to become Vicar of Townstal before the dissolution, and held on to his job there with a tenacity worthy of the Vicar of Bray through the religious changes of Henry VIII, Edward VI and Mary, before dying in 1554.

St Clare's Chapel in later years

After the building and consecration of St Saviour's in 1372, the main purpose of the chapel of St Clare disappeared, and it gradually fell into disuse. Though it remained the property of Torre Abbey until the dissolution, references to its being used as a chapel cease during the 15th century. In 1545, when Henry VIII had acquired all Torre Abbey's lands, it is listed amongst many other properties granted to George Rolle and Nicholas Adams as 'the *house* lately called St Clare's Chapel in Hardness in the tenure of Richard Prideaux'. [44]

20. Brass of a 15th-century lady.

In 1586, the Corporation of Dartmouth bought all the lands of the Rectory of Townstal, including the chapel, and it remained in their hands until 1850. In a deed of 1675 the house was said to have been 'late and now converted into a horsemill'.[45] In 1775 a parish poorhouse was built on its site, part of which was used as a school in 1820. In 1850 this was demolished to build St Clair's Terrace. It is not true that the building lay on the north side of Clarence Hill, as Watkin suggested after finding some old stones there which looked as if they came from the chapel.[46] These are more easily explained as having been taken from the site of the chapel when building work started in 1850 and thrown on spare land across the way.

Chapter Four

Traders, Privateers and Pirates

The Shipmen of Dartmouth

> A Schipman was there dwelling far by Weste;
> For ought I wot he was of Dert-e-mouthe.

So wrote Geoffrey Chaucer in the prologue to the *Canterbury Tales*. He goes on to describe the 'schipman' as an unscrupulous character engaged in the Bordeaux wine trade, who not only stole wine from his merchant master but after fights at sea thought nothing of throwing enemy sailors overboard. However, his knowledge of seamanship was unrivalled:

> But of his craft to reckon well the tydes,
> His stormes and his dangers all besides,
> His harbour and his moone, his pilotage, There was none such from Hulle
> to Carthage.

Chaucer had visited Dartmouth in 1373 as a trusted customs official of Edward III, to enquire into the seizure by the mayor and bailiffs of a ship and cargo belonging to a merchant of Genoa with whom the king wished to remain friendly.[1] The name of the mayor in that year is not known, but among the leading burgesses whom he must have met was John Hawley, one of the 12 parishioners mentioned in St Saviour's charter of 1372 and mayor in 1375.

For this reason, many people have assumed that Hawley was the model for the shipman. It is more likely, however, that he was a composite character based on many tales about the lawlessness of Dartmouth seamen which had reached court circles over the years. Chaucer knew that those who heard his poems would associate the port with piracy. Hawley himself in 1373 was not known to have been involved in anything but honest trading.

Chaucer would have been more likely to have heard of the misdeeds of William Smale — who had entertained Bishop Hugo — who was accused in 1346 of having, with 13 ships, plundered a Spanish merchantman of its wine and thrown its sailors overboard.[2] Smale was ordered to return the goods, but only because the king had recently arranged a marriage alliance with Spain and wished to be friendly with that country. Smale did not change his ways: in 1361 his seamen were accused of boarding a ship with a cargo valued at £20,000, going from Brittany to Flanders, and killing the master and 100 mariners.[3]

There was, however, a distinction between piracy — robbing at sea purely for private profit — and privateering. In all the wars of the time, the king issued licences to ships to become privateers, who were encouraged to capture the merchant ships of the enemy. The king took a percentage of the profit and the rest was shared between the owners, captains and crews as a reward for risking their lives. It was a kind of self-financing royal navy, and at that time the only one. All the other countries did the same thing, so merchants had to arm themselves and be prepared to fight off attacks from enemies. When the king wanted ships for his wars, he commandeered merchant vessels. When choosing leaders for his navy, who better than the masters who had been successful in these unofficial battles? Needless to say, such men were regarded as local heroes.

Protests were only made when neutral ships were captured, as in the case of Chaucer's Genoese merchant. The accepted maritime law was that, if a master suspected a neutral ship of carrying goods for the enemy, he could demand to search it. If enemy goods were found, he could order the ship to be brought into a harbour and remove them. If an enemy ship carrying neutral goods was captured, the merchant could demand his goods back. If a ship refused to be searched, it was treated as an enemy, and if captured became a lawful prize whether carrying neutral goods or not. Most of the cases heard in English courts involved disputes over neutral ships or goods and, since the accused could often argue that they had acted within the law, they often took years to settle. Only if the king was very anxious to keep on friendly terms with the country of the merchant concerned were they likely to win restitution.[4]

The Hawley Family in Dartmouth

The John Hawley who must have met Chaucer in 1373 was the second of that name. His father is reputed to have come to the town from the small hamlet of Allaleigh, near Tuckenhay, and the name may be derived from there. The father and his wife Elizabeth had by 1344 begun to build a warehouse and quay on the Foss, just south of the millrace, to which their small fleet of cogs returned after their trading ventures.[5] It became known as 'Hawley's Haw' (or Hoe), and a rhyme of the day ran:

> Blow the wind high, or blow the wind low,
> It always blows safe to Hawley's Hoe.

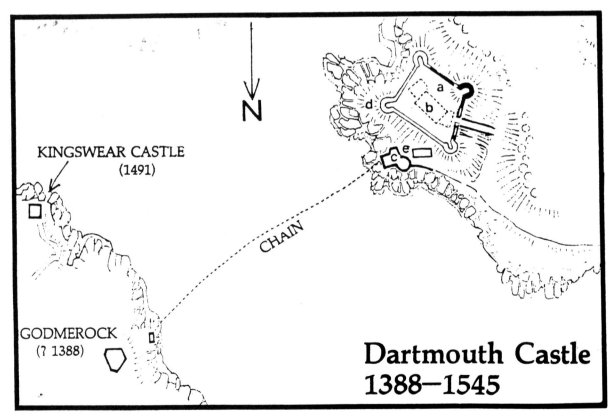

21. Plan of Dartmouth and Kingswear castles, showing the chain to Godmerock to prevent enemy ships entering the harbour. Letters correspond with the drawing opposite.

The first John Hawley never became mayor, though his name appears as witness on some borough deeds up to 1344. After that, no Hawleys are mentioned until 1372 when their son appears; he must then have been a young man about 30 years old. He was already a well-to-do merchant, one of the 12 leading burgesses. He remained active in town affairs from then on, serving as mayor 14 times before his death in 1408. His trading ventures were successful since he is listed in the poll tax return of 1377 as having four servants, the most belonging to any individual in the town. There were then 679 people over 14 years of age in Dartmouth and Southtown.[6]

In 1379, during his third term as mayor, John was granted a licence with Thomas Asshenden and Benedict de Bottesana to go to sea for a year with seven ships at their own expense to attack and destroy the king's enemies, the standard form of words for a privateer.[7] The war soon intensified, and in 1383 the 'men of Portsmouth and Dartmouth' destroyed a French fleet, slaying all but nine men. They later captured 1,500 casks of wine, sailed up the Seine, destroyed four ships and captured another four.[8]

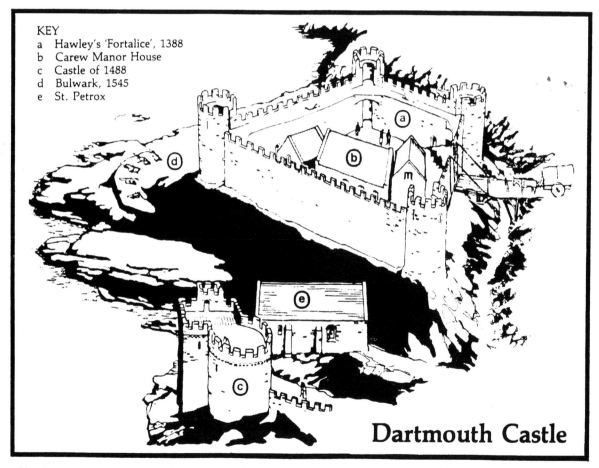

KEY
a   Hawley's 'Fortalice', 1388
b   Carew Manor House
c   Castle of 1488
d   Bulwark, 1545
e   St. Petrox

Dartmouth Castle

22. Imaginative view of Hawley's 'Fortalice' (1388) and the later castle of 1488, with the Carew's manor house inside the walls of the old castle.

In 1384 Hawley claimed to be the victim of an attack by Bretons, who were in theory the allies of England. Although he had papers giving him safe conduct from the Duke of Brittany, Hawley and Asshenden's ships were attacked in a Breton port, the goods taken, Hawley and the other seamen assaulted, and held to ransom. They appealed to the Duke for justice, but we do not know with what result.[9] This explains why Hawley had no love for the Bretons.

By 1386 Hawley was directing operations by a fleet of privateers who lay in wait off the coast of Brittany, attacking French and neutral shipping at will. He was often in trouble with King Richard: when he seized the cargo of a Zealand vessel he was ordered to restore the goods as its Duke, Albert, was a friend of the king.[10] However, he was not punished otherwise. In the thick of the war against the French, the capture of 32 Rochelle salt ships in one expedition by 'a Dartmouth owner', unnamed but probably Hawley, would have been regarded as a national success.[11] The French accused Hawley not only of piracy but of ravaging their coast, and as the tide of war turned in favour of France by the late 1380s there was well-grounded fear of French counter-attacks on the Devon coast.

The 'Fortalice' of Dartmouth

The government now looked to Hawley, again mayor in 1388, to organise the defence of the Dart. He was ordered to compel the burgesses, by force if need be, to build a 'fortalice' at the entrance to the port.[12] The town was granted the right to be the sole exporter of tin in 1390, possibly to provide revenues for the purpose.[13]

The 'fortalice' was the town's first castle, of which only one thick walled tower, part of its curtain wall, and a dry moat remain. Its likely appearance can be seen in plates 21 and 22. It was not finished by 1389, when a truce with France may have slowed the work, but it must have been ready by 1403 when war was renewed. On the Kingswear side a small fort called Godmerock was built, from which in time of danger a chain could be stretched across the river to keep out enemy ships. The site of the castle lay in the manor of Stoke Fleming, whose lords, the Carews, later built a manor house inside the curtain walls. Beside it lay St Petrox, which grew into the chapel used by the garrison, manor house, and people of Warfleet valley.

In 1402 John Corp, owner of much land in Southtown, was given a 'licence to crenellate' a house by the entrance to the port.[14] This is thought to have been Paradise Fort, on the north side of Warfleet creek, where a tower still stood until 1855. Corp was a leading figure in Dartmouth, appointed in 1393 Deputy Chief Butler, with the job of collecting the tax on wine for the king. He presided at his house — probably at Paradise — over a commission of inquiry in 1394 into charges brought against Hawley by the Bretons about his actions in 1386. Fifty-five seamen were brought as witnesses, who might be expected to support Hawley's defence.[15] There is no record of the decision in the case but, as Hawley continued to play his usual prominent part in the town affairs afterwards, one may assume he was acquitted.

There is a brass in Stoke Fleming church to a John Corp and what appears to be a young girl, Elyenore. The inscription in Norman French and Latin says that the girl died in 1391, and the man in 1361. It seems likely that the Corp who was a colleague of John Hawley had the monument erected to his father, John Corp the elder, who had died in 1361 and the girl Elyenore was his own daughter and heiress, the granddaughter of the elder John. The younger John took an active part in the affairs of the port and was M.P. twice in 1411 and 1413.

Meanwhile Hawley between 1388 and 1401 served as mayor nine times and as M.P. twice, which would have involved going to Westminster. He not only supervised the building of the castle, but was actively concerned with the enlargement of St Saviour's church. He

3. Paradise Fort, Warfleet Creek, in 1830. John Corp was given 'licence to crenellate' his house there in 1402. The house on the quay, left, was built by Nicholas Roope in about 1600.

4. Brass of John Corp (d.1361) and his grand-daughter Elyenore (d.1391), placed in Stoke Fleming church by John Corp the younger, father of Elyenore.

also had considerable business and family interests in the west country. In 1389 he began to buy from the crown the estates at Tresilian, Cornwall, and in the Scilly Isles of Robert Tresilian who was executed for treason in 1388. These included some tin works whose value would be increasing with the needs of war. In 1402 he was granted the custody of the lands of Elizabeth Tresilian, which had passed to the king's wardship because of the 'idiocy' of Elizabeth.[16] He must have been obliged to visit these estates while, during the same period, acting repeatedly as mayor of the town. In spite of all this, his most active days were still to come.

Renewed War with France: The Battle of Blackpool
Already by 1400 the truce was crumbling. Henry IV had deposed and murdered Richard II, which had angered the French as Richard's wife was a French princess. In the preparations for renewed war, Hawley, despite his age, was made deputy lieutenant to the Admiral of England for a time, and ordered to send ships to Southampton.[17]

However, he was soon in trouble with Henry for having seized and taken to Dartmouth a Flemish ship carrying a valuable cargo. The king was just negotiating a truce with Flanders, and Hawley was ordered to return both ship and cargo. He in fact only released the ship and crew, keeping the cargo until further irate demands arrived from the king. Even after the truce was signed, Hawley was included with other privateers in March and April of 1403 in a series of raids on Flemish and Dutch shipping, which prompted the Count of Flanders to retaliate by seizing English merchandise worth £10,000 in Flemish harbours. Henry ordered Hawley and 17 other privateers to be at Calais in person to answer charges against them, but all seem to have ignored the summons.[18]

In August 1403, claiming to be retaliating for many English attacks on their coast and shipping, the Bretons under their leader William du Chatel attacked Plymouth by night and burned the town. The king had to postpone his legal actions: instead, Hawley, John Corp and Edmund Arnold of Dartmouth were immediately commissioned to make war on the Bretons[19] and, with Dartmouth the most likely next target of attack, there must have been frenzied preparations to arm and equip the new fortalice to resist.

Hawley was made joint captain with Thomas Norton of Bristol of a fleet of west-country ships which in the autumn of 1403 captured seven merchant vessels from Spain, Lombardy and Flanders — all neutral countries — and carried them back to Dartmouth and Plymouth with their valuable cargoes. They had again angered the king who ordered them in the spring of 1404 to return the plundered goods.[20]

They had still not done so when the expected attack from the Bretons came in April 1404. Du Chatel with 300 ships, 2,000 knights and full supporting crossbowmen landed at Slapton, hoping to take Dartmouth from the rear. Hawley despatched an army to meet him, while he defended the castle against a possible sea attack. Some of Du Chatel's army had deserted to plunder some passing Spanish ships, so that when the two sides met at Blackpool, with a high tide swelling the stream between them which the English had fortified into a strong defensive position, he was without his usual screen of crossbowmen to defend his knights. Taunted by one of his knights for showing cowardice when he at first hesitated, Du Chatel determined to show his valour and attack none the less. In the hail of arrows and stones from the English side many of his knights were killed; some drowned when their armour dragged them down as they crossed the stream. One English chronicler records that women and peasants fought in their army. Du Chatel was mortally wounded after a heroic struggle, 25 high-ranking prisoners taken and those who were not killed fled. This defeat of a trained army by a collection of ill-equipped countrymen, none of them knights — for though Dartmouth men were renowned for fighting at sea, they had never before fought as a land army — astonished the Court in London, and Henry IV ordered a *Te Deum* in Westminster Abbey.[21]

Hawley superintended the ransoming of prisoners, a chance to make money for a good businessman. Du Chatel's brother wrote to Hawley begging for the return of his body and effects.[22] The king claimed a half share in two of the prisoners, and summoned Hawley to meet him to answer for them. In reply, we have the only surviving letter written by Hawley himself, in which he begs to be excused from coming in person, for 'I have been suffering from so severe a disorder on one of my legs for more than a month that I cannot ride, and am not well able to walk'.[23] He may have had gout, a common disease at the time. On the other hand, he may have been glad of an excuse not to meet the king when he had ignored so many of his orders to return captured cargoes to their owners.

25. Brass of John Hawley and his wives Joanna and Alicia, in the chancel of St Saviour's.

26. Hawley's house in Higher Street, second left, which was the Guildhall from 1494-1864, from a painting by Miss E. Hunt, 1839.

Hawley was still organising more privateering raids in 1405. The king now threatened the arrest of those who refused to obey his orders, with the confiscation of goods if they refused to release merchandise wrongfully taken. Hawley was in December 1406 imprisoned in the Tower of London, and kept there until he guaranteed to make restitution to some merchants of Barcelona, under a penalty of £10,000. Three west countrymen stood surety for him for £3,000, and he was allowed to leave the court. [24]

Even in the last year of his life, Hawley is listed among a group of shipowners who had captured 17 ships, contrary to treaty. Edward Courtenay, Lord of Norton, and John Corp were among those commissioners appointed to look into the charges. The impartiality of these commissioners may be guessed from the fact that John Corp in the same year was himself charged as part owner of a ship which had captured a Flemish vessel. [25] It would have been difficult for the government to find anyone local to judge these cases who was not himself guilty of similar offences.

John Hawley died in 1408 and was buried in the chancel of St Saviour's where his brass shows him in knight's armour, his two wives Joan and Alice on either side. Both had died before him. His son by Joan, John Hawley III, had been in the service of the king since 1395, while sharing in his father's business as merchant, landowner and privateer. He was many times M.P. for Dartmouth, often like his father accused of piracy but equally often asked to investigate the offences of others. In 1434 he went on a pilgrimage to St James of Compostella — it was by now a regular business in Dartmouth and Kingswear to provide transport for pilgrims — and he died in 1436. His son Nicholas did not long outlive him, dying in 1442 without children. Nicholas' sister Elizabeth, wife of John Copleston, inherited all the Hawley properties in Dartmouth and Cornwall. [26]

The Hawley family home in Dartmouth was a fine timbered house between Higher and Lower Street, where John's family went on living after his death. The Copleston family lived in Hawley's house for three generations, but some time before 1494 it was sold to the burgesses for a guildhall, replacing the first one which lay to the north of St Saviour's. It remained in use for this purpose for nearly 400 years, until pulled down for road widening in 1864. [27]

Hawley, then, was associated with the three finest buildings of medieval Dartmouth: St Saviour's, the first castle, and the Guildhall. Controversy will always reign about whether he was a privateer or a pirate, but in the midst of war few rules were kept, and saintly characters were rare on either side of the Channel.

The Exploits of Robert Wenyngton

Hawley was neither the first nor the last of the medieval shipmen of Dartmouth. Of the many privateers who continued in his tradition, the most notable in the 15th century was Robert Wenyngton. He was an important burgess, first mentioned in 1437, and was among those who signed the land documents of the town by 1438. [28] He and his wife Joanna bought 'an empty piece of land' on the east side of Lower Street, adjacent to the river, where they built a house by joining onto the wall of the one to the north, with the permission of the owners, the Bolt family. It probably stood on the site now occupied by Hawley Road.

In 1445 the Sheriffs of Devon and Cornwall headed a commission to enquire whether Wenyngton, among several others, had taken a ship sent by the king's French aunt to England, laden with wine, iron and other goods. They were accused of disposing of the cargo and beating up and killing some of the crew. [29] Only the charge survives, not the verdict. He must have been acquitted, however, as in a letter of 1449 to the Earl of Devon the king described him as 'my beloved squire Robert Wenyngton', which he would hardly have done if he still thought Wenyngton was guilty of robbing his aunt. [30]

Wenyngton during the next two years acted as town bailiff, witness to land transfers, in 1448 as mayor and in February 1449 as one of the town's M.P.s.[31] In April 1449 he was given a commission, with two prominent men of Kent who later became sheriffs of that county, to 'serve the king at sea' and 'clear the sea of pirates': there could be no greater sign of the king's trust in his abilities.[32]

He can have wasted no time in getting a fleet together, for six weeks later he wrote a long letter to Thomas Daniel, one of the king's ministers, describing a great naval engagement. First, his ships had taken two large ships of Brest which were coming out of Flanders. Expecting retaliation from the Bretons, he and his fleet lay in wait at sea to meet them. Instead, they saw a fleet of 100 great ships of Prussia, Lubeck, Holland, Flanders and other neutral states. Wenyngton came aboard the admiral's ship and ordered him to strike his sail in the name of the king of England — presumably demanding the right to search for enemy goods. The admiral refused: when Wenyngton threatened to oversail them he told him to 'do his worst' since the English ships were so small and few in number he did not fear them.

As the wind was in Wenyngton's favour, his lighter ships could sail faster and a fierce battle began. Wenyngton reported that they 'shot at us a thousand guns and iron crossbow shots without number', killing and wounding many of his company. The reference to guns is of interest. These were relatively new weapons in those days, and seldom used at sea since they were so large and cumbersome in the confined space of merchant vessels. Despite this, with a good wind, Wenyngton's fleet managed to oversail them. The next day the admiral sent a boat with a flag of truce, offering to give his vessels up, and agreeing to go with the English into whatever port they liked. Wenyngton then escorted them into the harbour of Wight, and claimed to have made the greatest capture for a century. His letter was to ask the king's Council urgently to send someone to tell him what to do with them. He claimed that the men of the captured fleet had done £2,000 worth of damages, and he 'was advised' to 'drown them and slay them' unless they had orders otherwise.[33]

Because they had refused to be searched, and had fought and inflicted great damage on his fleet, Wenyngton was by the laws of the day within his rights to threaten this action, but he was probably wanting to force the Council to agree to his taking compensation in goods and ships rather than exacting such a ruthless revenge. England was at that time losing the war in France, about to be driven from nearly all her land there, and the government may not have welcomed an action which would anger a group of neutral trading countries with whom they wished to do business in future. They would have been unlikely to agree to the wholesale slaughter of the seamen. Two years later they had to pay the Duke of Burgundy £4,666 in compensation for losses caused by Wenyngton's fleets.

England's failures in the wars were largely because Henry VI was mentally unable to govern, and rival groups of powerful nobles were battling for political power. No sooner had peace been made with France, at the price of losing all England's French possessions except Calais, than the country slid into the chaos of civil war known as the Wars of the Roses. One unpopular minister, the Duke of Suffolk, was impeached by the House of Commons in 1450 and fled overseas. His ship was stopped by one under the command of 'Robert of Caen', who seized and beheaded Suffolk. The patent roll entry of 1451 in connection with the compensation to Burgundy says that Robert of Caen was an alias for Wenyngton, who if so was the murderer of Suffolk.[34]

Despite his involvement in both these incidents, Wenyngton continued to be a leader in town affairs. In a second Parliament of 1449 he was one of the two members sent by Dartmouth to Westminster. He was made one of the two receivers of customs dues in Exeter and Dartmouth in 1455, a post of some trust in the gift of the government. He was mayor once more in 1456-7, when he was involved in negotiating an agreement with the city of St Malo about ransoms for masters and seamen taken in war.[35]

In the bloody power struggle for the crown between the rival houses of York and Lancaster, Dartmouth seems to have supported the Yorkists. After Edward IV, the Yorkist candidate, seized the throne in 1461, he awarded Wenyngton in the next year £10 annually out of the Exeter and Dartmouth customs dues, the equivalent of a pension in those days. This is the last we hear of Robert, who was dead by 1466.[36]

Chapter Five

Everyday Life in Town and Village

The Search for Medieval Dartmouth

Medieval Dartmouth lies around us and in some cases underneath our feet, but with a little imagination it is possible to re-create it. Much of today's town has been reclaimed from the sea over the centuries. As recently as 1985-7 another six metres was added to the embankment which was itself part of a 19th-century reclamation (*see* endpaper map). Therefore to understand the medieval town it is necessary mentally to wipe out about two-thirds of the modern one.

In the Middle Ages it consisted of two small townships on either side of a deep tidal creek, Hardness to the north and Clifton to the south, the water reaching west as far as Ford. Paths on the line of modern North Ford and South Ford roads led to this first crossing place. Undercliff would then have been on the edge of the water, which covered all the present town centre including the market place, Victoria Road, Foss Street, and the main car park. Clifton clung to the edge of the cliffs to the south of the creek, along the original shoreline, which was to the east of the present Lower Street.

The ancient route into the town from Totnes was on the line of the modern road from Norton until the junction with Yorke Road, when it followed what now survives as a footpath to Pathfields and Townstal churchyard. From there the route was along Church Road, and straight down by the shortest descent along Mount Boone and Ridge Hill to the river at Hardness. A right fork followed a lower contour on the south side, today Clarence Hill leading into Clarence Street, while a further right fork descended even more steeply as Browns Hill Steps. All these roads were too steep for wheeled vehicles, and until the building of Victoria Road after 1823 all inland transport was by packhorse.

Ridge Hill and Clarence Street joined up again by the river at Hardness, the suffix 'ness' meaning a headland, while 'hard' meant to sailors a firm beach, useful for repairing and building boats. Today at this point there is a public house called the *Ship in Dock*, which up to the 1930s used to look over small shipbuilding yards on the edge of another small creek, called Coombe Mud, since filled in to form Coronation Park. From medieval times onwards ships were built not only facing Coombe, but also on the south side of Hardness, now filled in to form Mayor's Avenue.

The two parts of the town were joined by 1243 when the Foss (dam) was built across the creek to harness the power of the tide to drive a mill (*see* plate 59).[1] This has given its name to Foss Street. The building must have caused the slow silting up of the mill pool to the west, as well as of the main river to the east. John Hawley's parents built a warehouse on the east side of the Foss in 1344, by which time a second mill had been built there.[2] The Foss soon became a short cut from Hardness to Clifton, saving the long walk round by Ford.

South from Foss Street the main path led past the first Guildhall and the priests' house towards St Saviour's church, one of the few buildings to survive from the 14th century. It stands on a little hill, and for many years after it was built the churchyard wall on the east was close enough to the sea for boats to tie up to it. In the lanes around the church, modern Church Lane and Church Close, were small houses whose foundations lie buried under the present buildings. The cemetery was once much larger than it is today: on several occasions when the road has been dug up to lay pipes to the west of the church human skeletons were

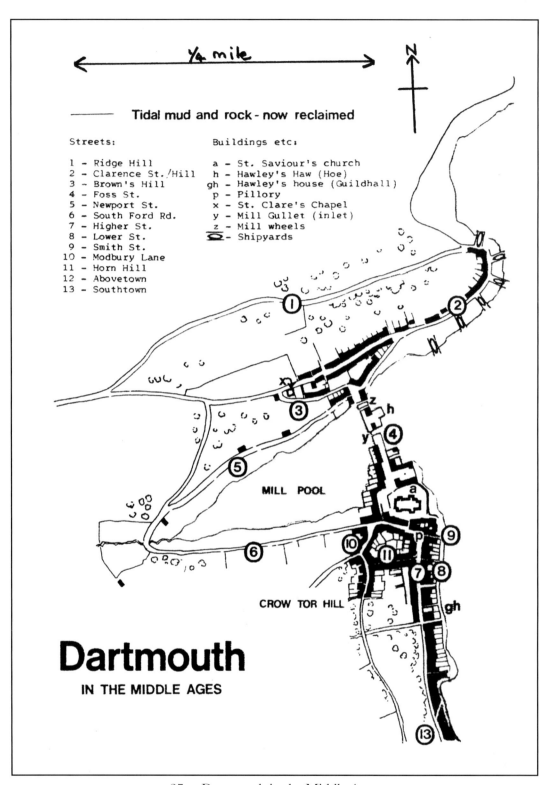

¼ mile

N

—— Tidal mud and rock - now reclaimed

Streets: Buildings etc:

1 - Ridge Hill   a - St. Saviour's church
2 - Clarence St./Hill   h - Hawley's Haw (Hoe)
3 - Brown's Hill   gh - Hawley's house (Guildhall)
4 - Foss St.   p - Pillory
5 - Newport St.   x - St. Clare's Chapel
6 - South Ford Rd.   y - Mill Gullet (inlet)
7 - Higher St.   z - Mill wheels
8 - Lower St.   - Shipyards
9 - Smith St.
10 - Modbury Lane
11 - Horn Hill
12 - Abovetown
13 - Southtown

MILL POOL

CROW TOR HILL

Dartmouth

IN THE MIDDLE AGES

27.   Dartmouth in the Middle Ages

found. The old path led through the cemetery, round the church, past the present *Seven Stars Inn* and under an archway to Higher Street. This archway once had living quarters above it, and was only taken down in the 19th century.[3]

Here, where Smith Street joined Higher Street and Lower Street, was the commercial heart of Clifton, and the most prestigious place to live in the 14th century (*see* plate 28). In 1358 William Bacon lived on the south side of the corner where Smith Street joined Lower Street, opposite a quay there, now gone.[4] There were shops, a market, breweries, bakers, butchers and craftsmen including Geoffrey the Goldsmith who lived here in 1310 and is thought to have given his name to the street.[5] Here stood the pillory, and the stocks — a warning to dishonest tradesmen — and in the churchyard was the cucking stool. The culprit was in this case tied to a chair suspended on the end of a mast, which was swung out over the churchyard wall and ducked into the sea at high tide.

28. Drawing of the Shambles and pillory, by William Henley.

29. Map orientated to correspond with
Plate 28, showing the medieval and
modern names of the three main streets of
Clifton-Dartmouth. The names of the
owners of the numbered houses, according
to 14th-century leases, were:

❶ Elena Glour. Demolished in the 1860s.
❷ John Rurde. Now on the corner with
Smith Street.

❸ Roger Pole. Now the Job Centre.
❹ Fourteenth-century owner unknown,
now the Cherub.

The roads in the earliest documents are
not given their present names, but were all
called 'the King's way' or street, though
there was always some description which
enables us to identify them. For instance, in
1308 Elena Glour granted to Richard and
Margery Gyllot a house described as:

> Between the King's way next the sea on the
> east, the King's way in which the pillory is
> situated on the west, the house of John Rurde
> on the south, and the way which leads from
> the sea towards the King's way on the north.[6]

This enables us to identify the house as
the left hand one of the three shown in plate
28, a corner house between Lower Street,
Higher Street, and what was known until
the 19th century as Pillory Lane. It was
pulled down to widen the bottom of Smith
Street, but the foundations could be seen
under the road during recent excavations to
renew the town's sewers.

By the 15th century, the current names
were in use. Higher Street was literally
above Lower Street, connected to it only by
steps until the later 19th century. Houses
might be entered from the ground floor on
Lower Street, and from the first floor in
Higher Street. Lower Street ran along the
edge of the sea, but by the 14th century plots
of land began to be leased using the phrase
'with as much as can be protected from the
sea' on the east side.[7] The lessees had to
reclaim the site of their house by throwing
rocks and rubble into the river until they
had raised it above the high-tide level. When
they had done so, they had a useful quay to
which they could bring their boats, so this
soon became popular with merchants.

Higher and Lower Streets continued
roughly parallel to Bayards Cove, then
known as Bearscove, a small sandy inlet
whose quay had not yet been built. Bayards Hill led up from the cove to Southtown, while
running parallel higher up the hill was Above Town. For those coming into Clifton from
Townstal, the way was along Waterpool Lane and down the steeply-sloping Crowthers
Hill.

Dartmouth was fortunate in having a good water supply, which came cascading down
the hills in streams. Pynnes Lane (now Horn Hill) was originally a watercourse, later
forced underground, and led to a conduit in Higher Street which can still be seen. The
convenience of having fresh water attracted some brewers to build their houses beside it.[8]
Two more conduits, both still there, served Crowthers Hill, at its junctions with Above

30. Higher Street looking south, in a 19th-century painting. From the left the buildings are now the Office Equipment Shop, the Chantry Bookshop, and the Cherub. On the right a boy is collecting water from the conduit which once stood there. All the houses on this side have since been demolished.

31. Foss Street looking towards St Saviour's church, from a 19th-century painting. The pillars leading to the Flavel church, built in the 18th century, can be seen on the left.

Town and South Ford Road. Both are shown on John Roope's map of the town drawn in 1619 (*see* plate 43), as is another one just north of the church. Many others can still be seen around the town. People collected their water from these conduits in buckets up to the beginning of the 20th century, as some still living can well remember.

Although much has been demolished, a few houses remain to show what medieval Dartmouth was like. The best preserved group is on the east side of Higher Street, from where it joins Smith Street south to the 'Cherub', which leans jettying out in a top-heavy way towards the shop opposite which once also had overhanging upper floors since cut back. Here one can see the narrowness of the original Higher Street, which once continued at this width southwards. Until 1925, a continuous row of 14th-century houses survived on both sides of the road (*see* plate 107).

The 'Tudor House', now the Job Centre, was rebuilt in the 16th century on the site of a medieval house for which leases survive back to the 14th century, as they do for the other houses in the block. When owners of the 'Cherub' stripped off the plaster which still covered its walls until 1960 they uncovered a rare 14th-century window along with the superb timberwork of the frame and ceilings. At the time the building was condemned to demolition: all similar structures on the other side of the road had already gone, destroyed not by bombs but by the local Council and local inertia.

Further south along Higher Street once stood Hawley's house, later the Guildhall, which stretched down to Lower Street. It is shown in a painting of 1839 (*see* plate 26), by which time it was already in decay, and it was demolished to make Newcomen Road in 1864.

Originally Lower Street contained some of the best merchants' houses, convenient because they could build warehouses backing on to the river into which their ships could unload their cargoes. Thomas Asshenden, a fellow-privateer with Hawley, lived in one such house on the site now occupied by the Masonic Hall. Deeds survive which call it 'Asshenden's Place' up until the 17th century, after which an even bigger house was built on the site by the Hayne family.[9] Robert Wenyngton, as already mentioned, built a new house and quay further north, probably on the site of the present Hawley Road.[10] Most of these old houses had to be demolished at the same time as the Guildhall to widen the road. The Harbour Bookshop and the Scarlet Geranium Restaurant are among the few which escaped.

Another was Agincourt House, fronting on to the last part of Lower Street to retain its medieval width. While the outside has been rebuilt, the inside, now an antiques shop, shows the layout of a merchant's house with an internal courtyard separating the living and shop area from the kitchen quarters at the back. Looking north from here along Lower Street to the Harbour Bookshop, one can imagine the line of the original Lower Street on the west side.

32. Agincourt House, Lower Street, a 14th-century house with an internal courtyard.

The churchwardens' accounts, which record money spent on the increasing number of properties given to the church, tell us that houses were built of stone side walls, with upper floors and fronts of timber, often slate hung, sometimes tarred and daubed. Roofs were slated, never thatched, which enabled the town to escape the terrible fires which often destroyed other medieval towns. Windows and chimneys — relative luxuries — were beginning to appear by the end of the 15th century. Chimneys, always of stone or brick, enabled upper floors to be added to single-storey dwellings. Building land was always scarce, so more people could be housed on the same site. We can picture the contents of a modest town house from the valuation of William Lee's goods in 1498.[11] His household goods included a table, two forms, one plank, one old carpet, a little table, one cupboard, the hangings (curtains) of the parlour, one coffer, three old cushions, one bedstead, one flock bed, two feather beds, three bolsters, three pillows and three candlesticks, as well as various pots, pans, ewers and basins. From the way the list is written, room by room, he seems to have had a dining room, parlour, and two bedrooms, one containing two beds, and a kitchen.

Keeping the Peace

In the countryside around the Dart valley, most of the people earned their living by farming and fishing, and had to share responsibility for law and order in their village or tithing. The system of frankpledge meant that all males over 12 years of age swore to keep the peace themselves and to keep an eye on neighbours. If one of the community committed a crime, the whole vill was punished, so it was in everyone's interest to catch the criminal.

We tend to imagine that people in these times were more law-abiding than those today, but that was not the case. In 1238, the cases brought before the travelling judges of the Devon Eyre, which dealt with serious crimes, included 10 murders for the hundred of Coleridge alone, as well as five sudden deaths which might have been accidents.[12]

Some examples of the crimes are of interest. Millers seem particularly prone to violence, to judge by this sample. Roger the Miller in Dartmouth burnt his own house, together with his wife and three children, and fled. He was outlawed. Dartmouth was held responsible and fined. He had no chattels — presumably all had gone up in flames — or they would have been confiscated. William the Miller, also of Dartmouth tithing, killed William the Baker and fled, leaving the town to be fined for his crime as well as,.presumably, being for the moment short of millers. Gilbert the Miller of Dittisham was outlawed for the death of William the Smith of Cornworthy, on the evidence of his wife Helen, so his village was fined. He had chattels worth 4s. 2d. which were confiscated.

Guy the Tailor, who lived in Ashprington, fled and took refuge in the church of Harberton, where he confessed to having killed a man in Somerset. By taking sanctuary in a church and confessing, he escaped being handed over for trial, but he was forced to leave the country on pain of execution if he returned. However, Ashprington was fined for not catching him first, and Harberton for failing to present the case to the county court earlier.

Thomas the Chaplain of Ashprington had killed a man and fled, so he was declared an outlaw, and his chattels worth 32d. were confiscated. Totnes, which was held responsible for him since the Priory there appointed the chaplain, was fined.

The early medieval records of the courts of Dartmouth no longer exist, but one case of murder is recorded. In 1390 the mayor, Richard Henry, was summoned before a court to account for his having executed a woman, Denys Beaumont, by burning instead of the usual method of hanging. The jury found that Denys had been guilty of poisoning her husband, and the mayor was pardoned after saying that he believed the borough's privileges gave him the right to have her burnt to death.[13] Criminals were hanged at Deadman's Cross, where Waterpool Lane crosses the present Yorke Road, and their bodies left to hang in chains to frighten other evil doers.

Where there was a dispute over the rightful ownership of land, it was decided as late as the 13th century by a duel fought between the rival claimants. One such case is recorded in East Cornworthy between disputing heirs of Judhael of Totnes. Roger de Nonant had inherited part of Judhael's lands, while the other part had gone to the Cantiloupe family, four of whose members were now headed by Milisent, daughter of William de Cantiloupe. Both sides however claimed various lands in East Cornworthy. The claimants, if women, could appoint a champion to fight for them. A duel was fought before the court at Westminster, after which Roger acknowledged the right of Milisent and her three relatives to the lands. The winners then paid Roger 400 silver marks for them.[14]

The port of Dartmouth must have attracted many villagers to move there in search of better wages as overseas trade flourished. As early as 1332, when a subsidy was demanded by the government on 'movable goods', which would include merchandise, it is noticeable that of all the people who had to pay the largest amounts, ten shillings and over, nine lived in Dartmouth and Southtown, one in Kingswear, four in Totnes, one in Cornworthy, and there were none in any of other surrounding villages.[15] No doubt those wishing to escape from the bare subsistence level of their village holdings could easily have found jobs as seamen on one of the many ships, and hope to win a share in prize money. However, to become a freeman and be eligible for such privileges as not having to pay petty customs to the Duchy of Cornwall, a man had to be elected by the mayor and burgesses.

Most of the laws of the borough were designed to ensure that unscrupulous tradesmen did not cheat the people or damage their health by selling rotten food. A miller was only allowed to keep three hens and a cock — to prevent his feeding his clients' grain to large numbers of poultry. If he gave short weight he was fined for the first two offences, but for the third he was put in the pillory. A brewer who sold ale short measure was fined twice, then ducked in the cuckingstool and put in the pillory soaking wet. A fishmonger who sold infected fish was fined twice, then put in the stocks. A cook had to sell no meat or flesh 'but it be good and wholesome for man', and must not bake any meat twice, or suffer the same penalties. An innkeeper was fined not only if he overcharged, but if he allowed his premises to be used as a brothel. For this, he was threatened not only with the pillory but afterwards would be expelled from the town. Taverners — who sold wine, not beer — had to have their measures checked and wares tasted by officers of the town, as well as the price fixed. They were forbidden to make their own wine, presumably to prevent mixing with the more costly imported variety.[16]

Breaches of the town's laws were dealt with in the regular mayor's court, held in the Guildhall, where all the free tenants were obliged to attend if required, or pay a fine, usually 4d. A Jury of Presentment was chosen, whose job was to make a list of alleged misdeeds.[17] The majority were concerned with keeping the streets clear of dung, a problem when everyone was responsible for dealing with his own and that of his animals. Most people kept a pig or two, chickens, and possibly a horse, and there were frequent complaints from neighbours such as: '1496 Johanna Jaket keeps a dunghill before the Brewhouse in Pynnes Lane'. When beer was the main drink even for children, no one wanted it to be polluted.

Another cause of complaint was of doing the washing at the town's public conduits. This was strictly forbidden, for fear of infecting the water supply. The place for washing was at the Ford, where there was a good spring of water and a field adjoining for drying and bleaching clothes in the sun.

The jury often accused the officials of not enforcing their own rules: 'the bakers are not making bread according to the statute' or 'the tapsters sell beer with measures unstamped'. They were accused of not providing a cucking stool on one occasion.

Some offences have no modern equivalents: the wife of Richard Stone was accused at various times of being a 'common scold', a 'common listener at windows' and a 'common gossip'. On another occasion, the brewers of Stoke Fleming were accused of bringing 'apple beer' (cider) into the town. Dartmouth, it seemed, allowed only beer and wine to be sold.

The prices of necessities were controlled by the Corporation, and there were penalties for 'regrating', that is, profiteering in times of shortage.

Diseases and Medicine

Other entries from the borough court accounts tell us about the medical services of the time, such as they were. A barber, John Cole, must have combined his trade with surgery since he complains he has not been paid by John Wells for 'healing and curing' John's wife's breast and John's knee, for which he was due 16s. 8d.[18] Another early medical man was Robert Savery, who sued the blacksmith Thomas Harry for 'so injuring his horse, value 30s., that it had to be destroyed, besides the great charge and cost of his leech craft, amounting to 13s.'.[19] Savery clearly needed a horse to do his round among the local villages as well as in the town, carrying his leeches with him.

Plague was brought to England at the time of the Black Death in 1348-9, and thereafter remained endemic with outbreaks every few years. As no parish registers go back this far, we cannot be sure how many died, but it is estimated that the population over the whole country was reduced by one third. We know that the vicar of Townstal died in 1349, and two new vicars were appointed to Stoke Gabriel in that year. Priests who ministered to the sick and dying were clearly likely to be infected. As a port frequently visited by ships coming from France and the Mediterranean where the disease broke out earlier, Dartmouth is likely to have suffered severely. It seems from the records that the mayor, Ralph Brewer, took over early that year, perhaps because his predecessor had died.[20]

Leprosy was another dread disease, also spread by traders, and the nearest leper hospital was at Totnes where the House of St Mary Magdalene had been founded to take up to 11 people. There are records of Dartmouth lepers being sent there at the expense of the borough as late as 1617. Charitable people often left money to the hospital in their wills, as did Walter and Agatha Thoresleigh in 1416.[21]

Work and Wages

Evidence of wages begins with the churchwardens' accounts from 1430, mainly for the building trades.[22] An experienced craftsman could earn 10d. a day, and he was usually assisted by a boy learner who earned 4d. or less. In 1441 a carpenter was paid only 8d. a day plus his 'beer and meat' which were reckoned to be worth the extra 2d. Some workmen were paid a piece rate: for instance, a mason mending the cemetery wall was paid 12d. a perch (5½ yards). Various women were paid 2s. a year for washing the church linen, and a penny each for mending three surplices.

Surnames often reflected the occupation of the worker. In 1438 Henry Clockmaker was paid 12d. for moving the clock from one bell tower to another. Another skilled craftsman was John Glover who in 1443 was paid 4d. for a calfskin for covering a book used in the church. Richard Goldsmith was paid 15d. in 1496 for 'mending the Cross, and for silver upon St Saviour's foot', perhaps a statue in the church.

Enjoyments

As already mentioned, there was an organ in St Saviour's by 1433, and music must have accompanied the miracle plays which were performed in the church. There is a payment to 'George, for painting the clothes for the play on Easter Day'. These plays were one of the earliest forms of English drama, and helped both to teach people the bible stories and to entertain them. A rare example of 15th-century musical notation appears in the form of the 'Dartmouth Magnificat', on the front of a court book (*see* plate 35).

Holy days such as Christmas, Easter, Whitsuntide and various saints' days were the only holidays people enjoyed, apart from Sundays. In most villages and towns men devoted their Sundays, after church, to practising archery, wrestling, fighting with staves and other manly sports by which they kept fit in case they should be called upon to fight against an enemy.

The weekly market was an occasion when villagers and townspeople met to buy and sell their wares. A port where returning seamen might bring foreign luxuries as well as foreign news would be a great attraction. There were also annual fairs in the towns to which country people would come, to buy goods brought by travelling pedlars, and watch jugglers, acrobats or other entertainers. These occasions would provide a chance for the young to meet marriage partners from outside their own village: husbands often took brides from other parishes. The average villager would be able to travel as far as he could walk, or go in a small boat, so that all those living on the banks of the Dart were part of one community. Seamen would know all the ports of southern England, including London, and those on the coast of France and Spain as well. Their tales of the marvels of foreign cities, trading adventures and sea battles must have entertained their families and more stay-at-home fellows during many a long winter evening.

Chapter Six

The Tudor Age I

New Castles

During the last part of the 15th century trade from the Dart declined as the merchants lost the preferential treatment they had enjoyed when much of France was owned by England. There was not even the consolation of real peace. When the rival claimants to the English throne were not fighting each other in the Wars of the Roses, they were trying to regain their former French lands. Fears of French counter-attacks, combined with new developments in artillery, made costly new defences necessary.

In 1462 Edward IV granted the burgesses £30 yearly out of the customs for the fortalice built by Hawley because of the 'continued expense in chains and boats for cables and pulleys for raising the said chains' — a clear reference to the chain across to Godmerock.[1] However, by 1481 Edward ordered them to build a '*new* tower and bulwark of lime and stone', which was to be furnished with guns and artillery. To encourage them, Edward granted them an additional £30 for four years.[2]

Some work must have already started but it cannot have gone very far. The new king Henry VII made an almost exactly similar agreement in 1486 but increased the annual grant to £40 yearly, and ordered them 'in all haste' to finish the tower and bulwark and provide it with guns.[3] It was only after 1488 that another round of work was begun.

The reference to artillery provides the reason for all this new building. Hawley's fortalice had become obsolete with the gradual introduction of heavy cannons in warfare during the last century. The whole technology was very new, and changing all the time. This was to be the first castle in England specially designed to have guns as its main armaments, with gunports splayed internally to enable turning to cover the field of fire. They were placed in the basement, as near the waterline as possible.

Long before the castle was completed guns were in place: in 1488 Thomas Gale, the Mayor, records paying £14 for 'two great murderers' (guns) for the castle, and a further £4 for 'binding and stocking' of them on to wooden beds.[4] Wheeled guncarriages were not then in use. In 1491 wagons were commissioned to carry 'divers ordnance and artillery from the Tower of London to the town of Dartmouth'.[5] These may have been the 'twelve serpentynes' for which the mayor William Fokeray paid eight pounds in that year. He also paid: 'For a bulwark that is begun in Kingswear side for the defence of the same port . . . £40'. This is the first mention of the building of the new Kingswear castle. A further round of building work took place between 1501-3, when Dartmouth's mayor John Rede paid £64 9s. to Sir Thomas Smith, parson of Modeley, for overseeing two years' work on it.[6] Stone for the building of the castles was brought in 'five great barges' from Charleton, near Kingsbridge; on another occasion five boats of Cornworthy stone were used.

On the Dartmouth side there is evidence of some changes of mind during construction. First, a round tower was built, then a square one which was joined on to it on the south. A chain could, as before, be carried across to Godmerock. The new castle at Kingswear was similar in style to the square tower of Dartmouth, and further out to sea. The two new castles were part of the same overall plan, designed to be able to fire at and sink enemy ships before they reached the chain. However, the castle at Kingswear was so exposed to the weather that Sir John Gilbert in 1583 asked that brass guns, which were more expensive, should be sent there as the sea would corrode iron ones.[7] By the late 16th century guns had

33. Dartmouth and Kingswear Castles in the 19th century, drawn by T. Allom.

been developed with a longer range and those from the Dartmouth side could cover the whole harbour entrance. After that Kingswear castle fell for a time into disuse, but was once more fortified to defend the harbour in the Civil War, 1642-5.[8] (*See* plates 21 and 22.)

Another castle was built about 1539 nearer the town, at the end of Bearscove, as an extra line of defence in case the enemy should breach the chain. No records have been found describing its building so its date is uncertain. It was certainly not there in 1522, when the Earl of Surrey lay off Dartmouth in the *Mary Rose* with the English fleet and described its defences as 'two castles . . . not two arrows shot' from the town.[9] It is most likely that Bearscove was part of Henry VIII's strengthening of the coastal defences in 1539 when Dartmouth is listed among many other towns as a place 'where fortification is to be made.'[10] The gunports are similar to those at the outer castles, with internal splays. It does not seem ever to have been used in war, and before long lean-to buildings were placed inside its walls for storage by local people.

The quay at Bearscove is first mentioned in the 16th century, and some houses built in this period, such as Port View House, can still be seen (*see* plate 80). However, the quay was not actually joined to the castle until after 1839, when the Council minutes record ordering its extension to provide a public way to it and a site for a house to be built immediately next to it.

Before the middle of the 16th century, the Carews, lords of Stoke Fleming who owned the site at the mouth of the river, built a manor house inside the walls of Hawley's fortalice. It was from this house that in 1552 Sir Peter Carew launched an attack on the castle next door, and seized it by force. The Corporation sent a petition to the Privy Council complaining that he:

> supposing the fort and tower to be built upon his ground, where indeed it doth adjoin the same, [he] hath lately with violence and scaling of the walls entered into the same and with force expelled your said orators and hath set new locks and keys whereby . . . they are interrupted from the keeping of the tower.[11]

The matter was cleared up by 1554, when Thomas Gourney was paid for spending a week in Exeter 'for making an end with Sir Peter Carew for our Castle' and a present was made to him of a hogshead of Gascony wine![12] After this the Corporation continued to garrison the castle as before.

Later Defences

Over the years Dartmouth castle was adapted to keep up with technical advances in artillery. In 1545 a battery known as Lamberd's Bulwark was built on the rocks outside the tower, to attack ships further out to sea.[13] The chain was used for defence against Spain in 1599, and again in the Civil War in 1643. When the Royalists occupied the town between 1643 and 1646 they built two earthwork forts faced with stone on the highest points on either side of the river. That on the Kingswear side was at Mount Ridley, and on the Dartmouth side at Gallants Bower, where the banks can still be traced among the trees, which were not planted until the later 19th century.

The battery outside the castle was brought up to date with advances in artillery in the late 17th and 18th centuries, while the castle itself was used as a storehouse, soldiers' quarters and occasionally as a prison. In 1861 the battery was completely rebuilt into its present form, because of renewed fears of a French invasion, to house five 64-pounder guns and a garrison. Its last use was in the Second World War, when a 4.7 in. gun was built on one of the platforms of the 1861 battery. This, with another battery on the Kingswear side at Brownstone, was designed to defend the area against air attack. In addition, in a variation on the old chain across the river, a boom carrying a steel mesh reaching down to the sea bed was floated across the mouth of the harbour to keep out submarines. This could be lowered to let in friendly ships, and raised when required.

For 600 years these fortifications have kept the Dart safe from seaborne attacks by foreign enemies. On the two occasions when the castles were seized by force, during the Civil War, it was by English armies which arrived over land.

The Water of Dart

In 1510 the new king Henry VIII leased to the Corporation of Dartmouth the rights over the river known as the waterbaileywick, which he owned as Duke of Cornwall. They had to pay £50 for the lease and a high annual rent of 20 marks (£14 13s. 4d.).[14] This gave the Corporation the right to charge dues known as 'petty customs', so called to distinguish them from the great customs which went to the king, on all goods shipped in or out not only of the Dart but of the whole area from Torbay to the Kingsbridge estuary. They appointed a waterbailiff to collect these dues, usually one of the leading burgesses. The grant had to be renewed at the succession of a new sovereign, often for a considerable cash payment, but in practice the Corporation held it almost continuously until 1860.

The town's trade by the early 16th century had fallen into a sad state. In 1521 Henry VIII wrote to the royal customs officers saying that because of the 'great ruin and decay of the town and port of Dartmouth' the revenues scarcely amounted to half what they had been in the time of his father, Henry VII. He urged them to help the mayor to search ships thoroughly to make sure that petty customs were paid.[15] While the income gained by the Corporation from petty customs was certainly useful, in many years it was not very large, after the high rent to the Duchy had been paid. This was largely because anyone who was a Freeman of Dartmouth, Totnes, Exeter and some other chartered towns was exempt, and these people included all the leading merchants.

However, in addition to the petty customs, the Corporation claimed all the other rights of the Duchy over the water which were similar to those of today's Harbour Commission. They could make laws, demand dues, inflict fines and generally regulate the river to suit themselves. They were the authority over land and water. They laid down the sizes and types of fishing nets to be used and issued fishing licences. They forbade the throwing of rubble onto the beaches or into the river, while doing exactly that themselves when they wished to reclaim land for building. They charged for digging a dock on the beach for building a ship — just outside the walls of St Saviour's cemetery, where the New Quay is now — and fined anyone who did not fill it in again when the ship was launched. Breach of any of these rules was dealt with at regular sessions of the Waterbailiff's Court.[16]

They could claim a percentage on the value of all wrecks sunk in the area under their control, and a share of all prizes captured and brought into it. The mayor had the right of first refusal of any turbot caught, rather as a sturgeon has first to be offered to the king. The Corporation claimed to own all land covered by the tide at high water, much of it soon to be reclaimed, and could charge for the right to build on it. The mud was sold as ballast to ships which had unloaded their cargoes. They made charges called quayage to help pay for the repair of the town's quays, anchorage for dropping anchor in the river, and groundage for grounding on the mud. One way and another, those who used the water had to pay.

Sir Thomas Carew, uncle of Sir Peter who later seized the castle by force from the town, was Vice Admiral of Devon in the 1520s and 1530s. This gave him the right to preside over the Admiralty courts in Exeter and Dartmouth. He began to act in such an extortionate way towards fishermen and other mariners that the Corporation sent a lengthy petition to the Council listing accusations against him.[17] He was challenging their rights as water-bailiffs. They said he demanded money from all the coastal towns and villages, imprisoning or seizing the boats of those who refused to pay. After suffering for years, the Corporation appealed to the Court of King's Bench, and the mayor, John Anthony himself, went to London for 65 days to plead the case. Among the many expenses he incurred was for 'a gallon of wine among the judges to discuss a matter — one shilling', which showed the manner in which justice was obtained. In the end, they won their case, and Sir Thomas' extortions ceased.[18]

Needless to say, many tried to avoid paying the dues demanded by the waterbaileywick, or to argue that they were illegal. The Corporation had to face all the expenses of fighting such cases in the courts of the land. One law suit concerned the tinners of Ashburton, who tried to claim that they were exempt. However, evidence was given that they had always paid dues in the past, and the Corporation won its case. Similarly, the fishermen of Salcombe tried to avoid paying, but were forced to do so after a lawsuit, as were three wealthy merchants of Kingswear.[19]

In this way, despite challenges, Dartmouth Corporation continued for nearly three centuries to keep a close control over the shipping of the port, and the revenues came to form a useful part of their income.

The Reformation in Dartmouth

In the 1530s Europe was in the throes of the Protestant Reformation, but there is no evidence that the people of the Dart valley were touched by its ideas. They went on, as of old, offering prayers for the souls of the dead, paying for candles and holy oil, and the clergy wore elaborate vestments, all practices which were condemned by radical reformers on the continent. When Henry VIII proclaimed himself head of the Church in England, and broke with the Pope, so that he could declare his marriage to Catherine of Aragon null and marry Ann Boleyn, most people had little option but to obey their ruler. They may have agreed with Emelina Petyfen, of Dartmouth, who was pardoned for saying 'The Devil take the King and his lady both!', but no one else dared to speak out.[20]

The last Abbot of Torre, Simon Rede, who was appointed to this post in 1523, seems to have foreseen trouble coming, for he began to sell off some of the monastic assets. The advowson to Townstal — that is, the right to appoint the vicar — was sold to Nicholas Kirkham of Paignton, who then appointed Rede himself as Vicar of Townstal in 1531. He remained Abbot of Torre as well. In 1538, when it was clear that the king meant to dissolve all the monasteries in England, Rede leased to William Adams for 10 years the Great Tithes of Townstal, in return for a rent to Torre Abbey, the stipend to himself and the chaplain of St Saviour's, and the responsibility for repairing the two churches. Great Tithes were on corn, and all other crops, animals and farm produce except for pigs, geese, butter and cheese, which were reserved for the vicar and known as Small Tithes.[21] When in 1539 the king's commissioners arrived at the gates of the Abbey to take it over, Rede moved to Townstal, where he had secured for himself an income, and a parsonage to live in.

The king now owned the lands of all the monasteries, and began to solve his financial problems by selling leases on them, at a high annual rent, to wealthy land-hungry gentlemen, who now had solid reasons for supporting him. Many of them became rich quickly by reselling at huge profits in a few years. In 1545 he granted for £300 all the property owned by Torre Abbey in Townstal, and over the river at Bowhay near Kingswear, to Nicholas Adams of Coombe, Dartmouth. The Coombe estate lay just west of Coombe Mud, now Coronation Park, where a large house in a walled garden existed up to the 19th century. Adams now gained the rents of 20 properties in Townstal and Dartmouth, including the 'house called St. Clare's Chapel', held by Richard Prideaux.[22] It is probable that Nicholas was the heir of William Adams, who already had the tithes, as by 1552 he acquired these as well as the above lands on a 21-year lease.[23]

Meanwhile, Protestant influence at Court led to orders that changes should be made to the church services. An English bible was put into St Saviour's, costing 16s.,[24] a new, more Protestant prayer book was introduced, and the cross and altar, both considered Popish symbols, removed. However, the last two were prudently stored in a coffer in the chapel. The Ten Commandments were painted on the walls of the chancel.[25] Townstal accounts have not survived, but no doubt the same happened there.

While the mayor and burgesses were prepared to follow royal orders about church services, they were very concerned to protect the considerable amount of property which had been given over the years to the chapel of St Saviour's. There were two sets of such property, known respectively as the High Store of the chapel, and the chantry, each accounted for by a churchwarden appointed by the burgesses. The revenues from them were used for church repairs and running expenses, for saying prayers for the dead, paying for chantry priests, special masses, repairs to houses and many other items. The first step taken by the Corporation was, in 1540, to change the oath taken by the churchwardens on their appointment. The words in brackets were omitted, and those in italics added:

Ye shall be true and faithful unto (Almighty God and the chapel of St. Saviour) *the Mayor and Commonaltie of the Town* and do the office of Churchwardenship of the said chapel (as other church-wardens have done before you, and see that all the jewels and other ornaments of the said chapel be well and safely kept unto the use and behoof of the said chapel). Ye shall see also that the tenements belonging unto the said (Chapel) *town* be well and sufficiently repaired . . . You shall also gather all the rents . . . that belong to the said (Chapel) *town* and account for the same to the Mayor and his brethren.[26]

Nothing could make it clearer that the wardens' prime duty was to the town, not the chapel, than the fate of the church jewels. These, listed in 1535 as 17 items mostly of silver gilt, including a cross, candlesticks, and two silver ships, were reduced in 1545 to only seven. Six of these were delivered to Mr. Newlond, the Mayor, and were placed as security for a loan of £16 2s. 3d. to pay a bill for gunpowder and the gunner's wages. They were later sold. A chalice was similarly sold for £5 to pay for the making of Lambard's Bulwark at the castle.[27]

They could have argued that they only just took them before the king. Between 1549 and 1552, Church Goods Commissioners were sent round by the regents of Henry's young son Edward VI to confiscate all the church valuables. They reported that jewels worth £22 10s. 10d. had been sold by the parishioners of St Saviour's, and there remained only one chalice, two suits of vestments, and five copes of cloth and tissue. At Townstal, 'a piece of cloth of arras wrought with silk and gold, worth 100 marks', had been taken from Townstal by Nicholas Adams, now of the Temple — the one who had bought the church property there and was now, it seems, living in London on his profits. The other churches in the villages lost all their treasures: from the hundred of Coleridge alone the commissioners collected nearly 90 items of church silver, all of which were sold to meet government expenses.[28]

The story was much the same with the church property. Over the next four years the two wardens' accounts were kept separately under their old names, but some of the money received was handed over to the Receiver (treasurer) of the town. For instance, £10 was given him in 1540, and a further £2 'for the buying of our guns' — hardly a normal church expense — and 13s. 4d. for the wages of the gunner.[29] In 1544-5 while the properties were exactly the same as before, both accounts were headed 'Certain lands and rents belonging to the aforesaid town'.[30] In 1547 the two accounts were joined together into one, and described as '*All* the lands and tenements appertaining to the Town . . . the gift . . . of divers burgesses of the same town *for the fortification and maintenance of the Port and Town*.' All mention of the church purposes of the original gifts was omitted.[31]

As with the church jewels, if this had not been done, all church land would have been confiscated by the Crown, and the town left with no means of paying for the church expenses for which they had been responsible since 1372. In 1547 the Protestant Regent Somerset passed a statute suppressing chantries and confiscating their revenues. After this there were no more chantry priests, whereas formerly there had been two or sometimes three in St Saviour's, and prayers for the dead ceased.

Six properties in Dartmouth were identified as having been given to the Chantry for 'superstitious purposes' — that is, 'for maintenance of a priest annually for celebrating mass in the chapel' — and sold for the enormous sum of £1,676 14s. 9d. to Giles Kelwaye of Stroud and William Leonard of Taunton.[32] Several commissions of enquiry later tried to find properties which had been concealed under this statute but, apart from these six, the Corporation kept hold of all the houses in the early churchwardens' accounts, which can be traced through into the 17th century and beyond.[33]

It must be said that the Corporation accepted their liability to pay out of their common fund for the repair of the chapel. Even before acquiring the church property they already had a considerable amount of their own, as can be seen from the number of surviving leases from the 13th century onwards, and they were soon to gain more as houses were built on new land reclaimed from the sea. All these were now combined on to the rent roll and over the years the church origin of some of the property was forgotten, until in the 19th century the whole affair was revealed and exploded like a long buried landmine in the face of their successors.

Meanwhile the churchgoers must no sooner have got used to the Protestant ways of Edward's ministers, who introduced a new Prayer Book in English instead of Latin, than the young king died and was succeeded by his half-sister Mary, a devout Catholic. Simon Rede was still at Townstal, though he died shortly after in 1554, asking in his will to be buried at Stoke Fleming church.[34]

At St Saviour's, Sir John Skinner, who had become a chantry priest in 1538 and stayed on as chaplain until 1574, had to restore the chapel to Catholic practices. The altar and reredos hidden in the vault were now replaced, the cross mended and put up again. The Ten Commandments were painted out. Catholic service books were replaced. The same mayor, Newlond, who in his earlier time in office had sold the church jewels, was summoned before church commissioners at Exeter and had to pay £20 'for the church plate'. They must also have disposed of the ceremonial copes and vestments worn of old by the priests, for they paid to buy new ones from London, and for their carriage from there to Totnes. It was a very expensive time.[35]

For Sir Peter Carew it was also very dangerous. Queen Mary was about to marry Prince Philip of Spain, an alarming prospect for Protestants as they might produce an heir who would keep England in the Catholic faith. Carew and several of his family were among those who supported Wyatt's plot to make the Protestant Lady Jane Grey queen. So was Sir Arthur Champernowne of Dartington, who owned lands at Kingswear. The Council was kept informed of who was involved locally by Sir Thomas Denys, the Sheriff of Devon, and they were among those proclaimed traitors by Mary in January 1554. The order went out to arrest them all, and Champernowne was taken along with two members of the Carew family. Sir Peter Carew escaped by sea from Weymouth to Antwerp, on a ship provided by Walter Raleigh (father of Elizabeth's favourite). He stayed abroad until Mary died in 1558, and returned to serve the Protestant Elizabeth for many years.[36]

When Mary died childless in 1558, her half sister Elizabeth reversed all her Catholic policies, while stopping short of the extremes of the most radical Protestants. The cross and altar were removed again. The new Elizabethan Prayer Book was introduced, and the English Bible. Everyone was obliged to go to church, or pay a fine of one shilling — enough to deter all but the rich from being absent — but the church was intended to be broad enough to accommodate all believers.

Some time in the second half of this century, a beautiful communion table with legs carved to represent the four evangelists was placed in the church. It is still there, but the four legs are now across the front, where all can be seen, and the table is used as an altar on which there is a crucifix. It must have been made during a Puritan period, when such tables were put in the centre of the church for commemorating the Last Supper of Christ.

34. Drawing of St John from the communion table in St Saviour's.

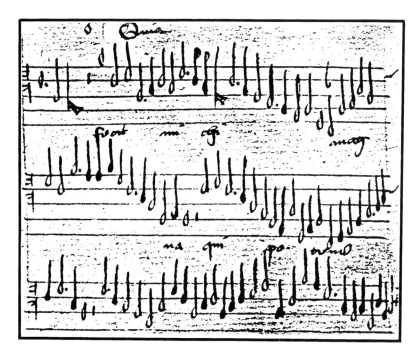

35. The Dartmouth Magnificat, written on a 15th-century court book in the Devon Record Office.

The tithes of Townstal remained with Nicholas Adams until 1571, with the obligation to pay the stipend of the vicar and chaplain out of them. However, they were then sold to a series of men who never paid these sums, while still collecting the tithes.[37] Eventually, in 1586, the mayor and burgesses bought both tithes and advowson for £500, subscribing the money out of their own pockets on behalf of the town.[38] The Corporation now appointed the vicar and chaplain, and could see they were paid. Their usual system for collecting the tithes was to 'farm' them out, often to one of the burgesses, for an annual rent. For instance, in 1591 Richard Drewe and William Langdon paid £40 a year to the Corporation, plus the vicar's and chaplain's stipends and the high rent, and were responsible for repairs to the chancel of Townstal church. Any surplus after this they could keep themselves. The Corporation could make sure they kept their part of the bargain.[39] The vicar was allowed a house near the church, on condition that he kept a school there.[40] It was probably in one of the houses just north of St Saviour's churchyard, in modern Anzac Street, where a school known as the Latin School was still held by the vicar in the 18th century.

Though most people accepted the Church of England, there were some Catholics and Puritans who hoped that one day their views would prevail, perhaps with a change of ruler when the queen died. The following years were to show that one church could not ever again hold together the whole range of beliefs.

Chapter Seven

The Tudor Age II

The Search for a Passage to Cathay

West-country ports, near to the Atlantic, were ideally placed to take advantage of the newly discovered continents of North and South America whose riches Spain and Portugal claimed wholly for themselves. As English seamen began to challenge this monopoly, Spain replaced France as the natural enemy, and religious conflict between Catholic Spain and Protestant England gave a spurious excuse for cruelty by both sides. In Elizabeth's reign English seamen defied the Spanish government's ban on trade with their colonies, where the people were quite ready to buy goods, especially slaves. In 1567 when John Hawkins' ships were attacked by a Spanish government fleet in the port of San Juan de Ulloa in Mexico, 100 English seamen were captured, of whom four were burnt as heretics, and the rest flogged, sentenced to row in the galleys, or imprisoned in Seville. Hawkins and the young Francis Drake, who was with him, brought the news back to Plymouth. After this, while England was officially at peace with Spain, the mariners of both countries conducted an unofficial war on the high seas.

The Gilberts, Raleighs and Champernownes

In the later 16th century the River Dart became the training ground for a famous band of sailors, all connected with or neighbours of the Gilbert family of Compton Castle and Greenway. They were to become leaders in the struggle with Spain, explore hitherto unknown sea routes and found England's first colonies. Soon after 1535, when the younger son Otho Gilbert married Katherine, daughter of Philip Champernowne of Modbury, a house was built for them at Greenway. There three sons were born to them: John, Humphrey and Adrian, each of whom had a distinguished career. When Otho died in 1547, Katherine married Walter Raleigh of Fardel, and had two more sons, the elder of whom later became Queen Elizabeth's favourite Sir Walter Raleigh and the younger, Carew, was also a leader of several sea-going expeditions.[1] Few women can have been the mother of so many famous sons.

Nearby in the parish of Stoke Gabriel in 1543 was born John Davis, who was to become one of the most skilled navigators and explorers of his day.[2] Of his father William and his family little is known. According to tradition they held some land on the Sandridge estate, which had passed from the Pomeroys to the Gilberts. As the name was not included among those paying the subsidy of 1543, when anyone earning over £1 a year was assessed, they must have been poor.[3] John went to sea at an early age, and became a well-educated man, with a knowledge of the writings of the ancient geographers, mathematics — so essential to a navigator — and a facility for learning foreign languages. He must have visited Dartmouth often enough to have used St Saviour's church, since he is recorded as having had a pew there in 1555.[4] When not at sea, he lived at Sandridge, probably at the Barton, while Adrian lived at the old Pomeroy manor house nearby. They remained close friends all their lives.

It is tempting to imagine the three Gilbert boys and Davis all learning to sail on the broad reach of the river between Greenway and Dittisham. All we know is that they all grew up with the ambition to find a new route to Cathay (China), by the north-west passage round Canada, which would lead to the riches of the east which even Columbus had not reached. When their younger half-brothers Walter and Carew Raleigh came to stay they too were imbued with the same ideas, as well as with the aim of founding an English empire overseas.

Katherine Raleigh's brother, Sir Arthur Champernowne of Dartington, was an active Vice-Admiral of Devon during the early part of Elizabeth's reign. He was the owner by 1555 of Godmerock Castle in Kingswear, and had a house in Dartmouth where he used to stay on his frequent visits to the port on official business.[5] He was involved, with William Hawkins of Plymouth, in the arrest in 1569 of some Spanish ships in Plymouth, carrying a huge quantity of plate and treasure sent by Philip of Spain to pay his army in the Netherlands, then fighting to crush a nationalist and protestant uprising under William of Orange. The Spaniards had taken refuge there to escape from French Huguenot (Protestant) privateers allied with the Dutch rebels, with whom English sympathies also lay.[6] Many English gentlemen, including Humphrey Gilbert and Champernowne's son Gawen, fought in their armies in France and the Netherlands.[7]

Champernowne supervised the transfer of the treasure from Dartmouth over land, guarded by 50 armed horsemen and 40 foot, to the Tower of London. The total filled 94 bags and amounted to not far short of 2,000,000 Spanish reales.[8] It had been loaned to Philip by some Genoese merchants who legally still owned it. When their agents in London informed the queen that they were as willing to lend it to her as to Philip she accepted the offer, kept half to spend on her navy, and sent the rest to William of Orange, the leader of the rebel forces fighting the Spanish army for whose arrears of pay it was originally intended. This was one of the many provocations of Philip by Elizabeth when the two countries were in theory at peace, but neither was yet ready for open war. The Spanish retaliated by seizing all the English shipping in Bruges.[9]

John Gilbert lived at Greenway all his life, and became a local administrator, serving the queen in a multitude of unpaid posts for over 30 years. He was knighted in 1570. He acted once as sheriff, and was in charge of mustering troops for defence when invasion was feared. He reported on the state of readiness of the castles, and acted as commissioner to stamp out piracy. He was in frequent correspondence with the Council in London. When his brothers needed supplies for their expeditions, he organised them. He played an active part in the Armada campaign, as will be seen later. He rarely left Devon, but gave both moral and financial support to his more adventurous brothers. He was accused by his enemies of lining his own pockets on many occasions, but he would no doubt have justified it by the great expenses the gentry incurred in many hours of unpaid work for the queen. Most of them took the chance to repay themselves from captured prizes when they could.

Sir Humphrey Gilbert

Humphrey, the most talented of the family, was educated at Eton and Oxford — as yet a rarity among the sons of Devon gentry. At the age of 18 he was introduced to the court through his mother's older sister, Katherine Ashley, who was the governess and close friend of the young Princess Elizabeth.[10] He seems to have been a natural courtier: his good looks and intelligence were such that Elizabeth 'had a special liking for him, and very often would familiarly discourse and confer with him on matters of learning'. After Elizabeth became queen, he fought in an expedition to capture Le Havre, and served several years in Ireland, where he was knighted at Drogheda in 1570 for his services. He was M.P. for Plymouth in 1571. He married Ann Ager, of Kent, one of the queen's ladies in waiting,[11] and set up home in Minster, in the Isle of Sheppey. He also owned Compton Castle, passed to him by his elder brother John who was childless.

However, his mind was always returning to the boyhood dream of finding the north-west passage. In 1566 he wrote *A Discourse on the Passage to Cathay*, with which he hoped to gain the queen's support, and in the following year he petitioned her for 'a licence and favour to enterprise the discovery of a passage to Cathay'. He also put forward a scheme for setting up 'Queen Elizabeth's Academy', a military and naval college for the training of royal wards and sons of the nobility and gentry to fit them for the army and navy. This idea, so far ahead of its time, was also ignored.

While Sir Humphrey did not yet have enough backing to finance an expedition of his own to test his ideas of a north-west passage to China, he was a shareholder in the voyages of Martin Frobisher, who made three attempts between 1576-8 to find it. Frobisher returned convinced that there was such a passage.

Sir Humphrey next presented to the queen a treatise *How to Annoy the King of Spain* suggesting, among other things, he might look for and take for the Crown new lands as colonies. This at last gained royal approval, and in June 1578 he was given the first Letters Patent ever granted authorising the planting of an English colony: to 'search out . . . such remote heathen and barbarous lands . . . not actually occupied by any Christian prince' of which he could take possession in the queen's name, and which he and his heirs could have and hold for ever.

Gilbert's First Expedition, 1578

With this official backing and help from friends and family, Sir Humphrey gathered together a fleet for this voyage which assembled in Dartmouth (*see* plate 49). He was clearly short of money, for in July he wrote to Walsingham from his home in Sheppey begging for payment of money due to him for the service of three ships in Ireland. He claimed he had been reduced to want as a result of his losses there. After all his service, he was subject to daily arrests, executions and outlawries and was having to sell his wife's clothes from her back![12] Walsingham became a chief shareholder, and the queen allowed one of her own ships to be used, but the plan may have been ruined by delays in the preparation. On 23 September, Sir Humphrey wrote to Walsingham that he had just sailed from Dartmouth with 11 ships and 500 men — apparently a formidable force, but it left far too late in the year for a voyage which ships usually made only in spring and summer.[13]

In fact, the expedition was a disaster from the first. Having left too late in the season, they were scattered by storms soon after leaving the Channel, and forced back to Plymouth. Quarrels broke out between Sir Humphrey and the leaders of five London ships who were with them, and the London ships departed. When the rest finally left again they sailed to Galicia, in northern Spain, and then to Ireland where they gave some help to the English commanders, but never went anywhere near Newfoundland or the north-west passage.

Gilbert's Second Expedition, 1583

Having lost a lot of money, it took Sir Humphrey five years to finance a second expedition. He was eventually paid for his service in Ireland in 1578, and he raised more money by selling shares in his rights of colonisation. Sir Walter was now a firm favourite with the queen at court, and she gave him to send to his brother as a sign of her approval of the whole venture a jewel in the shape of a golden anchor with a large pearl at the beak. She would not, however, allow Sir Walter to risk his own life by going with them, though he provided one ship for it.

The story of the voyage was later told by Captain Hayes of the *Golden Hind*, the only ship to survive.[14] It was a more modest affair than the first, with only five ships and 260 men, which sailed from Plymouth earlier in the season in June 1583. Sir John Gilbert sent the *Delight*, 120 tons, and Sir Walter the *Bark Raleigh*, 200 tons. There were also the *Golden Hind* under Captain Hayes, the *Swallow* and the *Squirrel*. They had on board, besides the usual shipwrights, carpenters and smiths, some mineral men including a Saxon refiner, to test any rocks they discovered as all hoped to find gold or silver.

The first setback was when the Captain of the *Bark Raleigh*, turned back to Plymouth, his men being sick. The remaining four reached Newfoundland, where in St John's harbour they found 36 ships, of various nations. They were shown Sir Humphrey's patent from the queen, and on the 5 August he claimed the country for England, and set up the Arms of England engraved in lead on a pillar of wood.

Hayes records that while some of the men repaired and revictualled their ships, others recorded the climate, native population, wild animals, geographical features and products on land and sea of Newfoundland and made charts of the coast. The Saxon refiner found first iron ore, then some ore he claimed contained silver. Others, however, were plotting to steal their ships while the captains were ashore, or hoping to return home on fishing boats. This is understandable in the light of Hayes' statement: 'Some were sick of the flux, and many dead', with numbers dropping daily. Gilbert therefore agreed to allow the *Swallow* to take home the sick.

He then decided to look for unknown lands to colonise, so he sailed south towards Cape Breton Island, using himself the tiny *Squirrel* because it could more easily explore nearer to the uncharted coast than larger vessels. Disaster struck when the *Delight* ran aground in fog on some shoals and was lost with more than 100 men. She carried most of the stores of food and clothing for the whole expedition as well as specimens of rock ores, plants and other products which Sir Humphrey had been collecting, all now gone, as were the descriptions and maps which had been made of Newfoundland. With winter approaching, and their stores of food and warm clothing lost, Sir Humphrey agreed to the men's pleas to turn for home.

Now, with only Sir Humphrey's tiny *Squirrel* and the larger *Golden Hind*, they reached a point north of the Azores, where they encountered such 'foul weather and terrible seas breaking short and high, pyramid wise', that men who had passed all their lives on it 'never saw more outragious seas'. The two ships stayed close together, and always carried lights at night.

Sir Humphrey's death
Sir Humphrey remained cool, to reassure his men, and after one occasion when his little ship was nearly swamped by the waves he was seen 'sitting abaft with a book in his hand' and cried out to the nearby *Golden Hind* 'We are as near to heaven by sea as by land'. That midnight, on the 9 September, the watchman on the *Golden Hind* suddenly saw the lights of the *Squirrel* disappear. In that moment, as Hayes graphically wrote, 'the frigate was devoured and swallowed up of the sea'. Hayes sailed his ship back to Dartmouth and went ashore to break the tragic news to Sir John Gilbert at Greenway.

Sir Humphrey had apparently achieved little, but his ideas inspired others. Davis took up the search for the north-west passage, and Walter Raleigh inherited his patent to look for colonies.

Sir Walter Raleigh and Virginia, 1584-7
Sir Walter financed, though he did not take part in, three expeditions which left from Plymouth, but are included briefly here as they followed directly from that of Sir Humphrey. In 1584, two ships left under Captains Philip Amadas and Arthur Barlow and landed at Roanoke Island, off the coast of modern North Carolina, which they named Virginia. They reported it was fertile, and well watered, with fine woods, game and fish, and that the Indians with whom they traded seemed friendly. They brought two of these 'savages' back to England, which may have made their Indian kinsmen less friendly to the next European arrivals.[15]

The following year, seven ships left from Plymouth under Sir Richard Grenville, and landed 100 householders — the first real colonists — at Roanoke. They were to be under the charge of Ralph Lane, with Captain Philip Amadas as deputy.[16] However, during the following winter they suffered terrible hardships, unable to feed themselves without help from the now hostile Indians. When Drake called in unexpectedly in 1586 they begged to be taken home, so that when Grenville arrived two weeks later with supplies he found the fort deserted. He left 15 people there to hold it. By 1587, when another shipload of colonists including 88 men, 17 women and 11 children arrived, they found the fort had been attacked by Indians and the 15 had vanished.[17] Because of the Armada campaign, these latest colonists were left until 1591 before a relief ship came. This found the site abandoned, with no indication of what had happened to the unfortunate settlers. Thus the earliest attempts to settle Virginia were a total failure. However, it is believed that one of the visiting ships brought back the potato to England in 1586, and Raleigh himself introduced it to Ireland soon afterwards.

Dartmouth and the Newfoundland Cod Fisheries

For many years some west-country fishing boats spent the summer months fishing on the rich codbanks off Newfoundland, but before 1580 the ships from other countries outnumbered those from England. No one was interested in claiming the land, which was bleak and inhospitable, and the fishermen returned in the autumn to sell their salted cod to Catholic countries in Europe where there was a ready market for it.

When open war broke out with Spain in 1584, the Spanish confiscated all the English shipping in their harbours, including those of the Netherlands. This gave the excuse for retaliation in an attack on Spanish and Portuguese fishing boats in Newfoundland, which were unprotected by the Spanish navy. Carew Raleigh, Sir Walter's brother, and Sir Bernard Drake — a distant and more nobly born if less famous relative of Sir Francis — led an expedition there which captured all the enemy vessels, taking 600 prisoners.[18] Spain was unable to defend the whole coastline of north and south America as well as fighting a war in Europe.

The prisoners were brought back to England, and put under the charge of Sir John Gilbert. Because of Spanish ill treatment of English subjects in Spain, the Council allowed them only 3d. a day per man for their keep, to be paid for out of the sale of fish taken from their own ships. The rest of the cargo was declared a lawful prize, to be distributed among the captors. Gilbert lodged many of them in Exeter gaol, which led to the notorious Black Assize. The overcrowded and insanitary conditions caused a massive outbreak of 'gaol fever' (typhus) which not only killed many of the unfortunate prisoners but also two of the deputy-lieutenants, several lawyers, and many gentry who happened to be in court.[19] It was also typical of Gilbert's inhumanity in dealing with prisoners, which was to be seen again at the time of the Armada.

However, as a result, the Newfoundland fishery was open to anyone who could afford to fit out a ship, unlike much of the trade under Elizabeth which was in the hands of rich London-based chartered companies who had bought a monopoly of a certain trading region. It favoured the small entrepreneur, with the profits divided into thirds for the owner, merchant and crew. Dartmouth was soon in the forefront of this industry, whereby all the ships left together in the spring. The master of the ship which was first to reach St John's, Newfoundland, was 'Admiral' for the season. Laws were laid down over the years, confirmed by the king in 1633. Of the crews, typically 24 would fish while 16 worked on shore, gutting, splitting, drying and lightly salting the fish. Others pressed oil from the livers to make the valuable 'trayne oil', used to light lamps and make soap. When the ship was full, it sailed for the Mediterranean or Iberian ports, where fish was in demand from Catholic countries even if England was at war with them. With the money from the sale another cargo was bought, such as wine, fresh or dried fruit, which was brought back to England. Some of the fish was later sold in the West Indies in exchange for new products such as sugar. It was the Newfoundland fishing industry which provided the wealth of Dartmouth for the next 200 years.

The Voyages of John Davis, 1585-7

By 1579 John Davis was a respected and experienced sea captain, who had somehow made enough money to consider undertaking voyages of exploration. He was a close friend of Adrian Gilbert, a scientist and mineralogist with interests in Devon tin mining, who also owned merchant ships. Both visited Dr. John Dee, who had at his house in Mortlake near London one of the best libraries in England of books about geographical exploration, as well as maps and charts and navigational instruments. Dee recorded the discoveries made by English seamen which gradually built up a body of knowledge about seafaring and navigation unrivalled at the time. Dee and Adrian had inherited Sir Humphrey's rights to lands north of Newfoundland, and together they began to plan another attempt to find the north-west passage. Walsingham, one of the queen's most trusted ministers, met Davis and Adrian at Dee's house and later subscribed to their voyage.[20]

John and Adrian were soon to be allied by marriage. In 1582 John married Faith Fulford, whose father owned the manor of Bozomzeal near Dittisham, while Adrian had already married Elinore, widow of Faith's brother Andrew Fulford. Both were now living at Sandridge, and making frequent visits to London to raise money for their expedition. In 1584, with the support of Walsingham and Raleigh, a new patent was obtained for all the trading rights in lands which might be discovered by this route. The Earl of Cumberland was a major shareholder, as was Davis' uncle William Sanderson, a London merchant, who may have had a hand in John's education.

In June 1585, Davis sailed from Dartmouth with two ships, the *Sunshine* of London, 50 tons, and the *Moonshine* of Dartmouth, 35 tons. The small size of the ships reflects the experience of the seasoned sailor Davis, who realised their advantage in exploring close to shore in uncharted coasts. Everywhere he charted the waters, coasts, rocks, currents and other features. They explored the waters between Labrador and Greenland, now known as the Davis Strait and believed the passage to China lay ahead, without any great problem of ice. He made two more voyages, in 1586 and 1587, all recorded with his usual thoroughness. He met many Esquimaux, and started a glossary of useful words in their language. On the third voyage he sailed up the Davis Strait to latitude 73 degrees, meeting huge cliffs of pack ice, and explored the coast of Greenland before returning. The names on today's map honour the expedition's financial backers: Sanderson's Hope, Cumberland Isles, and Cape Walsingham.

Davis reached Dartmouth on 15 September and wrote to his uncle Sanderson from Sandridge that he had been 'in 73 degrees, finding the sea all open, and forty leagues between land and land. The passage is most probable, the execution easy'. He had been further north than any man from Europe before him, and he thought the way to China was certain.[21]

He would no doubt have tried again in 1588, but in that year all England was preparing to fight off a Spanish invasion, and Davis was needed in the English fleet. He was master of the small pinnace the *Black Dog*, which acted as pilot and tender to the *Ark Royal*, flagship of the Lord High Admiral, Howard. He was with the *Ark Royal* in the engagement off the Isle of Wight when she was rammed by a Spanish ship.

In June 1589 Davis joined a large privateering expedition under the Earl of Cumberland which took many prizes off the Azores in which Davis had a share. As a result, he now had money to invest in another attempt to find the passage to the East.

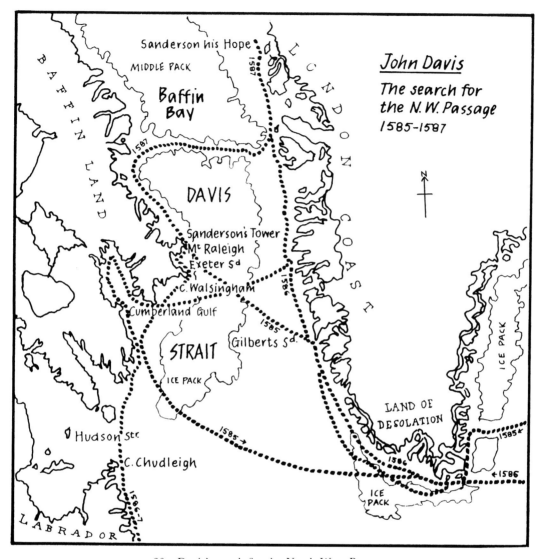

The figure:

Sanderson his Hope

MIDDLE PACK

Baffin Bay

BAFFIN LAND

LONDON COAST

John Davis
The search for
the N.W. Passage
1585-1587

1587

1587

DAVIS

Sanderson's Tower
Mt Raleigh
Exeter Sd
C. Walsingham

1586

Cumberland Gulf

STRAIT

Gilberts Sd

1585

ICE PACK

ICE PACK

LAND OF DESOLATION

1585

1586

←1586

Hudson Str

C. Chudleigh

1585 →

ICE PACK

1585-7

L A B R A D O R

36. Davis' search for the North-West Passage.

The Straits of Magellan, 1591-2

This time he joined an expedition to reach the Indies by the Straits of Magellan as second in command to Sir Thomas Cavendish, who had sailed round the world in 1586-8. Among his backers were George Cary of Cockington and his son. They left from Plymouth with four ships and a pinnace in 1591, Davis on the *Desire* and Randolph Cotton, a Dartmouth man, in command of the *Dainty*. The story of this journey was one of mutiny and appalling hardship. Cavendish turned for home with his two ships, and the crew of the *Dainty* mutinied. Cotton joined Davis who now had only one ship, the *Desire*, and the pinnace. While waiting for Cavendish, they were blown off course by a storm, and discovered the Falkland Islands. They passed through the treacherous Straits of Magellan to the Pacific, but when the pinnace was lost with all hands on the coast of Chile they decided to turn for home. By this time they were so close to starvation that they tried to kill and salt penguins, and ate a wild sage in the hope of curing scurvy, that terrible disease of ill-fed sailors. On the way home scurvy broke out again, and only 16 out of the original crew of 76 survived. Of these only five, including Davis himself, were able to work the ship.

Davis returned to Sandridge, having lost all his money, to find further disasters. His wife had deserted him and his three sons for a man named Milburne, who then made accusations against Davis. Raleigh wrote to Cecil in defence of Davis, explaining that Milburne was himself fugitive from justice accused of coining money and likely to be hanged at the assizes. Milburne had made Davis' wife pregnant while he was away at sea. He now hoped by making false accusations against Davis to prevent him giving vital evidence against Milburne on the coining matter, and thus taking revenge on him for seducing his wife.[22] The charges against Davis were dropped. No more is heard of Milburne, and the unhappy wife died shortly afterwards.

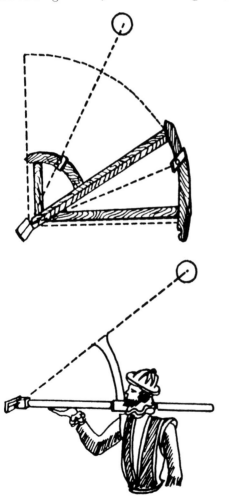

37. Quadrant and backstaff, invented by John Davis.

Davis tried to recoup some of his losses on his last voyage by going into partnership with Sir Walter Raleigh in a privateering venture in which a ship was captured and brought into Dartmouth. The goods included 25 bags of pepper and 'elephants' teeth' (ivory), and was said to be worth £20,000.[23] While at Sandridge in 1594-5 Davis wrote and published two works showing his unrivalled knowledge of seamanship. The first, *The Seaman's Secrets*, became the standard book on navigation for many years after. He described the use of the backstaff and quadrant, which he had invented, to measure the angle between the midday sun and the horizon and so work out the latitude in the open sea. The second, *The Worlde's Hydrographical Description* showed his knowledge of ancient and classical writers as well as publishing his own records, charts and notes on the places he had visited.

Davis' Voyages to the Spice Islands, 1598-1605

The Dutch were now planning an expedition to the East Indies, to break the Portuguese monopoly of the rich spice trade by the route round the south of Africa first pioneered by their sailors 100 years before. Davis went as a pilot for this expedition, which set

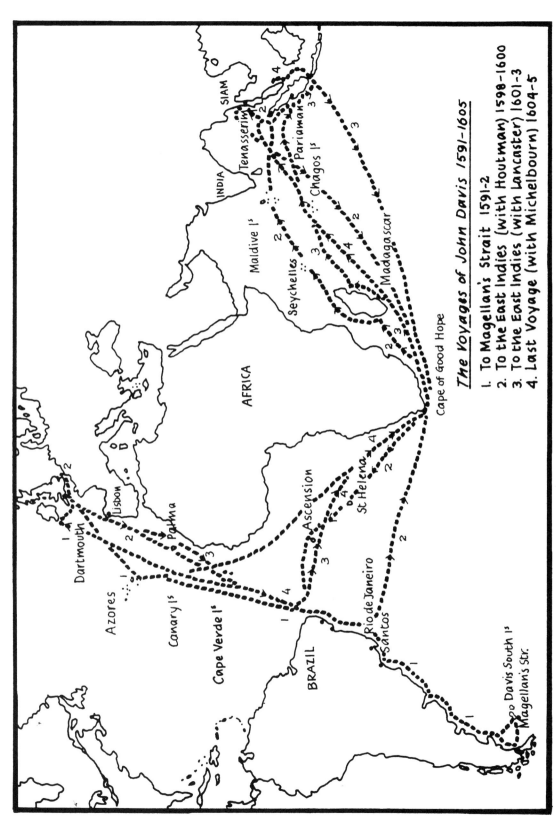

The Voyages of John Davis 1591-1605

1. To Magellan's Strait 1591-2
2. To the East Indies (with Houtman) 1598-1600
3. To the East Indies (with Lancaster) 1601-3
4. Last Voyage (with Michelbourn) 1604-5

SIAM
Tenasserim
INDIA
Pariaman
Chagos I⁵
Maldive I⁵
Seychelles
Madagascar
Cape of Good Hope

AFRICA

Lisbon
Palma
Azores
Dartmouth
Canary I⁵
Cape Verde I⁵
Ascension
St Helena
Rio de Janeiro
Santos
BRAZIL
Davis South I⁵
Magellan's Str.

38. Voyages of Davis, 1591-1605.

out in 1598 in two large ships, the *Lion* and the *Lioness*, under the command of Houtman.

With relatively little trouble they reached Achen, in northern Sumatra. Davis made hydrographical notes all the way which would be useful to his own countrymen later. The Dutch exchanged their wares for pepper, for which there was a ready market in Europe. At first the king of Achen seemed very friendly: he invited Davis to feast with him, and even arranged for him to ride to court on an elephant. There he met a Chinese merchant, with whom he talked in Spanish about possible trade there — the nearest he got to the China of his dreams.

However, the king was plotting to seize the Dutch ships by drugging some food he sent them. In a fierce battle in which Davis led the defenders, 68 Dutchmen including Houtman were killed, and the other captain was taken prisoner. Thanks to Davis the two ships were saved, and returned safely to Holland in 1600 with their valuable cargo.

He found the newly formed English East India Company about to start on their first voyage, and joined their five ships which left London in 1601, calling at Dartmouth for six days on the way. He served as pilot to the commander, James Lancaster, on the *Red Dragon*, 600 tons with 500 men. His knowledge of the route and markets made him invaluable. On reaching Achen, the king allowed them to set up a trading base there, and also in Bantam, Java. England now had her first foothold in the Far East, from which in later years her whole Indian empire was to grow.

Davis had made a good profit from this last voyage, and stayed at Sandridge for 15 months. He was now 60 years old — time, one would have thought, to retire. He became engaged to Judith Havard, and made a will dividing his property equally between her and his three sons whom she had apparently looked after. However, he could not keep away from the sea, and when ofered a chance to join another expedition to the Indies as pilot in 1604 he accepted. This was not with the East India Company, but with a rival group under Michelborne who had gained a charter from the new king James I. It consisted of two ships, the *Tiger*, of 240 tons, and a pinnace, the *Tiger's Whelp*. They reached Sumatra, and sailed south to the pepper markets where they exchanged their European goods for peppers and spices. Davis described each port, watering place, compass points, bearings and landmarks. At one place he described a break in a line of high land as being like the entrance to Dartmouth harbour, which he was never to see again.

The Death of Davis, 1605
Still searching for China, with which their charter gave them the right to trade, they sailed up the east coast of Sumatra. Here they met some Japanese pirates, whom they invited on board to try to find information about the route to China. Suddenly, hoping to seize the ship, the pirates attacked and Davis was killed in the resulting battle. He was buried at sea in December 1605, near to the island of Bintang. Michelbourne regained control of the ship by killing the pirates, and returned to England in 1606.

In this way died the most celebrated navigator who ever lived on the banks of the Dart. He never enjoyed the wealth which his skill had made possible for others. It was clear by the time he died that expensive expeditions such as this could only be financed with money from monopoly companies in London. Dartmouth could not compete, and by that time had turned to the less glamorous but more secure Newfoundland fishing trade as its best source of wealth.

Of the boys who had learnt to sail on the Dart, Sir John, Sir Humphrey and Adrian Gilbert had died before Davis. Sir Walter Raleigh had been thrown into the Tower of London in 1604 by James I under sentence of death for allegedly plotting with the Spanish to put Arabella Stuart on the throne. However, the next half century was to see yet more attempts by their successors to achieve their aims.

Chapter Eight

The Tudor Age III

Philip's Enterprise of England

After 20 years of unofficial war, open war with Spain began in 1584, when the assassination of the Dutch leader William of Orange on Philip of Spain's orders forced Elizabeth to send an army to help the rebels there. In 1585 Sir John Gilbert provided shipping for transporting 300 soldiers from Dartmouth to fight on the Dutch side, for which the town contributed £150.[1] The Mayor of Dartmouth wrote to the Council as early as December 1585, passing on a report from a returning merchant of an alarming build-up of ships and soldiers in Lisbon reputed to be for 'some great enterprize of England'.[2]

Philip's plans were delayed, but by the spring of 1588 he had prepared the largest fleet ever to put to sea, determined to conquer England. Where he would land was unknown to the English, but Torbay and Plymouth were likely targets.

Sir Humphrey Gilbert and Arthur Champernowne were both dead by this time, but other members of the family played a leading part. Sir Walter Raleigh was now a national leader planning the defences.[3] Sir John Gilbert, with George Cary of Cockington and Col. Edward Seymour of Torre Abbey, was in charge of raising an army to protect the coast from Exmouth to Dartmouth. They raised a local force of 800 men, all armed, while a similar number guarded the South Hams.[4] Each had a troop of horse. In every village and town the able-bodied men were mustered, and their weapons counted, for there was no regular army in those days. Dartmouth had 92 men, and Townstal a further 12 men. Kingswear mustered 37 men, Stoke Fleming 42 and Dittisham 49 men .[5] Some of those mustered were sent up to Tilbury to help guard Queen Elizabeth.

However, Dartmouth's main war effort was at sea, where she had always provided two ships of war, fully victualled, armed and manned. In 1588 her two ships were the *Cressant*, of 80 tons, carrying 70 men, Captain John Wilson and Master Christopher Waymouth, and the *Harte*, carrying 30 men. Both went to Plymouth in May to join the English fleet under the Lord Admiral, Howard, and the Vice Admiral, Sir Francis Drake, and served until the end of August.[6] They must have seen the whole of the action in that eventful year.

39. The *Ark Royal*, flagship of Admiral Lord Howard.

Copies survive of the accounts, showing exactly what provisions, weapons, powder and shot were supplied, and by whom, as well as a list of the crews, their various jobs, and how much they were paid. Each carried a surgeon, but Pultron on the *Harte* had his pay reduced to that of an ordinary seaman because he was such a bad one.[7] Many prominent men of Totnes and Kingswear, as well as of Dartmouth, were involved. The *Cressant* was hired from a group of five men, Richard Kelly of Kingswear, John Smith of Dartmouth, and John Trenheale, Leonard Dow and John Norman of Totnes.[8] To pay for all this, nearly £7,500 was collected from the hundreds of Haytor, Stanborough and Coleridge, organised by the Mayor of Dartmouth, Richard Drew and his Receiver Walter Dottyn.

In addition, nine more ships, carrying over six hundred men, were fitted out by the local gentry or merchants. Sir Walter Raleigh's *Rowe Bucke*, of 300 tons with 120 men, was with Howard and Drake throughout the Summer. Owned by merchants were the *Diamond of Dartmouth*, and the *Thomas Bonaventure*, which served six weeks.[9] Five others left the Dart in the thick of the fighting. Sir John Gilbert sent three, the largest being the *Samaritan* of 300 tons and carrying 150 men. Adrian Gilbert and Gawen Champernowne each sent one.[10] The *Elizabeth of Leistoff* with 30 men left at the same time.[11]

The Armada, long delayed by storms, was sighted off the Lizard on 19 July. Fire beacons, long prepared, flashed the warning along the coast from the hilltops.[12] Dartmouth watchers by their beacon on the top of Jawbones, still called Beacon Park, saw the signal from Prawle Point, and their flames were passed on to Firebeacon Hill, Dittisham, then to Torbay and on to London.

Howard and Drake, with no wind and an ebbing tide, skilfully warped the largest and best-armed English galleons out of Plymouth harbour. They led the main force south across the front of the Armada, then north-westward to take up position to its rear. The rest of the fleet left Plymouth later tacked close inshore and soon the entire English force was following the Armada up channel.[13]

The English ships which left Plymouth numbered 105, of which the official Royal Navy had only 16 ships of over 400 tons, and nine smaller galleons, backed up by eight small pinnaces. To these were added armed merchantmen, privateers and coasters. Sir William Winter later said of these smaller vessels 'we had been little helped by them, otherwise than that they did make a show'. However, in the circumstances, making a show was better than nothing.[14]

As the Armada passed Start Point, it was an awesome sight. The great galleons sailed in the form of a mighty crescent, with its points backward, and seven miles apart. Most were galleons, but some were galleasses, partly driven by oars manned by galley slaves. They numbered 125 ships, of which 70 were of 400 tons or more, and carried 8,000 sailors, 2,088 galley slaves, 19,000 soldiers, 1,000 independent gentlemen, 200 English and Irish Catholic exiles, and 180 priests. Philip's aim was to bring the heretic English back to the true faith. The plan was to sail to Calais, and take on a further 17,000 from the Spanish army in the Netherlands under the Duke of Parma, the best trained army in Europe. These were to be carried across to Kent, and if ever they had landed would have made short work of the inexperienced farmhands sent up to defend their country.[15]

When night fell, somewhere off Torbay, one could say the Spaniards scored two 'own goals'. In a tremendous explosion, a gunpowder barrel on the *San Salvador* blew up, setting fire to her. Later, badly burnt but with her main gunpowder store intact, she was captured and towed into Weymouth. More or less at the same time, the flagship of the Andalusian squadron, the *Nuestra Senora del Rosario* under Don Pedro de Valdes, collided with another ship and lost its bowsprit. Shortly afterwards in a further collision she lost her foremast. Left behind by the rest of the Armada, she floundered helplessly until morning.

At first light Drake arrived in the *Revenge*, along with the *Rowe Bucke*, his privateer's instincts having led him to slip away from the main fleet which was supposed to be following his light, and called on her to surrender. When he heard who his captor was, Admiral Don Pedro de Valdes, third in command in the Spanish fleet, and with over 400 men, surrendered without a fight on promise that their lives would be spared. Drake took Don Pedro and forty officers aboard, relieved them of 15,000 ducats, and ordered the *Rowe Bucke* to take the *Rosario* into Torbay.[16] Thus the only Spanish galleon in the whole Armada battle to be taken intact was brought into the shallow waters by Torre Abbey sands, towed by some

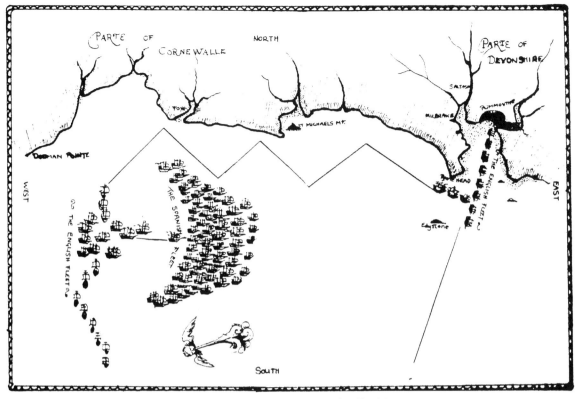

40.   The Armada off Plymouth, after R. Adams.

41.   The Armada off Start Point, after R. Adams.

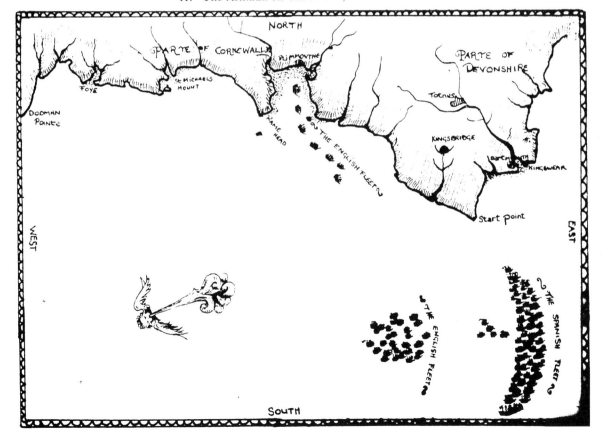

Brixham fishermen at the end. The *Rowe Bucke* then sailed round into the deeper waters of the Dart.

All the powder and shot and 10 brass cannons were unloaded from the *Rosario* and sent round to be loaded onto the *Rowe Bucke*, which then sailed to rejoin the fleet. The English fleet was so short of powder that without the quantity recovered from the *Rosario* and the *San Salvador* the whole campaign would have been in peril.[17] Gilbert's and the merchants' ships left the Dart on the same day, including the *Elizabeth of Leistoff*, all carrying more men, powder and shot for the navy.

The Spaniards, closely followed by the English, sailed up channel to Calais, where they dropped anchor in the exposed and shallow waters. Their plan was to pick up soldiers from the Netherlands for the invasion of England. However, seeing that the wind was blowing onshore, Drake ordered fireships to be sent in. With no time to send for hulks, some of the merchant ships were hastily prepared, loaded with barrels of tar and faggots, and that night carried by wind and tide towards the Spanish ships. The *Elizabeth of Leistoff* was one of those so used, and her owner later claimed £416 10s. for the loss of his ship and stores, which there was no time to remove.[18]

This was effectively the end of the plan to invade England: in panic the Spanish crews hastened to cut their cables and escape, driven north past the Netherlands, harried all the time by the English fleet. In the end they had to sail round the north of Scotland and west of Ireland, losing many of their ships on those rocky and unknown shores.

Meanwhile, back in Torbay, Gilbert and Cary were faced with the problem of what to do with nearly 400 Spanish prisoners, and an extremely valuable prize. The prisoners were for the moment put into the barn of Torre Abbey, owned by Sir Edward Seymour, and fed on the stores of food from their own ship. The local people were only with difficulty restrained from slaughtering them.[19] As for the ship, everyone thought it fair game for plunder, the gentry not excepted. However, Gilbert and Cary had instructions from the Council in London to keep the prisoners safe for possible ransom, and the ship itself was, by the law of prizes, to be shared between Drake and the queen. Gilbert and Cary then made an inventory of the goods on the *Rosario* — those that were left, for many casks of wine had disappeared. Cary later accused Gilbert of taking the best for himself, as well as much powder and a cannon for his own ship. The *Rowe Bucke* had taken many casks of wine, as well as 10 cannon.

At the end of August, the weather had improved enough to allow the *Rosario* to be towed round to Dartmouth by eight boats from Brixham. Over 200 of the prisoners had been moved from Torre Abbey to gaols in Exeter. The remaining 166 were put aboard their own ship in Dartmouth harbour.[20] Carey writes of their plight: 'Their provisions . . . is very little . . . Their fish savors so that it is not to be eaten and their bread full of worms . . .' Cary also reveals that Gilbert was using the prisoners every day as slave labour in his garden at Greenway. The Council in London ordered that 2d. a day should be used for food for them, but it had to be advanced by Cary himself as Gilbert refused to pay anything.[21]

Don Pedro had meanwhile been sent with the other Spanish officers to London, where they were well looked after in the houses of gentlemen, all hoping for a share in their ransom. He negotiated with the Council for the release and ransom of his crew, for 10 ducats each, and obtained permission to write to the Duke of Parma, the Spanish general in the Netherlands, for ships to be sent under safe conduct to take them away.[22] In May 1589 Elizabeth granted a passport for a Spanish envoy to come and pay the ransom. Don Pedro himself had to wait until 1593, when he was ransomed for £1,500 and the exchange of English prisoners held by the Spanish.

On its way back home, one more Armada ship was wrecked on the coast of Devon. Hopelessly lost and blown off course by a gale after rounding Ireland, the hospital ship *St*

Peter the Great foundered on rocks at Hope Cove in October. Cary was in Plymouth still trying to recover some of the guns taken from the *Rosario* by the *Rowe Bucke* when he heard of this. He rode to Hope to try to prevent pilfering there — too late, as the country people had seized the chance to take plate, ducats and jewels. He managed to recover some of the valuables, but not all. The ship itself was so wrecked, and soaked by storms as she lay on the rocks, that her cargo of valuable medical drugs was useless. One hundred and forty prisoners survived the shipwreck, and were also held to ransom.[23]

The *Cressant* and the *Harte* both returned safely after their four months' service — no doubt the mariners entertained their friends for years afterwards with tales of the great campaign. In the autumn, a meeting was called at Townstal of the owners of the two ships and of all those who had supplied anything to equip them, for the settlement of accounts.[24] The mayors of Dartmouth and Totnes were there, and everyone made their claims. It was revealed that, as a favour to the owners of the *Cressant*, it had been rated at 150 tons burden when it was in fact only 80, as they were paid at the rate of two shillings per ton per month. The merchants of Devon did not lose any opportunity of making money.

The Spanish War After the Armada, 1588-1604

The Spanish prepared three more Armadas which attempted to invade England in the 1590s. They firmly believed that many secret Catholics would join them: there were English exiles fighting in their forces as well as English Catholic priests being trained abroad ready to return if Spain was successful. A sailor reported he had heard the Spanish say that 'they have more friends in England than a bushel will hold of peppercorns'.[25]

One Dartmouth Catholic exile was William Randall, who was arrested in 1595 on a ship which was driven into Plymouth. He was accused of inciting shipwrights and mariners to serve the king of Spain, and of plotting to burn English ships with fireballs at Dieppe, Rouen or Chatham. He admitted — probably under torture --that he had shipped many priests and other Catholics to England from Dunkirk, where he was living in exile. It was said that many Catholic refugees had lodged at his house there, and even the Duke of Parma had visited him. After his capture, so anxious were the Spaniards to have him back that they offered to ransom him for 10 of the best English prisoners they held, or £10,000. His wife went up to London to plead for his life, and presented petitions in the queen's court. The Council were horrified to learn that she was lodging with the queen's shoemaker, fearing she might find some way of poisoning her majesty. Though the outcome of his case is not recorded, there seems little doubt that he would have been hanged.[26]

Four ships from each of Dartmouth and Totnes took part in an attack on shipping in Cadiz in 1596.[27] In November of that year the mayor of Dartmouth wrote to the Council that news had reached him that a Spanish fleet of over 90 ships was ready to sail, only waiting for provision galleys.[28] This second Armada lost 30 ships in a storm soon after leaving Spain, and the rest turned back. Another Armada of 136 ships reached the entrance to the Channel in 1597, but was again dispersed by storms. The last Armada to try to take England left in July 1599, when news that 200 Spanish ships were ready in Ferrol to sail for England was sent to the Council by Robert Martin, Mayor of Dartmouth.[29] Of these, 60 ships were reported by a merchant of Guernsey to be at Brest in August, while a French merchant who had spoken with the Spanish there said: 'Their design was on Dartmouth, and they said 30,000 Englishmen, already levied, would join them.'[30] Hortensio Spinola, an Italian spy for Spain, had earlier that year been captured with a survey he had made of all the defences of the south coast of England, in which he described the castles of Dartmouth, their armaments and the people. He suggested Torbay as being a good place to disembark, 'there being neither fortress nor people to hinder'.[31] With this information, there was a general mobilisation of forces, as in 1588, with 3,000 troops divided between

Dartmouth, Totnes and Torbay. However, the Armada was again dispersed by storms and never even came close to landing in Devon.[32]

Privateering: *The Madre de Dios*

In 1592, Dartmouth people had their first sight of the riches of the East Indies, when Raleigh's *Rowe Bucke* and a group of privateers brought in the *Madre de Dios*, a 1,600-ton carrack which would have dwarfed even the *Rosario*. It was laden with spices, amber, musk, pearls, gold, jewels, silks and treasures beyond their wildest dreams, and the locals began to pilfer the cargo on such a grand scale that Sir Robert Cecil himself was sent down to put a stop to it.[33] Raleigh had recently been put in the Tower for marrying Elizabeth Throgmorton without the queen's permission, but she had to release him to follow Cecil down to Devon to use his enormous local influence to recover the stolen property. When Cecil was seven miles from Exeter he reported he could smell the musk in people's bags, and some shops there were stocked with bags of seed pearls, jewels and other stolen goods. He intercepted letters written to friends in London inviting them down to share the spoil, and reckoned there were over 2,000 buyers there. He arrested a few, and ordered that anyone coming from Dartmouth should be stopped from returning to warn others of his coming. He complained he 'never met with fouler weather, more desperate ways nor more obstinate people'!

Sir Walter Raleigh, accompanied by his 'keeper' to see he did not escape, arrived in Dartmouth where his servants and mariners hailed him with shouts of joy. However, Cecil reported:

> (I) never saw a man more troubled to quiet them; but his heart is broken, as he is extremely pensive, unless he is busied ... The meeting between him and Sir John Gilbert was with tears on Sir John's part ... Whenever he is saluted with congratulation for liberty, he answers, 'No, I am still the Queen of England's poor captive' ...

Cecil questioned Gilbert on oath, suspecting that he too was involved in the looting, but was assured that since Raleigh's arrest he only came to the town once and was never aboard the ship. He concluded that while he was 'wronged in this, however in others he may have done like a Devonshire man'! The Council clearly knew their Devonians. On the principle of poacher turned gamekeeper, Gilbert was made one of the commissioners to hunt down the culprits.

With the help of Raleigh — who, with the queen, was entitled to a share in the prize — many of the stolen goods were recovered. Ten ships were loaded to take the treasures to London, where, including Chinese porcelain, ivory and ebony, they were valued at £140,000. The Corporation of Dartmouth offered £200 for the ship itself, after it had been in the harbour for two years, and promised to found a charity with the expected profits.[34] There is no record, however, that they actually did so. Her timbers would have been sold, and it is possible that many buildings in the area put up over the next few years may contain them.

The Growth of Dartmouth, 1570-1640

The Newfoundland fish trade was expanding rapidly, and becoming a triangular voyage. Salt from the Bay of Biscay was taken to Newfoundland for the fishing season. The salted fish and equally valuable 'train oil' was then carried back to be sold in the Mediterranean and Spain, in exchange for oranges, dried fruit and wine. Some fish was brought back to Dartmouth, where ships from France, the Netherlands and Scotland were waiting to buy it. In return was imported a growing quantity of timber, including masts and spars for ships from the Baltic, and wainscotts, the beautiful panelling used to line the walls of well-off merchants' houses. Locally-made woollen cloth was exported, while from Brittany was imported coarse canvas, used for sails, and lockram --a hardwearing linen cloth. One way and another, the merchants were doing well, and the port was flourishing as the 16th century came to a close.[35]

The realisation that Dartmouth would need better quays for the greater number of ships using the port, as well as more houses for a growing population, led the Corporation in 1570 to begin an ambitious land reclamation scheme to build on the mud of the river. It was financed by contributions from all the leading burgesses, as well as fines from the courts and payments for use of the graveyard. In 70 years, the appearance of the town was transformed by the building of the New Quay, Spithead and the Butterwalk.[36]

42.   Painting of the New Quay, Dartmouth, after R. H. Lancaster, c.1836.

Where once ships could tie up to the east wall of the churchyard of St Saviour's, a sea wall was first built, and orders were given that all the town's rubble was to be put inside it until the land inside was raised to fill the space behind it. On the river side this formed the New Quay, while the first six building sites at the south end for houses facing it were sold on 80-year leases in 1584 for an entry fine of £4 and a rent of 6s. 8d. a year. Covenants were enforced that the houses were to be well built, with thick party walls and slated roofs.[37] Leading burgesses were the first builders, including the mayor John Smith. In 1585

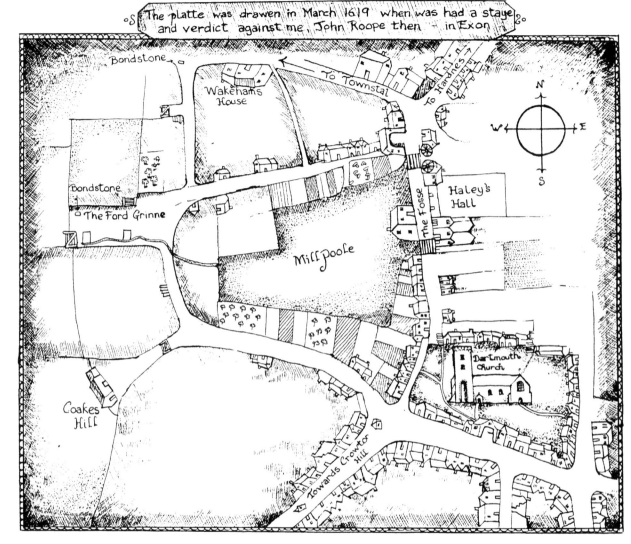

The platte was drawen in March 1619 when was had a staye and verdict against me, John Roope then — in Exon

Bondstone
Wakehams House
To Townstal
To Hardnes
Bondstone
The Ford Grinne
Haley's Hall
The Fosse
Mill poole
Dartmouth Church
Coakes Hill
Towards Crowton Hill

N
W — E
S

43. John Roope's map of 1619 was drawn to support his case that people had no right to use the mill bridges, which he owned. He lost his case, and Foss Street became a public way. His map gives more detail of the whole mill pool west to Ford. He marks two arches, one south of the church, the other by the north end of the Foss.

Thomas Plumleigh took the corner plot on Spithead, at right angles to the others. Soon these houses were the most prestigious in the town, where a merchant could watch from his window as his ships were being loaded or unloaded.

For the next 30 years or so there was a pause, during which in 1619 two maps were drawn which give a vivid picture of this stage of the town's development. The Corporation was involved in a law suit with John Roope of Little Dartmouth who also owned the mills on

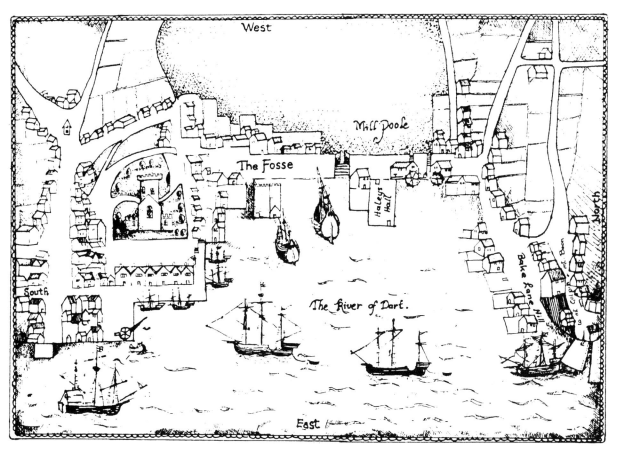

44. Townesend's map of the same date is drawn as if from a boat in mid-stream, looking west. It was commissioned by the Corporation to support their side in a law suit against John Roope over whether there was a right of way along Foss Street. Note the ships where the Butterwalk was soon to be built. The first six houses on the New Quay and two conduits can be seen. On the Foss the 'Flick hatch' allows the water to enter the mill pool, and it turns two mill wheels on the falling tide.

the Foss. He had been trying for years to stop the townsfolk using the bridges across his mills as a short cut from Clifton to Hardness, arguing that it was private property and they should take the long walk round by the Ford. The Corporation resisted this claim and eventually won, so ensuring that Foss Street became a right of way.[38]

Both sides produced maps to support their case (*see* plates 43 and 44). The Corporation's, drawn by Nicholas Townesend, is the more artistic, drawn as if he was sitting in a boat in mid-river looking west. The first six houses on the Quay are overlooking ships tied up to the sea wall, while round the corner more ships are on the mud where soon the Butterwalk was to rise. Nearby in the street was a free-standing water conduit, while another is shown at the junction of Smith Street, Crowthers Hill and Ford Lane. A crane is ready to unload

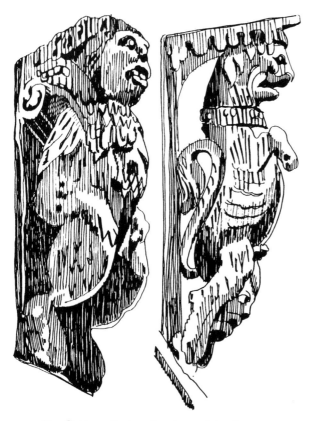

45.   Butterwalk: two drawings of detail.

at Spithead. The mill gullet, and the two mill wheels, lie either side of Hawley's Hall on the Foss. St Saviour's church has a high nave flanked by low, single-storey aisles, which 10 years later were to be raised to the same height as the nave. The churchyard is much larger on the west side than it is today, extending to Collaford Steps. On the Hardness side more ships can be seen on the mud where ship repair yards existed right up to the 19th century.

Roope's map omits the harbour, but shows the Foss with its mills and the whole Mill Pool west to Ford, with North and South Ford Lanes leading to it. He marks two arches, one north of the Foss at the entrance to North Ford Road, and one in Smith Street over the path leading to the churchyard. He marks a house not shown by Townesend on the west side of the Foss, just north of the mill gullet. The maps repay close study and comparison: Roope's has been compared with a modern O.S. map and found to be surprisingly accurate.

From about 1628 onwards the New Quay was extended northward and then turned at a right angle west. On the land so formed in 1639 four houses were built to continue the terrace already started in 1584. From south to north, these sites were leased to Joseph Cubitt and William Barnes — whose houses were in the 18th century to be converted into the *Castle Hotel* — with the next two both owned by Edward Spurway. He also owned two more adjoining houses round the corner in modern Duke Street.[39] All these men were leading burgesses and Puritans who supported Parliament in the coming Civil War. On the huge party wall which separated the houses of Barnes and Cubitt is carved the date and the initials of the men and their wives:

1639 B.W.M. Barnes, William and Mary.
C.J.J. Cubitt, Joseph and Johane.

On the reclaimed mud, at right angles to the New Quay, the Butterwalk was being built at the same time. The western part was leased to William Gurney in 1628 and the eastern to Mark Hawkings soon after. Both began to build, but in 1635 Gurney sold his part to Hawkings who completed the row by 1640 at a cost of nearly £2,500.[40]

No expense was spared in its building, with gables, slate hanging, and a riot of wooden beasts decorating the outside. There were originally 13 stone pillars where now only 11

46. The Tree of Jesse, the Butterwalk, now Killer's Chemist.

47. Pentecost scene, the Butterwalk, now in the 'Sloping Deck' restaurant.

remain: the 'walk' extended eastward under the adjoining building until 1880, as old photographs show. The pillars may be older than the building itself, and it has been suggested that they came from Hawley's Hoe which was being pulled down at this time. Inside the houses the main rooms are decorated with ornate plasterwork. One ceiling on the first floor over Killer's chemists shop depicts the Tree of Jesse, the ancestry of Christ. In the adjoining Butterwalk Restaurant there is a Pentecostal scene over the mantelpiece. The Borough Museum next door has rooms with superb wainscotting and ceilings of a naturalistic design. It was considered the finest room in the town in which to entertain Charles II in 1671.

However, Mark Hawkings did not long enjoy it himself. He must have been badly hit by the fall of trade in the port between 1639-41 to only half the volume earlier that decade, and owed debts of nearly £600. To pay them, in May 1642 on the eve of the outbreak of the Civil War, Hawkings was forced to raise a mortgage on the Butterwalk for this sum. With trade more or less at a standstill because of the war he failed to repay the loan, and the building eventually passed to John Plumleigh by 1653.[41]

48. The Butterwalk and great conduit, from a print of about 1850. The end building on the right was once Mrs. Hatton's Coffee House, then the Assembly Rooms, and was demolished in 1880. The National Westminster Bank is now on this site.

A lease of 1675 tells us that soon after it was built it began to subside — a common experience when reclaimed land was used — and that in 1657 extra walls had to be built in the middle, running north and south, to strengthen it. There was then a passage through the middle leading to the back, wide enough for a carriage to pass to reach the water's edge. Here there was a crane for the use of all the tenants for hoisting goods in and out of ships, which could be beached at the back door. They also had the right to use a brewhouse there to make beer, and to use the courtyard for washing of clothes and 'barking of nets' (coating them with preservative from bark).[42]

The conduit shown on Townesend's map (plate 44) was moved to the middle of the street beside the Butterwalk. It was known as Plumleigh's conduit, perhaps because it was adjoining his house. In 1799 it was moved again, to the edge of the quay, where it was a feature of many old prints until it was taken down in 1864.[43]

In the early 1630s there was also a major rebuilding of St Saviour's, where for a century very little had been spent. The whole cost came to £200, of which £111 was raised by public subscription and the rest paid out of Corporation funds.[44] The tower was rebuilt and increased in height, then the nave and both aisles, where the roof was raised to the level of the nave. On the roof of the north aisle are the initials of Alexander Staplehill, mayor 1633-4, while the south aisle bears those of William Gurney, mayor 1634-5. Beer stone was brought in for the walls and Rouen glass for the windows. On the floor of the chancel, next to the brass of John Hawley and his wives, lies one commemorating Gilbert Staplehill, father of Alexander, who died in 1636. Such brasses were condemned as immoral by the Puritans, and no more were made.

At St Petrox, too, the church was enriched mainly by the Roope family, with three fine brasses to John Roope, his daughter Dorothy Rous, and Barbara wife of John Plumleigh. Between 1636 and 1641 the church was enlarged. The two arcades and windows on the north side were added to the previous building, which consisted only of the present south aisle. A tower was built with a short, rather stumpy spire, which can be seen in prints of the 18th century (*see* plate 77). In 1856 it became unsafe and had to be removed. The date when the rebuilding was completed, 1641, is carved on the main door and pulpit. Unfortunately, both churches were barely finished before they found themselves in the front line of attack during the Civil War, 1643-6.

Chapter Nine

The Early Seventeenth Century

More Colonial Ventures

While the efforts of Davis and the East India Company had eventually opened up trade with the Far East, the surviving members of the Gilbert, Raleigh and Champernowne families concentrated their efforts on colonial ventures in America.

In 1595 Sir Humphrey's elder son, Sir John, went with his uncle Sir Walter Raleigh to Guiana, where they hoped to find the legendary El Dorado, or 'man of gold', who was thought to rule a kingdom rich in gold mines. They failed in this, but did discover in Trinidad a lake of pitch, which was probably not thought of much importance compared with what they were seeking.[1] Raleigh's aim was always to set up a permanent English colony in America. In 1602 he wrote to Sir Robert Cecil, the queen's Secretary, 'I shall yet live to see it an English nation'. The next few years were to make this view seem over optimistic.[2]

On the accession of James I, Raleigh was accused of treason and thrown into the Tower of London under sentence of death. He was kept there for 12 years, allowed to have his wife with him and sufficient books to enable him to write his *History of the World*, but not to follow up his dreams of empire. His second son Carew Raleigh was born in the tower.

Captain George Waymouth

In 1605 Captain George Waymouth sailed from London in the *Archangel* and called in at Dartmouth before setting off to explore the coast of New England. There he was kept for over two weeks, held up by an unfavourable wind. He took on more men, of whom Rosier, who later wrote an account of the voyage, said: 'few voyages have been manned with better seamen'. Waymouth's family had Dartmouth associations: Christopher Waymouth was captain of the *Cressant*, one of the two ships provided by the town for the fight against the Armada, and the name appears in the parish registers. The expedition was financed by Sir Ferdinando Gorges, a wealthy Devonian who had a lifelong interest in colonies, and Sir John Popham. They explored the coast and rivers of Maine, and described the Kennebec as 'the most rich, beautiful, large and secure harbouring river that the world affordeth'. They met and traded with many Indians, and seized five of them, with two canoes and all their bows and arrows, to bring back to England. On their return, they gave three of the Indians to Gorges and two to Popham, who both used them to learn more about their country and its possible sources of wealth. They were taken back with later English expeditions to act as interpreters and guides.[3]

Jamestown, 1607

It was these reports that encouraged the formation of a new Virginia Company, successors to Sir Walter's patent, in which his nephew Raleigh Gilbert (Sir John's younger brother), Gorges and Popham were among the members granted a patent by James I.[4]

One part of the company, setting off from London in May 1607, set up the first English colony at Jamestown, Virginia, among its first settlers the celebrated Captain John Smith whose life was later saved by the Indian princess Pocohontas. Despite untold hardships from hunger, disease and Indian attacks, so much so that of 900 settlers brought over between 1607 and 1609, less than 100 were still alive by 1610, the colony survived. John

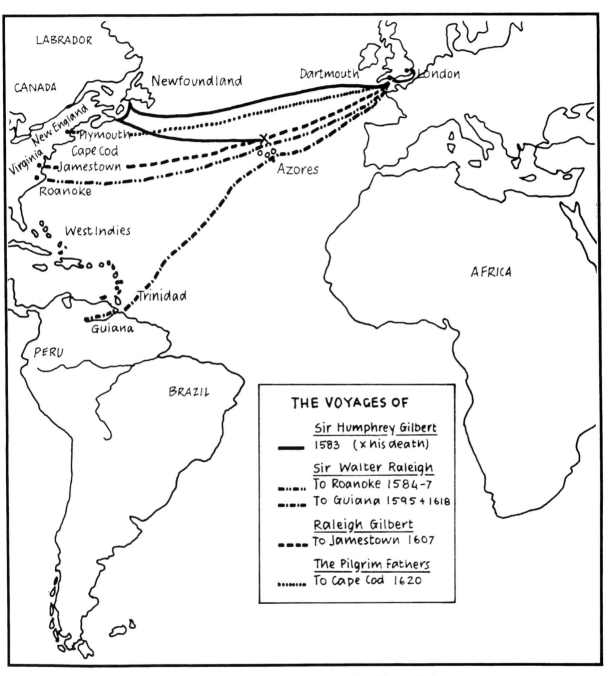

49. Voyages of Gilbert, Raleigh and the Pilgrim Fathers.

Smith made maps and wrote accounts of the richness of the land and sea around it which encouraged more settlers to go there.[5] The second or Plymouth part of the company, known after its port of departure, was inspired by Waymouth's descriptions of the beauties of the coast of Maine to send an expedition there, led by Captain Raleigh Gilbert and Sir John Popham themselves in 1607. The hardships of their first winter were worse than they imagined possible. In the spring a ship arrived from England with news that Gilbert had inherited the Compton estate on his brother's death. He decided he must return, and all the other settlers came too, not willing to face another winter there. Another attempt to found an English colony had failed.[6]

Raleigh's Last Voyage: The Guiana expedition, 1617-8

Sir Walter Raleigh languished in the tower of London, dreaming of ways to persuade the king to release him. James was always short of money, but anxious not to offend Spain. Raleigh put forward a scheme to search once more for El Dorado by sailing up the Orinoco river in Guiana. James agreed, but on condition that if any Spanish lives or property were harmed Raleigh would be executed. Since the Spanish already had settlers there who would be bound to resist English encroachments, this made the task impossible. Despite this Raleigh, now in his mid-sixties, took the chance as it meant he was released in 1616 to plan and equip the expedition. He left in 1617 with his elder son Walter, and sailed for Guiana and up the Orinoco searching for a gold mine. In a fight with Spanish settlers there the young Walter was killed, and the rest of the party failed to find any gold. Sir Walter, heart-broken by his loss and the failure of all his hopes, returned to England, where the Spanish Ambassador demanded his execution. He was beheaded in October 1618 on the old charge of treason for which he had been falsely convicted in 1604.

The Pilgrim Fathers, 1620

So far, would-be settlers had been attracted either by greed for gold, or a desire for land on which they could set up as independent farmers. From 1620 they were joined by those who were escaping from religious persecution at home.

In 1608, threatened with imprisonment for their Puritan beliefs, a group of people from Lincolnshire had fled to Holland, where they enjoyed religious freedom. However, by 1620 they had decided to found a colony in Virginia where they could retain their English way of life as well as worship as they liked. With money borrowed on harsh terms, they hired two ships and crews and set off, every penny they possessed invested in the venture.

On 12 August 1620 their two ships, the *Mayflower* and the *Speedwell*, slipped into Dartmouth harbour for repairs almost unnoticed by the locals. They had hoped by this time to be on their way across the Atlantic, and it was a bitter blow when the *Speedwell* was found to be leaking so badly that they had to turn back. The two ships were packed with food and all essentials for living for the first winter in the New World, and every day's delay meant they were using up precious stores.

They remained in Dartmouth harbour until 23 August, 'to their great charge and loss of time and fair wind'. One of the passengers aboard the *Speedwell*, Robert Cushman, wrote from Dartmouth to a friend that the ship was 'open and leaky as a seive [*sic*]'. The journey down the Channel had made him so ill that he was sure he was dying, and he made his will. He complained bitterly about the treatment they suffered at the hands of the captain, who would not allow them ashore in case they should run away. Cushman was convinced that, since they were already short of food because of the delays, if they did not perish at sea they would starve when they reached America.

The *Speedwell* was thoroughly overhauled and repaired in Dartmouth and after 10 days the two ships set sail for America. However, she began to leak again 300 miles off Land's

End, and they had to return to Plymouth. There it was decided to abandon her, transfer some of her passengers and cargo to the *Mayflower*, and to leave behind in England those who chose to stay. These included Robert Cushman. William Bradford, whose diary is the main source of information for the voyage, then revealed that the real problem with the *Speedwell* was her dishonest crew, who had been making holes in her to make it appear she was leaking in order to avoid going to America. They feared that on arrival there they would be left to starve by the crew of the larger *Mayflower*. The *Speedwell* sailed back to London leaving the passengers behind, and, curiously enough there were no further leaks. This story seems to clear Dartmouth shipyards of the suspicion that they did not repair her properly on her visit. The *Mayflower* with 102 pilgrims and 50 crew set off to cross the Atlantic. Only one man was lost on the nine-week voyage, but, blown off course by contrary winds, they reached Cape Cod, New England, far to the north of Virginia, their intended destination.[7]

Despite losing over half their number during the first winter through cold and disease, the Pilgrims' settlement, called Plimouth, survived. Over the next few years they were joined by many hundreds who left England because of religious persecution by James I and his son Charles.

Kingswear's Links with New England

In Kingswear by the end of the 16th century the cluster of 10 houses, wharves, quays and slips on the water's edge known as Kittery had among its owners the Champernownes and Shapleighs. During the 1620s Arthur Champernowne the younger owned several privateers, including the *Chudleigh* of Dartmouth, which had in 1622 been licensed by Sir Ferdinando Gorges' New England Council to trade fish on the coast of New England. It seems therefore that ships from the quays at Kittery were soon buying fish from the pilgrims landed by the *Mayflower* in New England, and no doubt bringing back descriptions of the country.[8]

Sir Raleigh Gilbert and Sir Ferdinando Gorges were still members of the Council in England for the Plymouth Colony, their part of the old Virginia Company. In 1636 Sir Ferdinand Gorges, who was related by marriage to the Champernownes, granted to Arthur Champernowne two large tracts of land each of 500 acres on the east of the Pescataqua river, in Maine. One was later known for many years as Champernowne's Island, the other as Godmerock after the castle in Kingswear which he also owned. Arthur used these to provide for his younger son Francis, who went out there in 1637 and became one of the leading inhabitants of New England for the rest of his life.[9]

Francis built his own farmhouse on a beautiful tract of land on the south side of the bay in modern New Hampshire where the scenery was similar to that he had known at home. He called it Greenland, perhaps after the dock of that name in Southtown, Dartmouth. He is credited with planting the English oaks still to be seen there.

Kittery is now famous as the earliest township in the state of Maine. It was so named by its first owner, Nicholas, son of Alexander Shapleigh, whose family had adjoining wharves to the Champernownes at Kittery in Kingswear.[10] As the Shapleighs were also important merchants in Totnes and Dartmouth, and Elizabeth Shapleigh married a Champernowne, Francis would have known them well both before and after they went to New England. Francis later moved into Shapleigh's home at Kittery, Maine, which like the property after which it was named in Kingswear has a beautiful site by the sea.

Francis was a strong Royalist during the Civil War, while neighbouring Massachusetts sided with Parliament, and seems to have returned to England to fight in the fleet for the king. He continued to play an active part in the affairs of the colony until his death in 1687. He and Shapleigh were among the first of many from the Dart valley who left home for

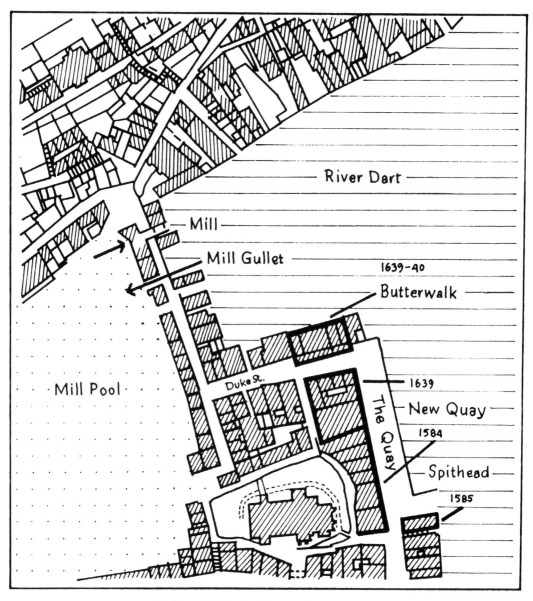

50. New building in Dartmouth, 1585-1640.

good and settled in America during the next three centuries, taking the names of their childhood haunts to the new world.

Civil War

The Seeds of Conflict

Trade with Newfoundland suffered in the reign of James I (1603-25) when he made peace with Spain and cut back the navy, just when piracy was a growing problem. The fishing fleets, exchanging their cargoes for other products in the Mediterranean, ran the gauntlet of the dreaded 'Turks' (Moslems) based near the Straits of Gibraltar, who not only robbed them but made slaves of any captured seamen. Dartmouth's mayor wrote to the Council in 1615 that Thomas Newman had lately lost a new ship of 120 tons to Turkish pirates within the Straits, while other merchants in the town had lost 10 more ships, the total value of which was £8,000.[11]

If they escaped this threat, other English pirates based in Torbay or Salcombe might attack them just as they reached home. These were often former privateers who had lost their jobs after the peace with Spain. One pirate ship had a crew of 30, of whom 16 were from Dartmouth and Kingswear. Thomas Norton of Dartmouth was said to have turned Mohammedan at Salee, Morocco, and after 'to exceed even the Turk's cruelty to his own men'. When these English pirates landed their plunder in England, a blind eye was often turned to their activities by the local vice-admirals or their subordinates, who were accused of taking bribes. Sir Richard Hawkins and Sir Richard Champernowne were both accused of this.[12]

In addition, James' court was notoriously corrupt, and those prepared to bribe his favourites could set up companies to buy monopolies to trade in a certain area, cutting out all other merchants. This made people reluctant to contribute to measures to combat the piracy threat.

In 1617, Sir Ferdinando Gorges, Governor of Drake's Island in Plymouth, wrote to the mayor of Dartmouth suggesting the two towns should offer to make a contribution equivalent to one year's customs receipts towards a fleet to attack the pirates' bases. While they were discussing this, a letter came from London restricting trade inside the Straits to the Levant Company, which had bought the monopoly. The town's dilemma was clear: if they contributed to a fleet to crush the pirates all their profits would go to this London-based company.[13] They could sell their fish to them, instead of exchanging it for what they could get in the Mediterranean countries.

In 1620 the town did contribute £89, raised by contributions from 178 ships which used the port that year, towards an expedition to Algiers to attack the pirate base.[14] The expedition was a complete failure, and the town's accounts continued to be full of payments to 'poor mariners, taken by the Turks', who passed through the port on their way home.[15] When the town was asked for another contribution by the government in 1622 they sent only thirty pounds, explaining the smallness of the sum:

> by reason of the loss of six ships of this port this year taken and carried away by the Turks ,.. each of them of a burden 150 tons and upwards, all laden with fish and merchandise, and in them 130 men now remaining captive in Algiers, many of them being of this place whereof wives and children are now left for most part to be relieved by the town . . .[16]

In fact in 1621 the town rate book shows that it had already contributed to the government three subsidies, each of over £200, which involved payments ranging from £10 to £3 from each of those who paid,[17] so this additional demand must have been very burdensome.

Royal Tyranny and Natural Disaster: The plague hits Dartmouth

Charles I, who became king in 1625, took advice from his inefficient favourite Buckingham,

51. Drawing of the borough arms in St
Saviour's, after the rebuilding of 1634.

whose bungles angered Parliament. To try
to influence elections to secure more pliant
members, in 1627, when a new Parliament
was being called, the Lord President wrote
to Dartmouth asking the burgesses to choose
as their representative 'a servant of mine,
Robert Dixon'. The burgesses rejected this
offer, saying that 'by their ancient custom,
they have usually made choice of men, free of
the Corporation, and well known to them'.[18]
This stand to support the rights of an independent Parliament foreshadowed their actions
in the Civil War.

Buckingham persuaded Charles to declare
war on Spain, and fitted out an expedition at
Plymouth to attack Cadiz. To save royal
money, 100 soldiers were billeted in Dartmouth at the town's expense, waiting to em-
bark.[19] The expedition left with rotten ships
and stinking food, and failed with great loss
of life. In addition, soldiers were frequently
carriers of disease. In the spring of 1627, 14
of them died of plague, which rapidly spread
to the overcrowded houses of the poor among
whom they were billeted.[20]

At the first sign of plague, according to a
letter sent by the mayor, Andrew Voisey, to
the Council in London, 'most men of ability
in body and purse have left the town', even the
bailiffs.[21] Voysey and the Receiver William
Plumleigh were left, desperately trying to
stop the disease spreading, and to deal with
those already stricken. The Vicar, Walter
Wylshman, recorded deaths from the plague
with a 'P' beside them in the burial register.

Voysey's day-by-day battle with this dread
disease is recorded in special accounts he kept
of the money spent by the town, while Plumleigh kept separate accounts for the people in
the almshouse where many more were ill.[22] He was responsible for issuing shrouds, so many
yards of cloth, according to the size of the body. The 'goodwives' who had billeted the
soldiers were the next to catch the plague, and soon it was everywhere. Ignorant of the
cause and without any cure, the only hope was to isolate the victims. People from other
villages were warned to keep away.

The mayor ordered the building of two special 'pest houses' up Crowthers Hill, which
were put up in a week, of timber, at a cost of £18 5s. 6d. In one, Goodwife Franciss looked
after 20 people at 1s. 6d. each, while in the other the Widow Cockwill looked after a further
ten. Week after week these two unsung heroines were paid 2s. for caring for the patients and
lived to tell the tale. The almshouse, built not long before, was used as a hospital, while
another pest house was built at Townstal. People suspected of having the disease were
boarded up in their own houses unless they went into one of these.

Dogs and cats were believed to spread the infection, and the order went out to kill every one of them. William Martin was paid 1s. to kill 40 dogs in one day, and that was just the beginning. The rats which really spread the infection had lost their main natural enemies.

Only the St Saviour's register has survived from this date, and records 55 deaths from plague. Other names are mentioned in the accounts, assumed to be from the missing registers of Townstal and St Petrox. In all, probably over 90 died, out of a population of about three thousand. Dartmouth's relative isolation by road, along with Voysey's prompt action, may have saved her from a worse outbreak. In Ashburton 450 died in an epidemic at about the same time.

The Civil War

Relations between the borough and the government of Charles I grew worse in the 1630s. The king had renewed the lease of the water-baileywick to the Corporation for a high entry fine of £80 in addition to the usual annual rent; however,

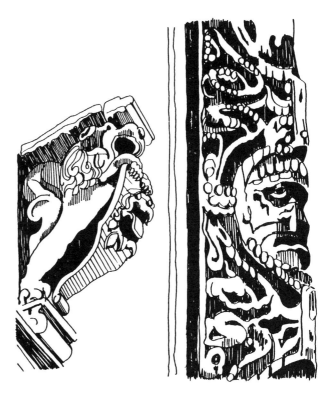

52. Two 17th-century carvings on a house in Clarence Street.

in 1630 the crown claimed the right to wreck of the sea and prizes, both of which the town had enjoyed as part of their lease. They had to sue in court to establish their rights to these.[23] While the early 1630s were peak years for trade, enabling much new building to be done, they were followed by a sharp fall in 1639-41, when wool exports from Totnes through Dartmouth fell to only one third of the earlier volume.[24] Blame was put on the granting of a monopoly to a London company.[25]

Anger at this and many other grievances increased when Charles after 1629 ruled without Parliament. When he was forced by the need for money to summon one in 1640 the members who met were determined he should never again rule alone. Dartmouth's members in the Long Parliament were Roger Matthews, a local merchant, and John Upton, who owned estates at Lupton near Kingswear. On his death in 1641, Upton was replaced by Samuel Browne who belonged to a group supporting John Pym who led the opposition to the king in the Commons.[26] Charles' attempt in 1642 to arrest the Five Members, including Pym and William Strode — another Devonshire M.P. — ensured that Dartmouth, like Exeter and Plymouth, supported Parliament in the struggle which followed.

However, families and communities were often divided in their political beliefs. Ambrose Roope of Little Dartmouth supported the king, while his cousin Nicholas fought actively for Parliament. All now realised that the issue would be decided by force, though no one really wanted war. For the whole of 1643 the town prepared its defences for the expected attack by royalist forces. All expenses were recorded by the mayor, Alexander Staplehill, and his receiver John Plumleigh. Later those who had contributed to the defence of the town drew up accounts, listing every amount spent or lost by them, in a 50-page book making total claims of £9,733 19s. 3d., which they hoped Parliament would repay to them.[27]

Nicholas Roope was present at the fight at Modbury in February 1643, when the Royalists were defeated, and then took 200 men with him to Plymouth, arming them at his own expense at a cost of £300. They spent the next three years there helping the city to hold out against the royalist siege, while Roope's Dartmouth and Stoke Fleming properties were left open to attack.

Thomas Newcomen, grandfather of the inventor of the atmospheric engine, had moved to Dartmouth from Stoke Fleming where his father was rector, and had become a ship owner. He was sent to London by the town, where he bought 36 barrels of gunpowder for £162. He paid for billeting 43 soldiers from the Modbury army, supporting them with 'bread, bisket and butter'. Roger Matthews, Plumleigh and Staplehill paid for iron costing £224, used for making 'shot, turnpikes, mattocks, pickaxes and ironworks for the forts'.

Both Dartmouth and Kingswear castles were manned day and night, with the chain carried ready to stretch across the harbour, and guns put in position. All the ships in the harbour were armed and guarded. Guns were mounted on top of St Saviour's new tower, as well as on St Clement's at Townstal, and the narrow roads into the town were blocked with anything they could lay their hands on. Henry Penny the blacksmith supplied 'ironwork' to all the forts, and spars were taken from the shipbuilders. Old weapons were dragged out: swords, bandoliers, muskets and even cross bow bolts.

There were road blocks at Mount Flagon, where Browns Hill joined Clarence Hill. Mount Boone — called after its owner, Thomas Boone — was defended with 127 'deales'. Ten guns were set up at the Mill end outside the 'North Gate', and six demiculverins on the New Quay. Other road blocks were made across Crowthers Hill and above Warfleet Mills, while the old Paradise Fort was strengthened with ironwork.

Exeter fell to the Royalists in July 1643, and Prince Maurice, Charles' nephew from the Rhineland, was sent to be in charge of the king's forces in the west. He decided to attack Dartmouth before going on to Plymouth. He offered the town generous terms, but it refused to surrender. Maurice camped outside the town for a month, in wet weather, before finally assaulting it from the Warfleet valley on 4 October 1643. The road block above the mills fell and Paradise Fort was seized, from where Maurice's guns could command both the town and the castle by the mouth of the river. The defenders fought hard, but had to surrender with the loss of 17 men.

The Vicar of Townstal, Anthony Harford, wrote his last entry in the parish registers a week after the town fell, and then a strange hand took over for the next three years. It is likely that Harford was of Puritan leanings, and left Dartmouth, though his wife remained behind to bear him a daughter in March 1644. He returned after the town was recaptured.[28]

Maurice had set up his headquarters at Milton Farm, near Townstal, where as might be expected his army celebrated its victory. The mayor, John Budley — who had only just begun his year of office as the fighting began — records how he had to deliver to the Prince's quarters nine barrels of the best sack or claret, and 24 hogsheads of beer.[29]

The effect of the town's resistance was to delay the attack on Plymouth, which Parliament had time to reinforce before Maurice reached it. Whereas the town might have fallen had he gone straight there, now it braced itself to hold out. Maurice had not crushed it by Christmas, and it was still not taken three years later. By keeping large numbers of royalist forces tied up in the besieging forces it played a crucial part in securing the ultimate victory of Parliament.

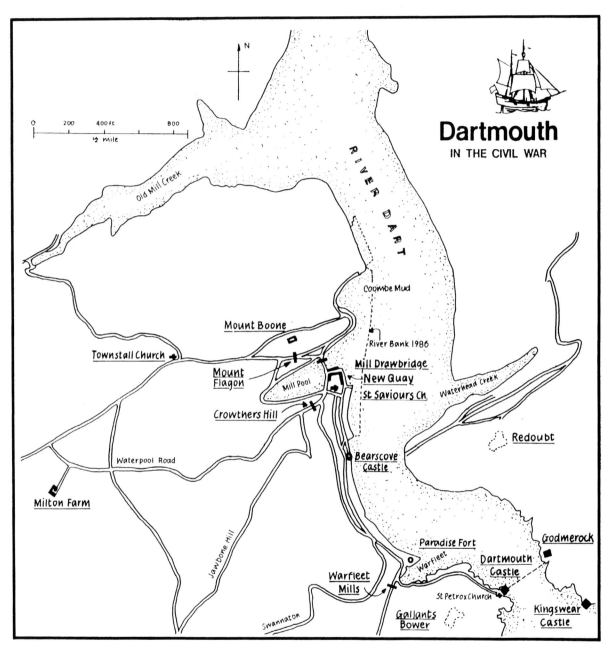

53.   Dartmouth in the Civil War.

Edward Seymour of Berry Pomeroy became Governor of Dartmouth, which remained under royalist occupation for three years, and those who were open opponents suffered in property and person. Lawrence Wheeler, who refused to take an oath of loyalty, was sent to Exeter gaol, his estate confiscated, and his wife and children turned out into the streets. Thomas Newcomen's ship the *Desire* was taken over by the Royalists. because it had fired against the Prince, when she was fully victualled and manned ready to set off for Newfoundland. Another of his ships, the *Olive*, was 'ripped up before my own door in despite of my wife'.[30] He lost a third ship, the *Tamsin*, on her way from Newfoundland to Portugal, to Irish pirates. While such actions by the cavaliers were bad enough, he sorrowfully reported that Parliament's army which recaptured the town in 1646 also plundered his house, and he could get no restitution from them.

The man who lost most was Nicholas Roope, who was in Plymouth for the next three years and claimed that his losses amounted to £2,525.[31] They included:

At Warfleet, 3 ships with their guns and all other provisions; at one other house in the parish of St. Petrox, in sails, ropes, fish and guns   £500

Plundered at my house in Dartmouth, 3,500 Newfoundland fish, lead, 74 muskets, 4½ barrels of powder, gold, gold rings, ambergrese; the spoiling of the house; the plundering of the household stuffs   £350

Plundered at Week . . . 10 horses, 6 oxen, 4 kyne, 4 young bullocks, 140 sheep and 200 fleeces of wool; 3½ acres of peas . . . with the house burnt to the ground   £250

This gives some idea of the range of goods a wealthy man might own; Roope was a farmer and a millowner as well as a shipowner and merchant.

Seymour built the earthwork fort at Gallants Bower above the castle to strengthen his land defences on the west side of the Dart, and a similar one at the Redoubt, Kingswear, which was guarded by the royalist Sir Henry Cary of Cockington. Seymour was always short of money, so was glad of the customs duties on any ships which entered the harbour. The first to do so was the town's Newfoundland fleet which arrived just after its fall to the Royalists, unaware of its fate.[32] However, Parliament was able to use its navy to blockade the harbour which greatly reduced its usefulness, and prevented help reaching the Royalists from the king's French relatives.

Seymour had many problems: how to feed his garrison and the town, to prevent any uprising against him, and keep his men armed and paid despite constant demands from Maurice to send more arms and money to Plymouth. To feed the soldiers, all the villages were ordered to send food to Dartmouth, to prevent the soldiers from 'plundering and outrage', and the names of any who refused were to be listed for punishment.[33] Even those who contributed their quota of food were hard hit. Harberton villagers were still owed £200 for billeting soldiers, who had left them with a 'very great sickness', when it was demanded that they billet a further troop of 68 horsemen. In desperation they attacked the soldiers with clubs and drove them off.[34]

The Royalists were losing the war elsewhere, and news reached Seymour of their defeat at Marston Moor. Sir Hugh Pollard had now taken over as Governor of Dartmouth, with Seymour and the Earl of Newport under him. By January 1646 the siege of Plymouth was lifted, leaving that town undefeated. With the royalist army in disarray, Fairfax in the same month decided to recapture Dartmouth. He was helped in planning his attack by the local knowledge of some of Roope's soldiers, now released from Plymouth.

Fairfax relates how he first sent two regiments of foot to march to Dittisham, and two to Stoke Fleming, both held by Royalists.[35] It was decided to attack the town in three places:

The first post was on the west gate by Col. Hammond: on the north end of the town by Lt. Col. Pride, and on Townstal church and works by Col. Fortescue. The time resolved on was in the evening; our men fell on with great resolution . . . Col. Hammond entering the west gate where four guns were planted, and two upon the Mill Pool upon his flank. The enemy firing his great guns but once, his men . . . did very gallantly . . . and went freely on and beat off the enemy, and possessed one fort after another, viz. Mount Flagon, West-gate, Paradise fort, and beat off the main guard; where were taken four Lieutenant Colonels; and so possessed the town from the west gate to Little Dartmouth.

In the interim, Lt. Col. Pride attempted the north part of the town, called Hardness, where beating off the enemy he entered it, and took about 80 prisoners in it, and by it possessed all the north part of the town unto the drawbridge, which divided the north part from the rest of the town; where Col. Hammond's men and his met Col. Fortescue with his men, attempted Townstal church, which was very well manned with above a hundred men, and having in it ten guns. His men after some dispute, with good resolution entered the place and possessed it, so that the enemy was beaten out of all except the great fort in the east side of the river called Kingswear fort, and the castle with the fort which lay over the castle at the mouth of the harbour called Gallants Bower to which last the Governor with the Earl of Newport, and as many as escaped us, fled.

Sir Hugh Pollard decided to go by boat to see what was happening in the town, and was wounded in the thigh by a musket shot which passed through the side of the boat as well as both thighs of the man next to him. He retired to the castle. Meanwhile Kingswear castle, defended by Sir Henry Cary, was attacked. This was described as 'a very strong bulwark, strong enough to have made troublesome resistance', and well armed with guns and powder. However, Cary came to terms and was allowed to march his men away, leaving all their arms and provisions behind, on their promise not to take up arms against Parliament again. The next day Pollard too surrendered, the officers being taken prisoner with a promise that their lives would be spared. Nearly 1,000 soldiers of lower rank were sent home. Fairfax captured all the guns, ammunition and food stores, as well as two of the royalist boats in the harbour. The horrors of war for the ordinary soldier were revealed later in the story of Roger Mogridge, one of those guarding Gallants Bower, who from lying on bare ground in the extreme cold of that January night had to have his hand amputated because of frostbite.[36]

After the fall of Dartmouth a Puritan mob sacked the house of the royalist rector of Dittisham, who barely escaped with his life. He, like the rector of Stoke Fleming, was replaced by a Puritan minister. Their church paintings were defaced and memorial brasses damaged. Anthony Harford, vicar of Dartmouth, sided with Parliament. He fled during the royalist occupation and returned when the town was recaptured. It did not save his church from vandalism, as Hawley's brass lost part of its frame and shields, and the paintings on the screen were badly defaced.

Fairfax went on to crush the Royalists in Cornwall, and to relieve Exeter in April. By mid-1646 Charles was defeated, but what to do next was the question. Few who had fought for Parliament wanted a republic: they wanted a king who would rule *with* parliament. Charles even in defeat tried to evade promises to do so, and after a short second Civil War Cromwell set up a court to try him for treason.

Thomas Boone of Mount Boone, though a friend of Cromwell, refused to be one of its judges, as did Fairfax. When it ordered the execution of the king, many who had fought against him were horrified. Both the Dartmouth M.P.s, Browne and Matthews, were among the moderates excluded from Parliament by Col. Pride's 'purge', an attempt by the extreme Puritans to secure a body which shared their views. Matthews was imprisoned in the Tower of London and fined £1,000 as a delinquent, despite his plea that he had supported six soldiers and two sons in Parliament's cause. He died in 1652, the fine unpaid and his property still confiscated, until his widow managed to have it reduced to £666 and paid in order to reclaim the rest of her estates.[37] These included Matt's Point, the headland just west of Blackpool Sands, which was named after the Matthews family.

Rule by the Puritans

The next 11 years saw persecution and hardship for those who had fought for the king. The royalist gentry were heavily fined: some, like Sir Henry Cary, who had to sell all his Cockington estates to pay, lost all their family lands. Sir Edward Seymour and his son, who had defended Dartmouth for so long, were taken prisoner to London and also had to pay heavy fines. The gentry were angered that Cromwell tried to rule without them, suspecting them quite rightly of being disloyal, so that they were not asked to do the thousand and one local jobs which they had willingly and freely done for the monarch in the previous century.

Cromwell tried to rule the country through Major-Generals, appointing his brother-in-law Desborough over the South-West. The Newfoundland trade gradually picked up again, with the aid of naval convoys across the Atlantic to defend them against royalist privateers.[38] Thomas Boone became influential in the town through his friendship with Cromwell, though he was often absent. He was sent by Cromwell as an envoy to the kings of Denmark and Sweden, and visited Russia.[39]

The leading members of the Corporation were William Barnes, Joseph Cubitt, Edward Spurway and Lawrence Wheeler, all Puritan merchants and shipowners. When the vicar, Anthony Harford, died in 1654 there was a dispute between the Corporation and Thomas Boone as to who should succeed him. Boone wanted John Flavel, whom Cromwell himself was said to favour, while the Corporation wanted Allen Geare. Desborough was asked to settle the matter. He ruled that both should be appointed, Geare to St Saviour's and Flavel to Townstal. The two men seem to have worked amicably together for the short time left of Puritan rule.[40]

When Boone became M.P. for Dartmouth in 1658-9 the Corporation challenged his election on the grounds that it had been by 'all the inhabitants' instead of, as was customary, by the freemen alone. They spent £121 in legal expenses fighting the case, but the Commons Committee upheld Boone's election by a narrow vote. Clearly Boone was more popular with the townspeople than the narrow circle of the freemen.[41] However, the death of Cromwell in 1660 was soon followed by the return of Charles II, and Boone's political career came to an end. His reputation in the town was perhaps summed up by the saying of the time that 'although he had but one eye, he saw further than those with two'. He returned to Dartmouth and took no more part in local affairs, though the hill on which his house stood has been called Mount Boone ever since.

Chapter Ten

Village Life Through the Centuries

Village life changed little from the beginning of the 17th until the early 20th century. The lords' estates were gradually broken up as newly rich merchants bought properties in the country and became landed gentlemèn. For the farm labourers who worked for them the difference would hardly have been noticeable. It was still true in the 19th century that, for instance in Dittisham, the rector as lord owned every house there. The early parish schools existed only in order to keep the lower classes in their place, not to enable them to advance. Boys were apprenticed at eight or nine years old to farmers or millers, and girls as domestic servants. A boy might escape to sea, as many did, but nothing changed for those left behind. The memories of old people today show that in their childhood there was little that would have been different from that of their forebears 200 years ago.

Stoke Fleming

It is rare to have a complete picture of a whole manor in the early 17th century, but a rental which has survived among the Seale papers enables us to construct one for Stoke Fleming between 1600 and 1615.[1] It shows a typical manor at the close of the feudal era.

When George Southcote inherited Stoke Fleming and Southtown along with four other Devon manors from his father in 1600 he was already a wealthy man, having married the heiress of Buckland Tout Saints where he now lived in the comfortable manor house there. He was therefore an absentee landlord, who appointed an agent to collect his rents.

The Carews, who had held Stoke for nearly 300 years, once lived in a stone manor house which they built in the village, just north of the church. In the 16th century they built another house inside the walls of Hawley's old castle (*see* plates 21 and 22), as part of their efforts to seize control of the port of Dartmouth, and the house in the village was abandoned by them. Their old manor house is listed in the rental as the 'mansion house', held by John Cole with 15 acres. No traces of this house now remain, but Milles in 1750 reported seeing some pointed arches from it lying to the north of the church. This would have been much the most convenient place to hold the court, and Cole may well have been the agent who did this for George Southcote.

The rector of Stoke at this time, from 1594 to 1614, was Elias Newcomen, great-grandfather of the inventor Thomas Newcomen. One of the holdings for which rent was paid for a cottage with 38 acres was described as 'was Parson's'. The glebe land held by the church in 1841 at the time of the tithe apportionment shows a considerable holding near the centre of the village.

Stoke village was farmed on the open field system at least up to 1362, when a manorial survey showed that 400 acres there were held in common, but by the 16th century these lands had been enclosed to form individual holdings. Now, houses and land were let out on terms of 99-year leases on the lives of the lessee and two other people, usually his wife and children, who never in practice lived for the full term. The lease laid down various feudal dues owed to the lord. One of these was 'heriot', usually the lessee's best beast or its value in money, to be paid on the death of one of the people named as 'lives'. The lessee might have to provide the lord with a capon at Christmas, and to pay 'suit of court' — attend at the manorial court when the business of the manor was dealt with. More rarely, 'suit of mills' was demanded, whereby he had to have his corn ground at the lord's mill.

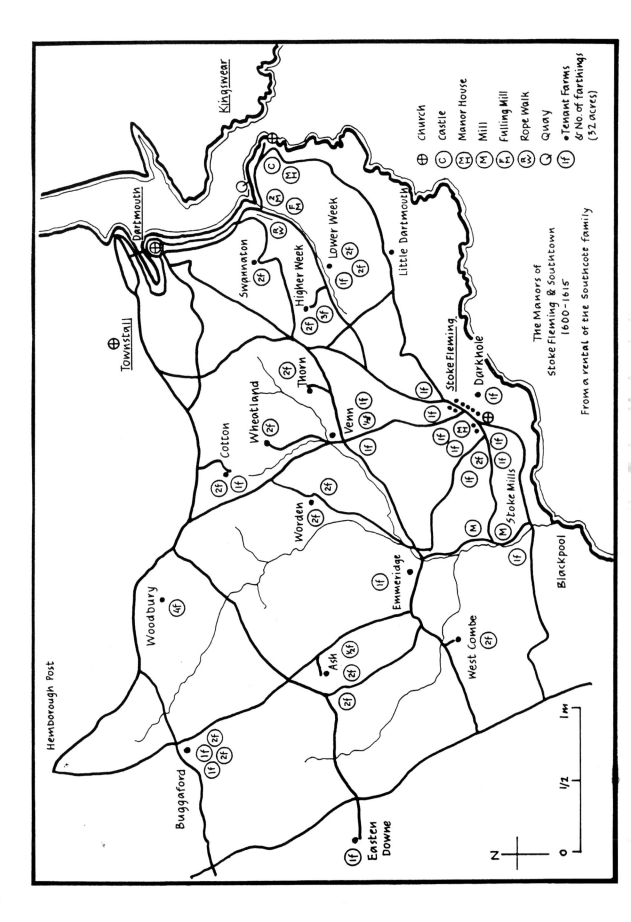

Hemborough Post

Kingswear

Dartmouth

⊕ Townstall

Swannaton ②f

Little Dartmouth

Lower Week

Higher Week

Cotton

Wheatland

Thorn

Venn

Stoke Fleming

Darkhole

Stoke Mills

Woodbury ④f

Worden

Emmeridge

West Combe

Buggaford

Ash

Blackpool

Easten Downe

The Manors of
Stoke Fleming & Southtown
1600-1615

From a rental of the Southcote family

Church — ⊕
Castle — Ⓒ
Manor House — Ⓜ
Mill — Ⓜ
Fulling Mill — Ⓕ
Rope Walk — Ⓦ
Quay — Ⓠ
Tenant Farms — ●
& No. of farthings — ①f
(52 acres)

N

0   1/2   1m

In addition to all these dues, he paid an annual rent. In Stoke, 42 people owed suit of court, but only two owed suit of mills; 11 had to give capons at Christmas and 12 to pay a heriot.

These feudal dues were already becoming irksome, and many people had by this time become copyholders, which meant they held by the same three-lives' lease but paid only a money rent.

In the village of Stoke, 24 cot-tagers are listed as copyholders, most of them with only a small garden, and paying a rent of from 2s. to 4s. a year. However, seven people held one or two 'farthings' of land in Stoke, the old Saxon unit meaning one fourth of the hide. It was usually of 32 acres, although it could be as much as 45 acres. The rents paid varied widely, from 3s. 6d. to 20s. for a farthing. These farthings probably represent the dividing up of the former open fields, with the occupants of the landless cottages forced to be labourers for their better-off neigh-bours. There was also a small vil-lage at Embridge, where Alice Lidston held a farthing of land.

Sixteen farms are mentioned by name in this rental: is it a coinci-dence that Domesday Book listed exactly this number of small-holders in Stoke in 1086? These tenancies may reflect Saxon or even earlier farmsteads. Like the village lands, they were calculated in far-things and held by copyhold, pay-ing rent but no feudal dues. Woodbury, the largest in one hold-ing, had four farthings, 132 acres, and paid 28s. rent. All the others, though referred to under one name, were by this time subdivided be-tween two or more tenants. The amount paid in rent for two far-things, which usually amounted to 64 acres, varied from 10s. for Westcombe to 40s. for Cotton.

55. Village street in Stoke Fleming, late 19th century.

Nicholas Roope and his family were among the wealthiest people in the manor, in the absence of a resident lord, with property in Warfleet, Southtown, and the Week valley, while his brother John owned the adjoining estate of Little Dartmouth, as well as the mills on the Foss in Dartmouth. In St Petrox church there are two brasses, of John Roope and his daughter Dorothy Rous.

There were two mills in Blackpool valley, owned by Arthur and Walter Wotton, one described as 'newly built'. All the beer used in the village would be made locally. A group of 12 feoffees paid rent for the 'church house' and the 'church brewhouse'. In many Devon villages these became inns: if this is the case in Stoke, the *Green Dragon* is in the right place to be the old church house. There were two other brewers and a malthouse in Stoke parish. Fishing went on from Blackpool beach, where Edward Langman rented a cottage and garden on condition he brought fish to Dartmouth.

The manor of Southtown included Warfleet, Bearscove, and the fields west of Above Town. Most of the tenants here had to pay some feudal dues, including suit of court in Dartmouth as distinct from Stoke. In all, 25 tenants from Southtown were liable for suit of court in the manor courts and George Southcote could look forward to receiving from them six capons at Christmas.

Warfleet was then a small hamlet, where the Roopes were the most important people. Nicholas Roope the Younger had built what was described in the rental as 'a very fair house and quay with a garden at Warfleet' where ships could land with their merchandise. This house, later pulled down, can be seen in an old print (*see* plate 23). George Deymont had a house, garden and rope making place at Warfleet, referred to in a map of 1749, which was along the side of the valley above Week Road (*see* plate 76). With the Roopes' ships coming in regularly to their quay, there would be a constant demand for new ropes after every voyage.

John Holligrove held Warfleet mills, described as two watermills and one horse mill, with a garden and orchard. He paid £19 a year for them — the largest rent in the book — and they would have served the farms in Week valley. Henry Robins had a fulling mill as well, paying 32s., to wash and dress woollen cloth for the local weavers to make it more windproof. It was an indication of the importance of this local industry.

George Davie, the castle gunner, lived in a small cottage nearby and several more cottages were clustered along the valley near the mill. Paradise Fort, somewhat decayed but still capable of being fortified in times of danger, stood on the north point of the creek. St Petrox, by the castle, was the parish church used by the inhabitants of both Warfleet and Southtown.

During the Civil War the royalist rector, Richard Reynolds, though over 80 years old, was evicted and a Puritan William Bailey replaced him until 1660. In that year Reynolds, now nearing 100, returned to end his days as rector of his old parish.[2]

George Southcote, son of the lord of 1600, did quite well out of the war. He and his son Thomas fled to Exeter during the war 'to avoid the violence of the soldiery'. In 1646 they took the covenant swearing loyalty to Parliament, and were said to have given great assistance to Parliament's friends. Unlike most gentry, they were fined only a small sum, and were able to buy up lands in Lincolnshire which other Royalists were forced to sell. In 1654 George was made Sheriff of Devon.[3]

Ashprington

Ashprington manor and church were given by Judhael of Totnes to Totnes Priory, which was itself a cell of a Norman abbey. The church still belonged to it in 1288, when the rector had to pay half a mark yearly to the priory. The site of the churchyard is raised above the surrounding land and looks like an earthwork. Since the church itself is dedicated to St David, the patron saint of Wales, and there was once a holy well also dedicated to him, it may be that a small chapel stood here on an already ancient earthwork in Celtic times. There is a Norman font of red sandstone, earlier than any surviving part of the church. The oldest part of the present church is the tower, while the body of the church is of 15th-century style.[4]

At Painsford there was a private chapel, which was licensed in 1419. It was bought by the Somester family, and later by the Kellands who rebuilt the chapel in 1687. There are memorials to both families in the parish church.

At the dissolution of the monasteries, Ashprington, which still belonged to Totnes priory, was granted to Francis Knowles for £553 10s., and a few months later he sold it to John Giles of Totnes. His son Edward later bought Sharpham, then not the fine house which is there today.[5]

After the Civil War, the rector was deprived of his living by the Puritans for being an Anglican and using the Book of Common Prayer, and his wife and children were turned out of the rectory. He was compelled to hide in Sharpham woods from the roundheads for two weeks, before finally escaping to Cornwall, and he died in 1655 before the Restoration. His Puritan successor, John Burgess, was in his turn forced out in 1662 after the Restoration.[6]

After the passing of the Elizabethan Poor Law in 1601, all parishes had to look after their own poor. Sir Edward Giles, a descendant of John Giles who bought the manor in 1539, gave an almshouse for six poor people of the parish on his death in 1622. Ashprington has a particularly good series of Overseers of the Poor Accounts, complete from 1689, which tell us a great deal about how this small village met its responsibilities. It can serve as typical of other places where records have not survived.[7]

In 1689 much money was spent on the almshouse, which was completely rebuilt, the poor people apparently being moved out for seven weeks. Nathaniel Ferris was paid for keeping two of them, and for 'fetching the almspeople home to his house'. A number of people were paid 4s. to 7s. a month in outdoor relief, that is in their own homes. A horse was provided to take one woman to the doctor, probably in Totnes. There are payments for shoes, a shift, a neckcloth and a cape; and for a new kettle, a coverlet, a bolster and sheets for the almshouse. The overseers provided plants to be grown in the almshouse garden, and bought a pair of weaving looms so that the poor could keep themselves busy. Poor children were fostered, and all children of the parish were apprenticed out from about nine years of age to learn a trade.

In 1721 there are several entries which suggest that the almshouse was used for childbirth. Mary Cloke's bed was specially carried in there, and she was provided with bread, drink, sugar, soap, candles, flesh and 'other necessaries for laying in', including wood for a fire, and a woman to deliver her child. She did not normally live there, as she was given a small amount of money when she left. As soon as inoculation against smallpox was discovered, the parish paid for all poor children to receive it.

The cost of all this was met by a poor rate, paid by all householders, who are shown in the lists of ratepayers. By the 18th century there was no one lord who owned the whole manor but several who lived in a few big houses. The Trists owned Bowden, and the Kellands Painsford. Landowners from other places such as the Holdsworths of Dartmouth and the Yardes of Churston owned property but did not live there. In 1765 Philip Pownall owned Sharpham, which his son Captain Philemon Pownall inherited. He was in the navy and during the American war made £70,000 in prize money which he used to start building the mansion on the estate. He was killed in 1780, leaving his unfinished house to his daughter Jane. The story goes that Edward Bastard fell in love with Sharpham, and determined to marry the heiress to obtain it. He persuaded her to elope with him, and hired all the horses in the neighbourhood so that there would be none left for any pursuers.[8]

The population of the village is given as 619 in 1821 when a census was recorded in the accounts. The amounts paid in poor relief amounted to £16 in 1690, and had reached £406 in 1821, by which time nearly all the villagers were receiving supplements to their wages out of the rates. In an effort to break the habit, under the new Poor Law of 1836, all local almshouses were closed, and paupers were sent to the Union Workhouse in Totnes. Outdoor

56. Sharpham House, Ashprington.

relief in theory stopped, but in practice continued, as these accounts show, for people who were sick or old.

At Tuckenhay nearby a paper mill was built in about 1825 which went on working until after the Second World War. It made very high quality paper, used for artists' drawings, writing paper and envelopes, and a special kind for foreign bank-notes such as those of India and Ceylon. All this was made from rags, which had to be 'thrashed', when metal parts like hooks and eyes were removed, then boiled for hours with alkali, and bleached. It was very labour intensive, employing as many as 60 people in busy times, including many women and girls. The fuel used was coal, brought in by river boats which could only get alongside the quay on the high tide. Like the lumpers in Dartmouth, men were paid a piece rate of 3d. a ton to unload it, and it was then taken by horse and cart to where it was needed, for private houses or the corn mills at Bow.[9]

Cornworthy

Cornworthy, after the dissolution of the monasteries, was bought by the Harris family. Only the remains of the gatehouse of the canoness's priory survive. The church is a beautiful, simple building, with an elaborate canopied tomb of Sir Thomas Harris in lawyer's robes and his wife Elizabeth, dated about 1610. The Norman font, as elsewhere in the Dart valley, shows that there was an earlier church on the site than the present one, which is mainly perpendicular in style. There are squints on each side, a reminder of the days when lepers had to stand outside to share in services.[10]

The Charity Commission report, 1821, records that Dame Elizabeth Harris gave a mill at Gitcombe 'then lately built', with a house and garden around, the rents from which were to be used for the relief of the poor. By 1821 they said no trace of any working mill remained, only houses.

The money was used to support a schoolmaster in a school for the poor. That schools were meant to keep the lower classes in their proper place is made all too clear by the Charity Commissioners:

57. Tuckenhay papermill.

58. Tuckenhay quay.

All the children of the parish have a right to attend school. They are taught reading and arithmetic, and a few of the older boys are taught writing. The girls are taught knitting and sewing by the schoolmaster's wife. The children usually attend the school between the ages of 5 and 9 years, it being the custom of the parish to bind them apprentice at the latter age.

The parish also had a poor house, described in 1865 as consisting of four dwellings adjoining the churchyard, partly used as a schoolroom. It was sold after the opening of the Totnes workhouse and was opened as a National (Anglican) school in the same year.

In the 18th century, John Seale who bought Mount Boone in Townstal also acquired much land in Cornworthy parish and during his many struggles with the Holdsworths in Dartmouth he preferred to come to Cornworthy church despite being much closer to Townstal. This explains why he was buried there in 1777, and his son put up a marble classical-style memorial to him on the wall.

Stoke Gabriel

Stoke was a small village in a very large parish, which included what are really sub-manors at Sandridge and Waddeton. It belonged to the Bishop of Exeter, and it is very likely that the church existed before 1066. The ancient yew in the churchyard is variously estimated at between 1,000 and 1,500 years old, much earlier than the present church. Since it was traditional to plant such yews in holy places, this suggests the site is older than the building. The Bishop of Exeter gave the church to the Chancellor of Exeter Cathedral, who then appointed the vicar. However, he neglected to maintain the church, which in 1338 was said to be nearly fallen to the ground, and the present church dates mainly from the later 14th century.

The old tidal mill on the dam across the creek was still standing in the 1860s, but when it was built is unknown. The lands around the village bear many traces of having once been farmed on the open field system. Away from the village centre, near Waddeton, some strips were marked on the tithe map of 1841, named in the apportionment 'Beastly common' and 'Shrop Down Common', which seem to be the last vestiges of such a system.

A fine row of Tudor buildings near the church includes the old school house, the sexton's house and the *Church House Inn*. The stocks used to stand outside these buildings.

There was a private chapel at Waddeton from at least 1323, possibly earlier, when it was owned by the Fishacre family, and it was used by people of the hamlet of Waddeton, which is some way from Stoke Gabriel. The old mansion lay beside the chapel, but in the 19th century when a new house was built by the Studdy family the chapel was rebuilt nearby.[11]

In the 16th century John Davis the navigator was born at Sandridge, and grew up to be a friend of the Gilbert family in Greenway. Sandridge manor was by then owned by the Pomeroy family, and Davis probably lived in the barton.

By the 19th century, the natural beauty of the parish attracted many wealthy residents. Sandridge was bought by Lord Ashburton, A. W. O. Holdsworth and Henry Hunt both lived at Maisonette at different times, and Sir R. L. Newman also had property there.

In 1866, Stoke Gabriel was hit by a serious cholera epidemic in which 21 people died in one month. Other villages on the Dart had cases too, Ashprington and Dittisham especially. The outbreak occurred before an even more serious one in Brixham, where 61 people died. These villages were picturesque, but the drains left a lot to be desired.[12]

Kingswear

Kingswear, though always much smaller than Dartmouth, had a similar trade pattern. Many merchants lived in the cluster of houses along the shore called Kittery. Just behind, possibly on the site of the modern house 'The Priory', in the late 16th century, lived one of the most prominent merchants, Richard Kelly.[13] He was a part owner of the *Cressant* at the time of the Armada. He and his business partners John Trenhele and John Norman all

59. Tidal mill of about 1860, Stoke Gabriel.

60. *Church House Inn*, Stoke Gabriel, and a row of cottages which once included the old village school.

61. Kingswear waterfront, *c.*1840.

refused to pay petty customs to the Dartmouth Corporation, but after a long legal wrangle were forced to do so.[14] Kelly owned at least six ships, according to the 1587 waterbailiff's account, and was trading in canvas, oil, iron, and kerseys, a locally-made cloth. In 1592 his ship the *Mermaid* left for the Guinea coast of West Africa with a cargo which included: '2 hogsheads of brandy, $1\frac{1}{2}$ gross of Kerseys, 2 barrels of manacles of brass, 63 pans and basins of brass,1 trunk of counterfeit bugles and glasses, 1 chest of 10 doz. hatchets, 5 doz. axes and 2 doz. saws, 1 bundle of 13 hats'. Even the ship's pinnace was filled with seven tons of iron and one firkin of pewter, which would have made it difficult to launch in a hurry. These goods were to be exchanged with the West Africans, who might be deceived by 'counterfeit bugles', and wanted iron and brass goods. The 'manacles' could have been for holding slaves, caught in inter-tribal warfare, and sold to Europeans for shipping to the Spanish colonies in America. Another of Kelly's ships in the same year returned from the Cape Verde Islands with a cargo of '4,000 Guinea hides and 200 elephants' teeth' — the skins of exotic African animals and ivory.[15]

There was no love lost between Kelly and Dartmouth Corporation. He owned a quarry at Godmerock, and was sued by the Corporation for allowing his workmen to throw rubble from it into the harbour. The lawsuit, as usual, went on for years, and led him to counter-claim that he had not been paid his due for the *Cressant* at the time of the Armada, now 20 years past.[16] The Corporation won on both issues. When Kelly died in 1633 he left money for charity to be paid to the poor of Dartmouth, Kingswear and Stoke Gabriel.

In 1604, Kingswear was hit by a fearful epidemic of plague. In one year, 145 people died, almost all marked by the vicar with 'P' in the burial register. The average number of deaths annually in this small community was 10, so it was a major disaster. Any port was likely to be hit if a ship came in with an infected person on board. Dartmouth had had a much smaller epidemic in 1590, when Kingswear escaped, and there were no Dartmouth cases in 1604, so the river served as a barrier to infection. As people knew that isolation was the only hope of stopping it, orders went out immediately to stop travel in or out of a town or village affected.

Kingswear was occupied by the royalist Sir Henry Cary during the Civil War, and the Redoubt earthwork faced with stone built above the village. The merchants must have suffered a severe loss of trade during the war when the port was blockaded. When Fairfax recovered Dartmouth, Cary surrendered his arms and provisions, but was allowed to leave with his troops.

In 1698 John Fownes bought Nethway House, which he rebuilt in the following year, and in 1717 the whole manor of Kingswear including the buildings at Kittery. He added a Georgian front to an old building, later called Kittery Court. It was used by younger sons of the family. Thomas Fownes, his younger grandson, became vicar of Brixham and lived at Kittery House. He gradually bought up and pulled down the adjoining properties to form gardens. The elder grandson, Henry, inherited Nethway and the rest of the estates. In 1747 he married Margaret Luttrell, the heiresss to Dunster Castle in North Devon, and took the name of Fownes-Luttrell. He lived mainly at Dunster, but the family owned the village and most of the land around Kingswear until a sale of 1874.

The result of all this was that from about 1700 Kingswear ceased to be an active trading port, like Dartmouth, and was a residence for a wealthy family. When the ferry from the New Ground in Dartmouth to Hoo Down started, probably after the opening of the turnpike in 1765, Kingswear was by-passed as the road went along the north side of Waterhead Creek, where the *Passage House Inn* was built to serve travellers.

Kittery Court, as it became known by 1803, was sold by the family in 1830 and was owned for a time by the Roopes, before passing to the Hine-Haycocks. Even before the arrival of the railway in 1864, the exceptional climate and views from this coastline near the mouth of the river led to the building of other fine villas such as Holdsworth's Brookhill and the Beacon.[17] Many followed when more land for building was released after 1874, and it became a highly desirable place for holidays for families of yachtsmen.

Dittisham

There was probably a church in Dittisham in Saxon times, of which no trace remains. A stone Norman church replaced it after the conquest, of which only the tower is left today. Between 1328 and 1333 the church was almost completely rebuilt, and Bishop Grandisson himself came to dedicate it on completion.[18] A painting of a medieval tonsured priest has been found on the wall in the chancel, perhaps one of many which used to decorate the church. There is a Norman font, and a very fine 15th-century carved pulpit.

A smaller manor within the parish of Dittisham was Bosomzeal. It was originally called Hele, but passed into the hands of the Boson family whose name was combined with Hele to form Bosomzeal. They had a medieval manor house with its own chapel, which still survives in the present building. In 1450 Sir John Boson's daughter took the manor with her in marriage to Sir Baldwin Fulford, whose family owned it for the next hundred years. As already mentioned, Faith Fulford married John Davis, the navigator from Sandridge. The Fulfords built a fine Tudor living with an enormous stone fireplace onto the medieval house. By the 19th century this manor had been bought by the Seale family, who later sold it to the Raleigh Estates.

Dittisham itself passed by the late 16th century to the Rouse family, who appointed Sampson Strode as rector of the church in 1583. Later, the Strode family of Plympton bought the manor with the advowson from the Prouses, but never lived there.

62. Dittisham church and village, from a 19th-century print.

Most people worked on the land, for very low wages, but those who lived beside the river could hope to supplement their diet and income by fishing. By the 16th century Dittisham had some men who owned boats and were involved in both fishing and trading overseas. When the Corporation of Dartmouth in 1532 complained about the extortions of Sir Thomas Carew, they said he was demanding dues from fishermen for using tucking nets both in the river and in the open sea, which had always been free to all men. Thomas Reynolds of Dittisham suffered greatly at his hands: for not paying the fines demanded he was arrested and his boats seized.[19] After the Corporation's protest, Sir Thomas's actions were stopped.

63. Dittisham ferry and the postmistress with a donkey.

By 1587, a waterbailiff's account reveals that two Dittisham ships were trading to La Rochelle regularly for salt, used both for salting local fish and meat, or increasingly for the Newfoundland trade.[20] They also imported French wine. The owners of the cargo were from Totnes and Paignton, but the ships were probably owned and manned by Dittisham men.

By 1632 William Strode, who had inherited the manor, gave it to the benefice, which meant that the rectors were also lords of the manor. They did not, however, own the advowson. William appointed his kinsman John Strode as rector. On the eve of the Civil War, William Strode was one of the five M.P.s whom Charles I tried to arrest in the House of Commons, and became a leading Parliamentarian. John Strode of Dittisham, however, was strongly for the king. It was said he not only preached against rebellion in his own parish, but also in Dartmouth, where there were many supporters of Parliament. When that town fell to the king, Dittisham was forced to supply food for the royalist army, under a threat that all who refused would be punished.[21] When Fairfax's soldiers recaptured the town in 1645 Strode suffered severely at the hands of a mob who came from Dartmouth, plundered his house and burnt his books including all the church registers. They searched for Strode himself, declaring that if they found him they would kill him and 'hang his quarters before his gate'. He managed to escape, but they turned his wife and children out of his house. It seems likely that the same mob damaged the church's painted panels and a memorial brass which was ripped from the floor.

A Puritan, Edmond Tooker, was appointed to the church and stayed until 1660. John Strode then returned, although weakened by the hardships he had suffered, and remained rector until his death in 1668.

By 1723 the advowson to the rectory had been inherited by Sir John Hobart, who became the Earl of Buckinghamshire. A daughter of that family at the end of the century took the advowson with her on her marriage to the Earl of Mount Edgcumbe. The earls remained patrons of the living until 1959.[22]

The rectors appointed by these patrons remained the lords of the manor, and an 18th-century manor court book shows that the lord's clerk held a court at the Parsonage house. It dealt with all transfers of property from one tenant to another. Lower Dittisham was always referred to as 'Wales'. Tenancies were usually for three lives, with an entrance fine for renewal, and then an annual rent. Tenants had to swear fealty to the lord. It would be possible to work out every family in the village from this book. In 1768 a new rector, John Hutchings, arrived who had 13 children. The old parsonage house in Manor Street had been burnt down, and Hutchings built for his family the large house to the south of the village with a path down to the waterside. The court book shows that Hutchings gave his children many of the houses in the village, from which they would have drawn the rents.

The End of Village Life

Villages were never completely closed communities: some people always went off to seek work elsewhere, and the population changed even if some families continued in residence for hundreds of years. The whole system was brought to an end by the opening up of opportunities of education and travel by the end of the 19th century. The First World War dealt the old ways their final death blow. The board schools, and their church school rivals, had a more open attitude which brought out the hidden talents of their children. Those keen to learn could go on to secondary schools after 1902, though fees had to be paid.

The experiences of Ewart Hutchings, of Dittisham, which he described in *A Village Boys' Story* may serve to illustrate what was happening here and elsewhere.[23] William Hutchings, his father, went to the village school in Dittisham, leaving at the age of 12 to work on a farm for 2s. 6d. a week for 60 hours' work. In 1850 he took a ship from Plymouth to join in the Australian gold rush, later going on to New Zealand. He must have been successful, and, unusually, returned to Dittisham to live. There he brought up his family of seven children, selling farm produce and fruit to Paignton. He and his wife crossed the river to Greenway on the horse ferry, with a pony and trap laden with goods which they took round to hotels and shops in Torbay. They caught salmon with nets, which they stretched out to dry on the beach by their house. Ewart went to the village school, where he did well, and his elder brother in the Navy paid for him to go to a school in Upton, Torquay. This involved a ferry trip to Greenway, a walk to Churston, then a train to Torquay, and a walk of a mile to Upton. Later he went to a school in Plymouth, living with his brother in term time. With this education, never before available to a village boy, he went on to college to

64.   The family of Ewart Hutchings with salmon nets drying on Dittisham beach.

train as a teacher. Despite the interruption of the First World War, he eventually became a headmaster and ended his career as Principal of a College of Education.

   The pattern in the present century is increasingly that, if you want to get on, you have to leave the village for the wider world. On the other hand, those who have 'got on' seek the peace, quiet and beauty of village life. Thus in today's villages, only a minority have ancestors who have lived there for centuries. Most of the inhabitants have moved in, having earned enough elsewhere to choose to live in a beautiful rural environment. The gross poverty which marred the countryside in previous centuries is fortunately a thing of the past, but the descendants of the old villagers cannot afford houses in their own area. Ironically, cottages once used as almshouses now change hands at exorbitant prices.

Chapter Eleven

The Restoration and After

Anglicans and Dissenters

The 'happy return' of Charles II was greeted with much rejoicing even by the Puritan mayor, Lawrence Wheeler, who proclaimed his arrival with trumpeters, church bells and the firing of guns at the castle. The new king's arms were carved and painted, and put up both in the church and in the guildhall.[1]

Before he was invited back, Charles had promised forgiveness to those who had fought against his father, with the exception of those who had ordered his execution, and religious toleration if this was the wish of Parliament. However, the new members elected to his first Parliament were mostly Anglicans, and so hostile to Puritans that they passed a series of laws excluding from all church or public offices anyone who refused to take communion or accept the Prayer Book of the Church of England. Thomas Southcote, son of George and now the Lord of Stoke Fleming, was chosen as one of the town's M.P.s, and proved to be a High Anglican.

The Great Divide

It was a time of triumph for Anglicans, despair for Puritans, now known as Dissenters. In 1662 John Flavel and Allan Geare were among 2,000 clergy who gave up their livings rather than conform to the new laws. They were also forbidden to live within five miles of a town, or to act as schoolmasters. In the same year George Diggons, mayor of Dartmouth, and eight leading burgesses were forced to resign. All the most prominent families of the previous 20 years — Newcomens, Barnes, Cubitts, Plumleighs and Wheelers — refused to go to the Anglican church.[2] James Birdwood, who had been curate at St Petrox, was ejected in 1662.

In all the villages Puritan ministers, like William Bailey of Stoke Fleming, Edmund Tooker of Dittisham, Daniel Getsius of Stoke Gabriel and John Burgess of Ashprington, refused to conform and were ejected.

For the next 150 years Dissenters were barred from the government of the town. Neither could they serve as members of Parliament, go to university, or be customs officials. They faced financial penalties as well: dissenting merchants, since they could no longer be members of the Corporation, had to pay petty customs on their imports and exports from which their Anglican rivals were exempt. Faced with these hard choices, many over the next few years conformed, including Emmanuel Woolley who later became mayor. The rest tended to become a poorer section of the community. While some remained merchants, the majority were tradesmen, craftsmen or labourers, although a few became doctors or attorneys since these professions did not in those days involve going to university.

However, other families were content with the Anglican church, and we find Staplehills, Newmans, Spurways and Jagos taking a leading part as they had done before the Civil War. Any gaps on the Corporation were soon filled by new faces. Nicholas Battersby became vicar of Townstal and St Saviours', and Benjamin Spurway took over at St Petrox.

John Flavel's Adventures

From now on, Dissenters organised their own religious services in secret, sometimes in their own houses, always threatened with arrest. John Flavel's subsequent story reads like a real-life *Pilgrim's Progress* — a book written about this time by another Dissenter, John Bunyan,

112

when in prison for his beliefs. Flavel was a gifted preacher and prolific writer, his published works running to six volumes. Flavel's father, another ejected minister, was arrested with his wife in London for holding an illegal service in his house, and put into Newgate prison in 1665. Though allowed out on bail, both died of plague, which was rife in prison. Flavel left Dartmouth and for many years preached secretly at the homes of friends all over south Devon. One meeting place was on a flat rock in the middle of the Kingsbridge estuary, which was uncovered only at low tide: another was in a wood three miles from Exeter. On one occasion he rode to Totnes disguised as a woman, riding on horseback behind a man, to baptise a child. On another he escaped from pursuers by riding his horse into the sea from one cove at the mouth of the Dart and swimming it round to the next one.

In 1672 Charles II, still himself hoping for religious toleration, announced an 'Indulgence', and Flavel was able to return to Dartmouth openly as a licensed preacher. However, this did not last long and he was forced to leave for London by sea. His boat was nearly wrecked by a storm near Portland. He stayed in London for many years writing books and returned to Dartmouth when James II also granted an 'Indulgence'. Many people thought that this was only a step by James, known to be a Catholic, towards forcing England back to Rome, and Dissenters were accused of being his dupes. Flavel was attacked, his effigy carried through the streets of Dartmouth and burnt. However, his followers were able to set up a proper meeting house in Foss Street for the first time. They were known at different times as the Independents, Congregationalists, and now the United Reformed Church. Flavel died in 1691, on his way to a meeting in Topsham to try to bring together two rival sects. His body was brought back to Dartmouth, across the ferry at Kingswear, followed by mourners all the way, and buried in St Saviour's chancel — a proper place for one who had been vicar — as his followers had no burial ground of their own. By the time of his death, freedom of worship had been granted by William III, but Dissenters were still barred from public office. In 1709 the Corporation ordered the removal of the brass inscription put up in St Saviour's by his followers praising his virtues. This was then put in the meeting house in Foss Street, from which it was taken to the present Flavel church when that was completed in 1895. In 1885 a replica of the inscription was put up in St Saviour's by a less intolerant age.[3]

The Baptists, Huguenots and Quakers

Dissent remained strong in the town throughout the 18th and 19th centuries. Flavel's followers were estimated to number 'several hundred families' by the vicar of Townstal in 1774. There was also a group of Baptists, who had their own licensed preacher, Robert Steed, by 1672. Steed was one of those listed in 1663 as absent from church, and living in Southtown: it can be presumed that his Baptist group existed before this date, to have established itself so far. The Baptists numbered the Newcomen family among their members, and in the 18th century the inventor Thomas Newcomen was one of their preachers who held services in his own house. Their membership appears to have declined in the mid-18th century, when they joined the Flavel group's services and some families such as the Atkins and Lidstones appear on the registers of both churches.[4] By 1788 they had established a meeting house up the steps of Chapel Lane in Southtown, where it was described as 'lately erected' in an indenture of 1824, but where they met before that is not known.[5]

A group of French Huguenot refugees from the persecution of Louis XIV arrived in St Petrox parish after 1685. The stories that these people brought with them of their sufferings at the hands of Louis' dragoons aroused much sympathy, and £25 was sent to Dartmouth from a general subscription for their relief.[6] It all helped to fuel anti-Catholic feelings when there were fears that James II would try to follow his cousin Louis' example to force people back into the Catholic church. The Huguenots, being followers of Calvin, had similar religious views to Flavel's, but quarrelled amongst themselves as to whether to conform to the Anglican church or to remain a separate sect. Their first Pastor, Andre de Sante from Poitou, wished to conform, and withdrew when his congregation opposed him. The next Pastor was Jean Pentecost, in 1691, who led them as a small independent group of Dissenters who had a meeting place somewhere near St Petrox. Successive pastors were appointed to the French church, the last being Jean Maillard in 1737. Other French names in the St Petrox registers include Ongier, Gentel, and Chaille. Some of their descendants, who later joined the Baptists, were still in Dartmouth up till the 19th century.

There were also small numbers of Quakers, who usually worshipped with their friends in Kingsbridge. One of them, Walter Prideaux, became town clerk to the Dartmouth Corporation, the first of several of his family to hold this post over the next 60 years.

Thomas Newcomen and the Atmospheric Engine

Barred from taking part in the town's affairs by his Baptist beliefs, Elias Newcomen carried on his father's trade as a merchant and shipowner, and by his first wife Sarah had two sons. The younger, Thomas, became an ironmonger and inventor, who can truly be said to have changed the course of world history by his development of the atmospheric engine. Of his early education nothing certain is known, but his two surviving letters are written in a literate hand and reveal not only deep religious faith and biblical knowledge but also acquaintance with European politics of his day. His training as a practical ironmonger would have included work with all kinds of metal — brass, tin, copper and lead as well as iron — and his career shows he must have read about earlier experiments to harness steam power.

By 1707 Thomas was living with his wife in a house described in the town rental as 'next the Guildhall'. It ran through from Higher Street to Lower Street. He is also listed as owning several other properties in the town, and cellars used as workshops. He served his fellow Baptists as a preacher for 20 years as well as earning his living as an ironmonger. His work included not merely selling but making all kinds of iron goods, for which records show that he imported nearly 25 tons of iron in 1698-9. In his spare time, with his fellow-Baptist partner John Calley, he worked to develop an engine which was to be one of the major advances in the Industrial Revolution.

His job gave him a reason to visit the many tin mines then existing in Devon and Cornwall. He would have seen at first hand the problem which was troubling miners everywhere: how to get rid of the water as mines became deeper. Thomas Savery had patented a steam engine in 1698 but it was not able to pump water from the depth required. Newcomen developed an engine which used a vacuum caused by condensing steam in an iron cylinder which was connected by chains to a large rocking beam. Steam entered the cylinder from a boiler below, pushing the piston up; water was then sprayed inside the cylinder creating a vacuum and the piston was forced down again by atmospheric pressure. The other end of the rocking beam was connected to the mine shaft and operated the pumps.[7] Because Savery was richer and better known, Newcomen formed a partnership with him, and was able to use the balance of Savery's patent up to 1733, but Savery's engine worked by entirely different principles and was not effective.

Newcomen and Calley had perfected a scale model of the engine in a workshop in Dartmouth by about 1710, and the first full-scale engine was completed near Dudley Castle in 1712, in the heart of the South Staffordshire coalfield. Newcomen was introduced to the coal mining interests of the West Midlands through his Baptist connections. The records of the Netherton Cinder Bank church record as a visiting member in 1710 Elias Newcomen, probably Thomas' nephew who worked with him in his business. A Baptist church existed at Netherton, about a mile from where his first engine was built. When a new Baptist

65. Lower Street in the 1860s, by William Henley. The building on the left is the back of the Guildhall, with Newcomen's house next door. Some of its plasterwork, with that from other houses also demolished in 1864, was removed to Newcomen Cottage, Ridge Hill, by Thomas Lidstone.

meeting house was built in Bromsgrove in 1719 Thomas Newcomen of Dartmouth was one of the trustees. All this suggests that the Newcomens knew and stayed with Baptist friends through whom they would become familiar with the problems of water in coal mines in the area. After the success of the Dudley engine, similar engines were soon built in many coal mining areas. It was obviously economical to use coal to fire the engine which could then enable the coal to be mined at greater depths. However, they were also built in the tin mines of Cornwall, far from any coalfields, where at least five were in operation by 1727. Newcomen's later years were spent more and more away from home organising his business.[8]

While he was completely ignored by the ruling faction in Dartmouth, he soon attracted notice from mining engineers overseas. A Swedish engineer reported seeing his engine in

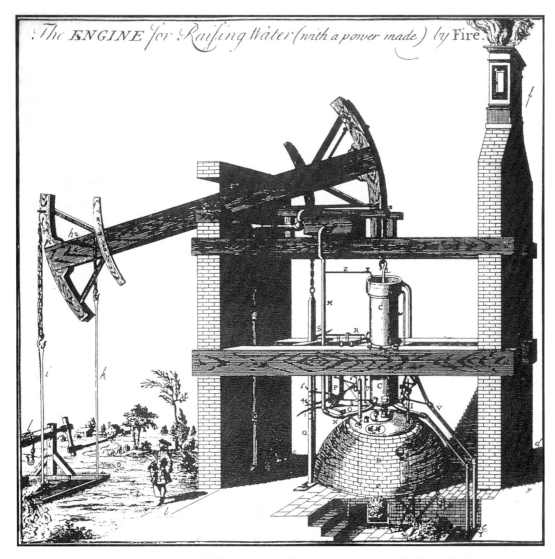

66. A drawing by Henry Beighton, 1717, of an early Newcomen engine at Oxclose. Used for pumping water out of mines, these engines led to an industrial revolution based on steam power produced by burning coal.

1720, and John Calley died in 1725 in Holland where he was negotiating for a patent. By the time of the expiry of the patent in 1733, four years after Newcomen's death, there were over 100 engines working on sites all over England and Scotland, as well as in Sweden, Hungary, Belgium, Germany and Austria. Newcomen died in London, aged 67, at the home of a Baptist friend Edward Wallin, and was buried in a non-conformist burial ground. James Watt, 50 years later, improved on one of these engines when he was asked to mend one, and later adapted it to turn a wheel. After that, the applications of the new power to industry, as well as to land and sea transport, were limitless, and the world moved into the Age of Steam.

It was not until the 19th century that Dartmouth recognised its native genius, but that did not stop his house in Lower Street being pulled down for road widening in 1864. Thomas Lidstone, an architect and surveyor, whose ancestors had been close friends of the Newcomens in Thomas' day, wrote three pamphlets on his life. When his house was demolished he bought much of the plasterwork from it, along with some from other houses, and built these panels into a new house he was building for himself on Ridge Hill.[9] Arthur H. Holdsworth had already, before 1841, bought the wainscoting from his sitting room to put in a summer house at Brookhill, from where it was later removed to the Borough Museum. Other panels which Holdsworth also removed have, sadly, since been destroyed. In 1963, to commemorate the bicentenary of his birth, Percy Russell and the Newcomen Society arranged for one of his surviving engines to be brought to Dartmouth and erected in a special building in the car park, where visitors can see it working.

In the long run, steam power spelt the end of prosperity for places like Dartmouth, far from the coal fields. Even when the rotary engine was adapted to the locomotive, the hills around the Dart valley made the building of railways formidably expensive so that they were late in reaching the town. For a while in the late 19th and early 20th centuries steam ships provided a burst of prosperity but eventually their increasing size made them move to larger ports.

67. Drawings of plasterwork now in Newcomen Cottage, Ridge Hill, removed from houses in Lower Street in 1864.

The Borough and its Government

The new Corporation were delighted to welcome Charles II when he arrived by ship on 23 July 1671. They entertained him lavishly in the panelled room in the Butterwalk, now part of the Borough Museum, and the mayor, Emmanuel Woolley, contributed £36 6s.8d. in gratuities to his gentlemen, ushers and other servants.[10] There is in St Saviour's church a stained glass coat of arms to Charles FitzCharles, the bastard son of the king, whom he created Earl of Dartmouth (according to local legend) because he was conceived on his travels in Devon on this occasion. The boy died young. Charles was rowed to Kingswear and continued by road to Exeter. The Hody family who then lived at Nethway House have a record that he spent the night of 23 July there.[11]

In 1671 there appears the first mention in the town accounts of the building of the New Ground, originally called the 'new town'. There are a lot of entries for 'carrying ballast' there, to build up the sandbank which appeared at low tide to form usable ground.[12] The original intention may have been to build on it, but the ground proved unstable and on one occasion was nearly washed away. There were already problems with the Butterwalk foundations, and in the end a strong stone wall was built around the reclaimed land for use as extra quay space for ships to tie up. A stone bridge was built to join the New Ground to the north corner of the Quay, which can be seen in many old prints. The land itself became a recreation place, used amongst other things for bonfires to celebrate national victories, coronations and the like. Some time after it was completed, a new ferry was started from the New Ground to Kingswear at Hoo Down, where a more level road led along Waterhead Creek towards Torbay. The old ferry route from the end of Bearscove to Kingswear village continued to be used for local traffic.

Although so many of the townsmen were excluded by religion from any share in the borough affairs, the burgesses who were eligible soon began to dispute within themselves for power, twisting rules and customs to suit themselves. The ancient custom was that there was a mayor with 12 senior councillors called magistrates.[13] Another 12, a sort of second team, were under them and called common councilmen. Finally there was a wider body of freemen, from whom all councillors were chosen. Their numbers were never laid down and varied in practice from 30 to 60. To choose a new mayor the retiring mayor and magistrates nominated two of themselves, from whom the whole body of freemen chose one. After serving for one year, he could not be re-elected again for three years, except in the case of the death of a mayor in office, when his predecessor took over for the rest of the year. To become a freeman the basic qualifications were to be the son of a freeman, or to have served an apprenticeship in the town and, of course, to be an Anglican. However, the choice from those eligible was made by the mayor and magistrates, who chose their friends, relations and business partners. The advantages of being a freeman included exemption from paying petty customs, and the right to vote for mayors and members of Parliament; the duties were to attend at such elections, and to be available to serve on juries.

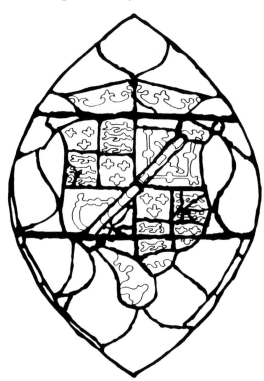

68. Drawing of the arms of Charles FitzCharles, showing the 'bend sinister' of bastardy, from a window in St Saviour's.

There were frequent conflicts between rival groups, each prepared to use any means to install its candidate. In 1680 Arthur Holdsworth, the outgoing mayor, forcibly installed his candidate Jago as his successor, though the freemen had voted for John Whitrow. Even when ordered by the Court of King's Bench to swear in Whitrow, Holdsworth refused to hand over the keys of the money chest or the borough seal, in an attempt to bring the affairs in the town to a halt. Here, the Common Council did step in, and declared all actions by Jago illegal, including the making of freemen.

As Charles II's life drew to a close, his heir being his openly Catholic brother James, Duke of York, tension throughout the country increased. Titus Oates' allegations of a Catholic plot against the king increased suspicions against ordinary Catholics. Among these was Sir John Southcote, who had inherited the manors of Stoke Fleming along with Buckland Tout Saints and others. He and his wife fled to France for a time in March 1679, amidst rumours that they were involved with the plotters.[14] There were equally wild rumours against the Baptists in Devon, who were said in 1682 to be plotting to 'fall upon the King

69. View of the New Ground, reclaimed 1670-80, and the high tide reaching to the back of the Butterwalk, in a print of about 1866. The railway, which reached Kingswear in 1864, can be seen. St Petrox's spire was taken down in 1855.

and all his Duchesses and whores, and the Duke of York and all his Duchesses and whores' to set up a Commonwealth again.[15] The newly-coined names of parties, Whigs and Tories, represented broadly the old parliamentary and royalist sides in the Civil War.

The Whigs tried to pass an Act excluding James from the throne, which Charles refused to sign. The king was already trying to influence the politics of town corporations by calling in their charters and reissuing them. Under Dartmouth's new charter of 1684, the royalist John Beare was made Recorder. He was a neighbour of Sir John Southcote at Buckland and a noted persecutor of Dissenters. In October 1685 he sent an address to the Council in London from the inhabitants of Dartmouth promising that they would never choose as M.P.s anyone who had voted for the Exclusion Bill, thus lining the town up firmly with the Tories.[16]

When Charles died, James succeeded to the throne but was soon faced by a challenge from the Duke of Monmouth whose landing at Lyme Regis attracted much support from the West Country. However, the Dartmouth Corporation loyally supported James, and lit bonfires to celebrate Monmouth's defeat and execution.[17] That a few at least of the humbler men were among Monmouth's supporters is shown by the fact that when they were hanged, drawn and quartered it was ordered the limbs of some should be displayed in the town.[18]

In 1687 James dismissed Edward Seymour the Recorder of Totnes and appointed Sir John Southcote in his place. The mayor and 33 of the 37 freemen refused to agree to this. Seventeen of them were dismissed by the king, who ordered them to admit others in their place, many of them known Protestant Dissenters to whom he had given toleration to win their support. Edward Seymour, who had fought loyally for Charles I, now joined the king's opponents. This must have created alarm in neighbouring Dartmouth, where Sir John had also been made a freeman.[19]

When James' actions aroused so much opposition from those with political power that William of Orange, his son-in-law, was invited to come to England, the Dartmouth Corporation was in a quandary. The accounts of expenditure simply do not refer to the landing of William at Brixham only five miles away, and the conclusion must be that they were waiting to see which side would win before risking their necks.

Nicholas Roope, however, whose father had lost so much fighting for Parliament's cause in the Civil War, had no doubts and was, he later claimed, 'the first gentleman who went to the King' when William landed. Unlike their cousin Ambrose of Little Dartmouth, the two Nicholas Roopes had not been members of the Corporation since 1662, and may well have been Dissenters. The elder Nicholas died in 1681. His son was rewarded for his early support by being made Governor of Dartmouth Castle by William in January 1689.[20] He held this post during the difficult year of 1692, when James, who had fled to France, was attempting with a French fleet to recover his throne. This fleet was at one time off Dartmouth, and Roope wrote in a letter to the Earl of Nottingham that he believed some in the town such as Sir John Southcote were likely to go over to James.

This was more than likely since, in June 1690, a warrant had been issued for the arrest on a charge of treason of Sir John Southcote, who again fled to France with his wife.[21] He later returned and lived quietly for the rest of his life at Buckland, where he had recently rebuilt the house there into a fine mansion.[22]

The Corporation of Dartmouth proclaimed William as king just as they had James, and continued with their internal power struggles. For the first time M.P.s were chosen from outside Devon, as Westminster party leaders tried to gain control of Parliament. The Tory merchant family of Herne from London, after at first failing to be elected in 1673, secured one or both Dartmouth seats for most of the years from 1689 to 1715 for five different members of the family, by methods which brought election petitions from their opponents in many cases.[23]

John Whitrow, who was mayor again in 1689, after the writ arrived for the election of the borough M.P.s, made 25 new freemen who had to promise they would vote for the election of George Booth against the Tory Josiah Herne. Herne successfully appealed to the Commons, who summoned Whitrow to London and arrested him for a time for his actions in this case. Since the Commons was at that time Whig and Herne was Tory, the fact that they found in his favour suggests he must have had a good legal case.

As Tories and Whigs wrestled for control in the town between 1699 and 1702, two rival mayors were elected, each of whom held elections for the two M.P.s. This was investigated by the House of Commons Committee, which revealed all sorts of irregularities. Some mayors had made freemen alone, or with only two or three magistrates, or, as in Whitrow's case, on the promise of voting a certain way. By 1706 the rules for making freemen were clarified: only the mayor and a *majority* of the magistrates could make them. However, out of 12, only seven might be present, and these all related by marriage or business partnerships, so in practice it was all too easy for a small clique to get its way.

Christopher Hayne, whose brother William had been M.P. for Dartmouth between 1689 and 1695, offered to stand for election in 1708. A merchant in the Spanish trade, now living in London, he wrote to another brother Cornelius in Dartmouth saying, 'My aim is for removing the scandal which the Corporation lies under. The very town's name is become offensive with the best sort of men'. His offer was ignored, and the Hernes, whom he blamed for this state of affairs, were still returned up to 1715. In 1714 he wrote again, saying that he refused to use his vote for any of the candidates. 'Those who have had the governing part have unfortunately been very much mistaken. The many monuments of ruin and decay are too obvious in their streets.' Hayne was by that time sufficiently well known in the city of London to be consulted by Horace Walpole and Lord Townshend about the terms they were then negotiating of a commercial treaty with Spain, on which he sent them a memorandum.[24]

After 1714 and the arrival of George I, the leaders of the borough began to support the Whig party, especially after Robert Walpole came to power, as its policies encouraged trade with the colonies which helped the town to become prosperous again. Control of the borough passed to the Holdsworth family for the next hundred years.

Chapter Twelve

The Holdsworth Era

The Holdsworth family dominated Dartmouth between 1715 and 1832. In 1650 the first Arthur Holdsworth came from Modbury and soon after married Joan Newman, the first of many marriages between the two families. Arthur lived at Mount Galpin (a name brought

70. Mount Galpin, Clarence Hill, home of Arthur Holdsworth.

from Modbury), though perhaps in an earlier house on the site of the present mid-18th-century building in Clarence Hill. The Newmans were already well established in the Portugal trade, and owned vineyards on the Douro from whose grapes they later made port wine. As well as the main Holdsworth line, there was also a younger branch descended from Robert Holdsworth. The first Arthur Holdsworth was soon a shipowner and merchant, taking a leading part in town affairs and serving as mayor three times between 1672 and 1685, but the family influence was not supreme until the 18th century.

By the 18th century the Holdsworths were linked by marriage or business partnerships with a small group of families, such as the Hunts, Roopes, Brookings and Teages, as well as the Newmans. Younger sons served as captains in the fishing fleet, or as factors at their various centres in Newfoundland, Spain or Portugal. Older sons were made freemen, and took their turn as mayors or aldermen. They married the daughters of the same set of families, so that the whole ruling group of the town became a close-knit old boy (and girl) network.

The Holdsworth family did not invent the system of controlling the Corporation, but they took advantage of it. The family, including the descendants of the younger Robert, was prolific as well as able. It never died out in the male line, even though in the mid-18th century each Arthur Holdsworth had in turn only one son — very risky in those days of infectious diseases. Between 1715 and 1830, a Holdsworth was Mayor for 49 years. If the related families are included, the total is 76. In the years between only those of whom the family approved were chosen, and no one opposed to them ever became a freeman. The family undoubtedly produced talented men over seven generations and was the chief employer in the town as well as controlling the borough and the church.

One wealthy family who did not become dominated by the Holdsworths was the Hayne family, also wealthy merchants with sons in Cadiz, Oporto and London. Cornelius Hayne

71. Silver punchbowl given by George Treby, M.P. for Dartmouth, to Arthur Holdsworth II before 1727. It was engraved by Paul Lamerie c.1720.

owned much property in Lower Street and built what came to be known as Hayne's Great House there. He also owned Fuge House, in Blackawton. His son Charles, who inherited great wealth, bought the Lupton estate near Brixham, where he rebuilt the house in 1750, and preferred the life of a country gentleman.

The first Arthur Holdsworth, who came to Dartmouth from Modbury and married Joan Newman, died in 1690. His son (1668-1726) became a close friend of George Treby, M.P. for Dartmouth from 1722-27, who gave him a beautiful silver punchbowl, now in the Ashmolean Museum, Oxford. This depicts on one side a dozen 18th-century gentlemen in tricorn hats, followed by their dogs, walking along a quay, with a row of columns on the left which may represent those of the Butterwalk, and a merchant vessel moored off shore. On the other side they are shown sitting at a table on which a punchbowl like this is prominent, under an inscription 'Prosperity to Hooks and Lines'. They are smoking long-stemmed pipes and drinking punch. The ingredients for these mayoral feasts occur regularly in the town accounts: an indigestible diet of lobsters, mutton and cheese washed down by punch made from rum, lemons and sugar.

These feasts were not held in the Guildhall, which by this time was used only for meetings of the Corporation and for court sessions, but in the 'Mayoralty House'. The Mansion House in Lower Street, built about 1735 by Captain Edward Ashe, contains a fine large room decorated with elaborate plasterwork full of classical allusions which is believed to have been used at one time for these feasts, though so far no documentary evidence proves

72.   Plasterwork in the Mansion House, Dartmouth. This particular example, on the walls of the stairs, depicts the labours of Hercules.

73. Widecombe House, Stokenham, the country house of the Holdsworth family.

this.[1] By the early 19th century the Mayoralty House was in the Hayne's 'Great House' in Lower Street where there was a large wood panelled room with a dais at one end on which the Corporation sat.[2] This is now the Masonic Hall.

The third Arthur Holdsworth (1701-1753) was made Governor of Dartmouth Castle in 1725, during his father's lifetime, the first of five Holdsworths to hold this post continuously until 1860. He bought the estate of Widecombe, in Stokenham parish, where he rebuilt the house there for his family, while he commuted to Mount Galpin in Dartmouth to run his business and the town's affairs.

The fourth Arthur Holdsworth (1733-1777), like his father, generally supported the Whigs in politics and was prepared to accept outsiders nominated by them as M.P.s. In 1761 he wrote to the Duke of Newcastle promising support for the two new candidates Howe and Jeffreys nominated by the Duke, assuring him that 'all my friends are unanimous in their behalf'.[3] The fifth Arthur Holdsworth (1757-87) who died young was himself M.P. for Dartmouth from 1780-87 and his widow, left with five children to bring up, was able to claim a pension from the government on the grounds that he had contracted consumption from living in London as his job had entailed. The sixth Arthur Holdsworth (1731-1807) was a cousin of the last, so to speak keeping the seat warm until the eldest son of the fifth

Arthur was old enough to take over. This was Arthur Howe Holdsworth (1780-1860), who was M.P. from 1802-20 and 1829-32, and who held the post of Governor of Dartmouth Castle until his death.

In addition to their grip on the borough, the family also controlled the church, of which the town held the advowson. Henry Holdsworth was vicar of Townstal from 1726 to 1763, to be followed by John Nosworthy who, though not himself a Holdsworth, had married Sarah, daughter of the third Arthur. Another Holdsworth, Robert, became vicar from 1808-1836, when he moved to become Vicar of Brixham which was also in the gift of the family. They controlled the advowson of Stokenham, as Lords of the Manor, where three Holdsworths were incumbents between 1739 and 1829.

The Challenge from the Seales

The Holdsworth grip on the borough by the middle of the 18th century was challenged by the new owner of Mount Boone, John Seale, who in 1724 bought it along with the whole estate of Norton Dawnay.[4] He was the grandson and heir of a wealthy London merchant who had lived and traded from the Channel Islands, and whose name appears in the Port Books as the owner of a merchant ship calling at Dartmouth with Jersey goods on her way to New England in 1712. The young John (1704-77), his heir, came to Mount Boone when just under age, and soon afterwards bought the estates of Coombe, adjoining the borough on the north, and Cornworthy. In 1733 he married Mary Hayne, daughter of Cornelius, who gave her a dowry. John became a friend of her brother Charles, who soon owned Fuge and Lupton. When Mary died, John married his second wife Elizabeth Fownes of Nethway, whose family were now the biggest landowners in Kingswear and around the east side of the Dart. Seale kept up some trading interests by shipping cargoes to the Mediterranean, but generally, like Charles Hayne, preferred to use his wealth to become a landed gentleman, and clearly expected to be welcomed into the ruling circles in Dartmouth. When he was not even chosen as a freeman, he began to create trouble for the Holdsworths.

74. Mount Boone and Clarence Hill from an old painting.

The Southcotes of Stoke Fleming began now to play a bigger part in borough affairs. Sir John Southcote of Buckland died childless, and by 1725 his property had passed to a distant relative, another John Southcote, who was a merchant of Dartmouth. He inherited Buckland, Stoke Fleming and all the other Southcote manors and built a small new Manor House in Southtown in 1727 (*see* plate 79). The Manor House, pulled down for road widening in 1905, can be seen in many old photographs and has left its name in the Manor Gardens. John was succeeded in 1744 by his son Henry Southcote, who became a friend of John Seale, and both seem very soon to have joined in opposition to the ruling Holdsworth group.

Coombe Mud: the Mud Trial, 1739-41
The first clash between Seale and the Corporation came in 1739. As owner of the Coombe estate which bordered the river, he claimed ownership of the mud to low water mark, and disputed the right of the Corporation to dig it up and sell it as ballast to ships — a practice which had for years produced a steady income. The case went to the Devon Assizes, when both sides drew a map to support their claims. It shows Coombe House and estate, Coombe Mud and the buildings, mainly shipyards, which fringed it on the south side, and the disputed pits. The Corporation claimed to own the mud below high water mark by their

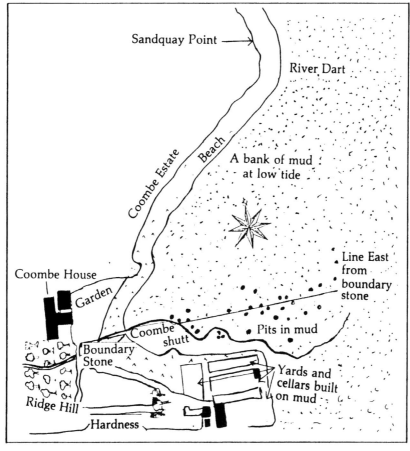

75. Map of Coombe Mud, 1741, drawn during the law suit.

lease of the Waterbaileywick. However, the court decided that this applied only within the boundary of the borough which was marked by a series of boundary (bond) stones, the most northerly of which stood at the southern end of Coombe Mud. The final version of the map, drawn after the case was concluded in April 1741, shows a line drawn due east from this stone, north of which the Mud belonged to Seale as far as low water mark.[5] In 1747 Seale ordered some fishermen, licensed by the Corporation as waterbailiffs, to stop drawing their seine nets on to Coombe Mud to land their fish. He even 'stepped into the water half a leg deep and with his penknife cut off 8 or 10 fathoms of the seine rope . . . and the fishermen by that means lost a fine draught of herrings worth upwards of £3 or £4, besides their rope worth about 10s.' He was able to show in the court case which followed that the fishermen had in the past given presents of fish to previous owners of Coombe — a feudal due admitting ownership — so again the Corporation lost their case.[6]

Southtown: Southcote's Trespass Case, 1749
Henry Southcote now joined the attack. It was the custom for the mayor, aldermen, bailiffs and any inhabitants, especially the boys of the town, to walk once a year in procession round the bond stones which marked the extent of the borough. In Southtown, which was part of the manor of Stoke Fleming but had been given to the borough to enable them to defend the castle, this involved crossing the lands of Southcote.[7] He accused them of trespass, and in 1749 stationed about 20 men armed with sticks to stop them breaking through a hedge to cross his field. This case also went to court, and a map was drawn which gives an interesting picture of Southtown at this date. It shows the roads of Southtown and Above Town, much as they are today, joining at the foot of Swannaton Road. The procession walked around Warfleet creek to St Petrox church, returning by the foot of Gallant's Bower to where two bondstones stood near Warfleet Mill. On the return route the boys and Constable went past the end of the Ropewalk and across two fields called Facy's Field and Facy's Hill. It was because they had to break down the hedge to cross these that Southcote objected. He ordered his men to stop the procession by force. The court in this case upheld the Corporation's rights. Perhaps it was just as well that Henry Southcote died in 1750, aged only 30, leaving an infant son, and the family's quarrels with the Corporation lapsed.

Sandquay, 1772-7
There were several minor lawsuits between the Corporation and Seale over the next 20 years, as they tried to challenge his manorial rights to Townstal and Norton, without success, and there was little love lost between them. In 1772 Seale began to build a large quay beyond Sandquay, about 90 feet long, and 80 feet out into the river, by dumping stones into the harbour. When the Corporation ordered him to stop, claiming he infringed their rights as waterbailiffs, another long and costly lawsuit began which was not decided until 1777. The first John Seale died in that year, but his heir, also John (1753-1824), carried on his father's policies with equal enthusiasm. The Corporation claimed the quay would ruin fishing, and would obstruct the shipping of the harbour. Seale showed that the quay was 13 feet short of the low water mark, and the 1741 trial had shown that he owned the mud up to that mark. He brought evidence from merchants and captains in the Newfoundland trade that the quay, far from being harmful to the harbour, would be of great use to them. Further, he pointed out that the Corporation had themselves, in their New Ground and New Quay, built further out into the harbour than he had, but now tried to stop others doing the same on their own property. A jury was brought to view the site, and the verdict went in favour of Seale, who was given damages of 40 shillings. The Corporation had to pay legal costs of over £600.[8] After this Sandquay was completed, and became a major shipbuilding area in the town for almost 200 years.

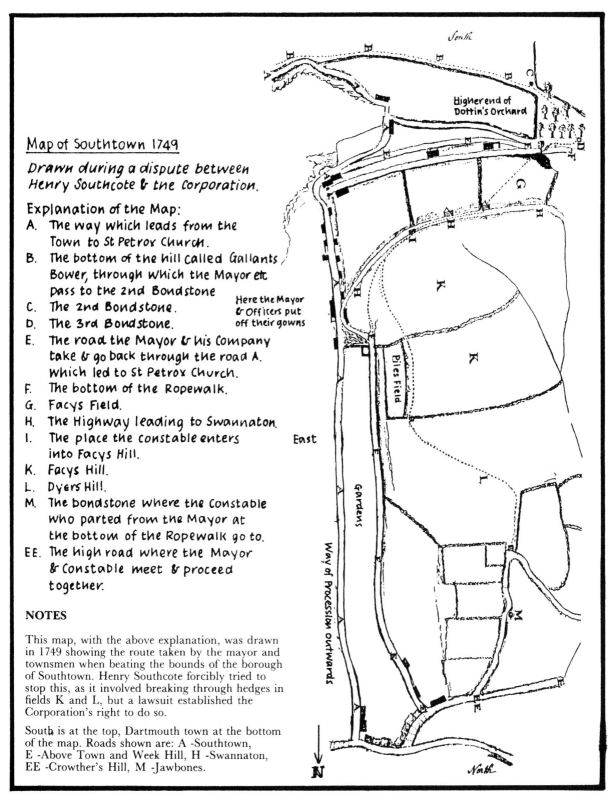

Map of Southtown 1749

Drawn during a dispute between Henry Southcote & the Corporation.

Explanation of the Map:

A. The way which leads from the Town to St Petrox Church.
B. The bottom of the hill called Gallants Bower, through which the Mayor etc pass to the 2nd Bondstone
C. The 2nd Bondstone.
D. The 3rd Bondstone.
E. The road the Mayor & his Company take & go back through the road A. which led to St Petrox Church.
F. The bottom of the Ropewalk.
G. Facys Field.
H. The Highway leading to Swannaton.
I. The place the constable enters into Facys Hill.
K. Facys Hill.
L. Dyers Hill.
M. The bondstone where the Constable who parted from the Mayor at the bottom of the Ropewalk go to.
EE. The high road where the Mayor & Constable meet & proceed together.

NOTES

This map, with the above explanation, was drawn in 1749 showing the route taken by the mayor and townsmen when beating the bounds of the borough of Southtown. Henry Southcote forcibly tried to stop this, as it involved breaking through hedges in fields K and L, but a lawsuit established the Corporation's right to do so.

South is at the top, Dartmouth town at the bottom of the map. Roads shown are: A -Southtown, E -Above Town and Week Hill, H -Swannaton, EE -Crowther's Hill, M -Jawbones.

76. Southtown in 1749.

Refusal to pay Petty Customs

One dangerous feature of this case for the Corporation was that many of the merchants, even including some younger members of the Newman family, sided with Seale. In 1772 we find the Corporation taking legal advice because merchants, encouraged by Seale, found they could evade paying petty customs by becoming freemen of Bristol and other places, which only cost them £10.[9] In 1784 the fifth Arthur Holdsworth, now M.P. for the town, was negotiating a new lease for the waterbaileywick with the Duchy of Cornwall. He claimed that the amounts collected in petty customs over the last 20 years barely exceeded the High Rent because of this. At the same time, John Henry Southcote, now grown up and an active lord of Stoke Fleming as well as friend of Seale, offered to lease the waterbaileywick for himself, which convinced the Duchy that it was much more valuable than Holdsworth claimed. Southcote, on evidence from retired collectors, wrote to them estimating the income at £80 a year, less £20 paid to the collector for his services. The Duchy therefore demanded a huge entry fine of £360. Holdsworth was horrified, but wrote 'If I pay for the business myself, Southcote must not have it'.[10]

The Corporation paid the fine, reluctantly, but the lease on inspection contained a clause obliging them to 'defend the rights of His Royal Highness against unlawful claims made by freemen of Bristol, Exeter etc.'. This caused even more consternation at the cost of law suits against the merchants and boroughs concerned, where Dartmouth freemen had similar exemptions. They demanded the erasure of this clause, to which the Duchy agreed; however, by an oversight in their office, it was not re-sealed after the erasure, thus making the whole lease invalid. This was only discovered in 1789, in the course of another legal battle with Seale, and when the news got out in the town no one would pay any dues at all.[11] The matter was eventually put right in a new lease of 1792, on the life of Arthur Howe Holdsworth, then aged twelve.[12] This proved to be the last lease granted by the Duchy to the borough, for when he died in 1860 they refused to renew it again.

The Right to Vote

As already seen, M.P.s were in effect chosen by the Holdsworth group, and were often men unconnected with the town. One eminent and popular number was Richard Howe, M.P. from 1757-82, a naval officer who became an admiral and served with distinction from the Seven Years War up to the end of the century. When he became an Earl in 1782 he moved to the House of Lords, so vacating his Dartmouth seat in the Commons. In the election of 1784, John Henry Southcote stood against Arthur Holdsworth and Richard Hopkins, claiming that the right of election belonged to the residents of Southtown, of which he was one. When the other two men were elected, he petitioned the Commons, but the Committee of Privileges ruled that only freemen of Dartmouth had the vote. John Henry Southcote was made Sheriff of Devon in 1785, a position of honour awarded to eminent landed gentry, and it seems ironical that he was not even able to vote in his own manor.[13]

Seale then stood for election in 1790, against the Holdsworth-backed candidates Edmund Bastard of Sharpham and John Villiers, again claiming the right of the inhabitants to vote. The freemen voted 35 for Bastard, 29 for Villiers and 8 for Seale. Seale marched 40 inhabitants of Southtown to the Guildhall but their votes for him were disallowed. He then petitioned the Commons on the grounds that bribery had been used, quoting cases where jobs, or renewals on leases for houses, had been promised in return for votes. Seale argued his case very effectively, demanding to see old Corporation records, and quoting the case of Thomas Boone's election by all the inhabitants in 1658 as a precedent. Both sides had to appear in London, when Walter Prideaux, the town clerk, was able to show that only freemen had ever had the right to vote. Seale lost his case — in those days there were far worse examples of corruption — with costs awarded to the Corporation. Prideaux, smarting

under previous defeats by the Seales, inflated these to £408, which Seale's lawyers argued
was exorbitant. They included transporting to London by post-chaise an old man, Thomas
Skinner, and his servant, so 'afflicted by the palsy that he could neither rise nor walk
without assistance', and putting him up in the best inns for the whole hearing.[14]

A group of Seale's supporters in the town formed a 'Committee of Privileges' which
included some of the younger sons of the ruling families, such as William Newman and
Roope Harris Roope who could expect to be chosen as freemen. The Council minutes record
a resolution that 'None of these shall on any account be elected freemen of the Borough'.[15]
There was little any of them could do as the law then stood. Seale made another attempt
to be elected in 1808, but after that devoted the rest of his life to campaigning for
parliamentary reform. He gave many speeches using Dartmouth as an example of the worst
kind of 'rotten borough', a phrase which in the end led to the Reform Act of 1832.

The Southcote Bankruptcy

John Henry Southcote had married Margaret Luttrell, of Dunster Castle, by whom he had
a son, also John Henry, and three daughters. They lived at Buckland Tout Saints, from
where he continued to take an interest in Stoke Fleming and Dartmouth affairs. However,
in 1794 he went bankrupt: Buckland Tout Saints and all his lands were sold. John Seale
bought the manor of Southtown, while Stoke Fleming was divided among many different
owners including Seale and Holdsworth. Southcote lived on until 1820, having regained
some money but no lands. Rumour has it that his children's extravagance was a cause of is
bankruptcy. In his will of 1806 he disinherited his three surviving children and left all his
money to two sons of a lady who one can only suppose was his mistress. His legitimate son,
John Henry, died childless in 1815 and the two surviving daughters, left with no dowry,
never married. The Southcote control of Stoke Fleming had ended.

Chapter Thirteen

The Newfoundland Trade

Prosperity to Hooks and Lines

Troubled Times, 1660-1713

After 1660, despite opposition from both the government and west-country ports, many people began to settle in Newfoundland and New England. The men began to catch and salt fish to sell to ships sent from England, who then merely loaded up and returned to sell their cargo in Europe. The French, in contrast, actually subsidised both men and women to settle in Newfoundland, where a sizeable community was established at Placentia to compete with the English for the fish.[1] While France was prepared to defend her colonists with warships, the English had none to spare.

The English needed the navy to fight two wars with the Dutch, in 1665-7 and 1673-4, both of which hit the Newfoundland trade. When the Dutch Admiral De Ruyter attacked the harbour of St John's in 1665 he was able unhindered to take all the ships and destroy cattle and houses. He said himself that six mounted guns there would have stopped him from entering. When the lease of the waterbaileywick was being renewed in 1673 the mayor petitioned that no entry fine should be charged as the profits were much lessened by reason of the 'utter decay of the Newfoundland fishing and the great loss of trade'.[2]

In 1676 laws were passed forbidding masters from taking more men than were needed for the fishing, and saying that every fifth man was to be 'green' (i.e. a new trainee), all supplies were to be brought from England, and no fishermen were to remain there over the winter. These laws were in practice ignored, and the number of settlers in Newfoundland slowly increased, as well as the numbers of men enticed away to New England where life was becoming more comfortable.

Since 1634 the government had ruled that in order to keep some sort of law and order in the fisheries, in the absence of a Governor, the Master of the first vessel from England to arrive at any harbour in Newfoundland after 25 March should be Admiral of that harbour for that season. Those arriving second and third were called Vice- and Rear-Admirals. The Admiral took over the best Fishing Room, and he had to adjudicate in any disputes which arose whether related to fishing or not. This system was confirmed by an Act of Parliament in 1698. There were frequent complaints against these Admirals by the settlers, who begged the government to appoint a proper Governor, a move vigorously opposed by the west country merchants.

In 1713, by the Treaty of Utrecht, the French part of Newfoundland was ceded to England. The French settlers, mostly Catholics, were allowed to stay on and keep their lands, or sell them if they wished to leave. Once England gained the whole of Newfoundland, it led to an enormous increase in trade from Dartmouth and other west-country ports during the remaining years of the century.

The Prosperous Years, 1713-1793

It is not surprising to find that a Captain Holdsworth was in 1700 a fishing Admiral in St John's. It was said in a report by Mr. Larkins that Holdsworth had brought out from England 236 passengers, mostly Bye boat keepers, that is people who owned a boat which they left all year in Newfoundland. Since he was Admiral — having arrived first — he put

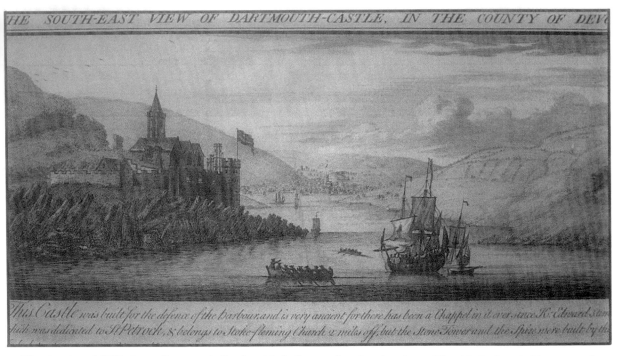

HE SOUTH-EAST VIEW OF DARTMOUTH-CASTLE, IN THE COUNTY OF DEVO

This Castle was built for the defence of the harbour, and is very ancient for there has been a Chappel in it ever since K. Edward 3tan
hich was dedicated to St Petrock, & belongs to Stoke-fleming Church 2 miles off, but the Stone Tower and the Spire were built by the

77. A print of 1734 shows Dartmouth Castle with St Petrox church spire above. The ship had probably returned from Newfoundland.

them into the best Fish Rooms and was accused of acting contrary to law on many occasions. In England his men used to frequent the fairs and market towns in Devon to gather recruits, offering them better terms than others, which he could afford to do since he could ensure that he had the lion's share of the business of the island. He built a large stone house in Ferryland, and the family had much property in St John's, where a street is now named after him.[3]

The master fishermen permanently living in Newfoundland were desperate for labour in the busy summer season, and both Holdsworths and Newmans had bases there. Young men were recruited by their agents in Devon and even Dorset and persuaded to sign on for two summers and a winter, or three summers and two winters, in exchange for a free passage, their keep while there, and at the end from £15 to £40 in back wages according to their length of service, age and fitness when recruited. Ships carrying these lads, or 'green' men, were warned not to call at any port after leaving in case they jumped ship.

Few of them came back, although free passage was offered. Some got into debt, and were forced to stay on to repay what they owed. Others were enticed away by masters of fishing vessels from New England. Some married the daughters of their masters — there must at an early stage have been women there. One way and another, despite laws forbidding settlement, the resident population had reached 2,611 by 1716, and 15,000 by 1765.[4] Many

Devon mothers must have known when their sons left home on these voyages that they would never see them again. Emigration probably explains why the total population of Dartmouth in the 1801 census was no greater than estimates based on the Hearth Tax of 1674.[5]

However, these settlers needed goods of all descriptions. By the mid-18th century ships were leaving Dartmouth regularly, filled with what the settlers had ordered. A typical entry in the Port Book for February 1744 records the following cargo for Newfoundland:

> Salt, molasses, strong beer, nails, tin ware, English soap, tallow candles, 50 sailors suits of clothes, 25 doz. shirts, 5 doz. rugs, 10 tons cordage, biscuit, pease, kersey, shagg, 640 ells English sail duck, twine, seynes, nets, lines, 1,000 pairs shoes.

Other ships carried cheese, dried whiting, wrought iron, lime, tools of all sorts, scissors, knives, barrels of port and casks of butter. Farmers, it seems, were exporting surplus food to America.

There were some re-exports — tobacco and oranges — but the great majority of the goods were produced in the villages around the Dart valley by hundreds of home workers in cottage industries. Devon cattle produced good hides, turned into strong boots and shoes in places such as Ipplepen and Broadhempston where an oral tradition of this industry still survives. Devon sheep produced the wool, spun, woven and sewn into all those sailors' suits in other villages. Ironware, tools, hooks, lines and cordage were made in Dartmouth itself, where they were already needed for the local shipbuilding and fishing industry. Considerable organisation was needed to go round the villages to place orders months ahead for the goods needed, to collect the finished articles, transport them by packhorse over country lanes and finally down steep streets still unfit for wheeled vehicles. Some may have come down the Dart by boat from the riverside villages. Eventually ships set out as early as January, laden with cargoes to meet orders placed in the previous September in Newfoundland. All this must been the main provider of work in the neighbourhood.

The Port Books show, however, that ships were trading with many other places as well as Newfoundland. Some merchants specialised in exports to Carolina, Virginia, Maryland and the West Indies, where settlers also needed goods.

78. Late 17th-century port bottles, known as 'cisterns', used in the port wine trade.

From Norway came a steady supply of 'deals', from Antigua sugar, from Rotterdam bricks, pantiles, wainscotting, empty casks and linen. Portugal continued to send lemons, oranges, raisins, figs and port wine. Jersey sent knitted stockings, breeches and even knitted petticoats.

All this stimulated the need for ships, which were built locally along the banks of the Dart around the shore of Hardness and Coombe Mud. Timber had to be imported from the Baltic to supplement local supplies, and local industries provided all the ropes, tackle, blocks, ironwork, sails and other necessities for them.

The Holdsworths and their allies were only the most prominent among the many merchants. There was an enormous increase in foreign-going shipping registered in Dartmouth in the 18th century, from a total of 825 tons in 1709 to 4,492 tons in 1770 and falling slightly to 3,648 tons in 1780 in the middle of the American War of Independence.[6] The borough as waterbailiff also collected dues from prizes captured in the many wars of the century.

The Last Age of Privateering

Privateers were encouraged after 1740 when the state no longer took any percentage of their profits from prizes.[7] In the War of 1739-1748 seventeen privateers were fitted out from Dartmouth with letters of marque against Spain or France.[8] Usually a group of eight or ten merchants, sometimes including the captain, combined to share the cost of fitting out such a ship. Holdsworths and Newmans, as might be expected, had shares in 15 ships, but the gentry were also involved. Each time the ships set out, a different combination of owners might take shares in her and the profits were distributed at the end of the cruise. Mariners had their shares, too, ranging from a half part for the cabin boy to six parts for the captain, to encourage them to risk their lives in this dangerous enterprise.

In 1745 two ships, the *Lyoness* and the *Tygress*, were set out by a group consisting of John Seale, Charles Hayne, Thomas Holdsworth, John Lydston, Richard and Robert Newman, Ambrose Penfound a local solicitor, and a London merchant William Poston, at a total cost of £5,295 10s.[9] These were large ships, of 300 tons, carrying 200 men and 20 guns. The *Tygress* made five cruises, and captured three prizes, one of which was worth £5,496 11s. 8d., but was herself captured by the French and carried into Martinique in 1746, according to *The Gentleman's Magazine*. As she was insured, this was not a total loss to her sponsors. However, Ambrose Penfound, a solicitor trusted by many of the local gentry to look after their money and rents, had used some of his clients' money to invest in the *Tygress*. When she was lost he went bankrupt and absconded. The financial mess he left involved most of the local landed families, and took over 20 years for the Court of Chancery to settle.[10]

A very successful privateer was the *Dartmouth Galley*, owned in 1744 by John Southcote, Arthur Holdsworth and four others. This was of 180 tons, and carried 200 men and 24 guns.[11] On a series of cruises she captured seven ships, most of which were brought back to Dartmouth. John Southcote died after two ships had been captured, and his son Henry was able to claim his father's share of the profits so far, amounting to over £2,865. Later this group sold the ship to other owners, and in 1745 she was herself captured by a French privateer and taken to La Rochelle.[12]

When a merchant ship was caught by a privateer, it usually surrendered without a fight, and the crews were reasonably well treated by the enemy privateer which mainly wanted the prize money. When two privateers met, however, it was a different story.

The largest privateer fitted out from Dartmouth in this war was the *Boscawen*, at 600 tons with 300 men, owned by Arthur Holdsworth, Nathaniel Terry and two London merchants. She captured a French privateer, *Les Deux Amis*, which was brought back into the Dart. An Admiralty court held in the *New (Castle) Inn* heard the French captain describe the three-hour long battle in which he resisted capture, many of the 49 mariners and 65 passengers on board being killed or wounded. However, he revealed that the *Boscawen* had missed a much greater prize since, on his way back from the Mississippi and West Indies with a valuable cargo of tobacco, sugar, hides and 60,000 pieces of eight, he had landed all but the hides at Corunna in Spain before he was taken off Bayonne. Even so, the remaining cargo and ship were valued at £10,000.[13]

After Canada was captured from the French in 1763 there was a great increase in the Newfoundland trade. However, when in 1776 the American colonies began their fight for independence from Britain, with help from the French, both sides of the Atlantic became extremely dangerous for trading ships. In this war no less than 58 privateers were fitted out from Dartmouth, and 35 ships were captured by Dartmouth privateers.[14] The *Exeter Flying Post* records almost every month either a prize ship captured and brought in, or its goods advertised to be sold, usually by 'Sales by the Candle' in the *Castle Inn*. The French were not idle either, and in October 1780 took two ships just off Dartmouth Harbour. In April 1781, the privateer *Lady Howe* — named after the wife of Dartmouth's M.P. Viscount Howe — brought in a Dutch prize valued at £30,000.[15]

One interesting privateering exploit which led to a long court case was that of the *Snapdragon* under Captain Thomas Goldsmith, bought and fitted out by John Seale and his agent Peter Ongier, which claimed to have captured a Dutch ship, the *De Liefde*. However, another English privateer, the *Bird*, claimed also to have captured her. The prize was brought into Dartmouth, where evidence was taken from its captain and crew as to exactly what had happened. As might have been expected, in view of their long-running quarrel with the Seales, the *Bird*'s version was supported by the Holdsworths. Ongier alleged that they had tried to bribe the Dutch crew to give false evidence, which they refused to do. Evidence was given that men from the *Snapdragon* first boarded her and were taking her papers when they saw a strange sail bearing down on them without any colours to indicate nationality. Suspecting a foreign privateer, they left the ship, which was then taken by the *Bird*. The court considered this unfair play on the part of the *Bird*, and awarded the prize to the *Snapdragon*. Its value was said to be over £3,600.[16]

New Building in Dartmouth, 1660-1800
When the Newfoundland trade was prospering, money was spent on new buildings. When times were hard, they were allowed to fall into ruin. This explains why few new buildings can be firmly dated to the period 1660-1715. St Clare's chapel in a lease of 1675 was described as 'late and now converted into a horsemill'.

The main effort of the Corporation was the reclaiming of the New Ground, but with trade in depression their income was reduced. In 1693 they imposed a toll on wheat sold in the market because they had to meet the great expenses of repairing all their quays, and their income from trade had been badly hit by the wars with France in the 1690s.[17]

After 1715 many new houses were built, or rebuilt on old sites, some of which can still be seen. The Mansion House in Lower Street has already been mentioned, built by Captain Edward Ashe in 1736, adjoining 'fishmarket slip'.[18] John Southcote built the Manor House in Southtown in 1727, the date being deduced from that on a sundial, now in Dartmouth Museum. Many of the houses on the opposite side of the road there are in an architectural style or bear dates showing rebuilding in the 18th century. Stokecliff was in existence by 1749, being shown on Southcote's map of that year.

On Clarence Hill (not yet so called), a row of houses is shown below Mount Boone House in a mid-18th-century painting owned by the Seale family, and Mount Galpin must have been built about this date. Mount Boone itself was rebuilt and enlarged, with an extra storey and a castellated roofline added. Many houses were built in Clarence Street for sea captains and shipbuilders, as the ship building and repair yards lay just below. On

79. The Manor House, Southtown, built about 1727, is shown here on the left, above the flagpole, before its demolition for road widening in 1905. After 1868 a coastguard house was built on the quay; behind the flagpole, and the leading light for shipping was fixed to the wall.

80. Bearscove, where the Customs House (right) was rebuilt from four smaller houses in 1737. The two houses on the left were also rebuilt at about the same time, to judge from their style, which is quite different from that of the older houses nearer the castle.

81. Mount Boone House, home of the Seale family from 1724 to 1871.

82. Portrait of Sir John Henry Seale.

Bearscove, four small cottages were made into the new Customs House in 1737 by John Seale, who then leased the property to the Customs.[19] Other houses there, such as Morocco House, seen to be of the same architectural style, though no deeds have yet been found to prove it (*see* plate 80).

In 1739 Arthur Holdsworth bought the mills in Foss Street from John Pollexfen. He had acquired them by his marriage to Julian Roope whose family had owned them for about two centuries. Holdsworth then conveyed them to the Corporation. The mill pond was slowly silting up, but the mills still worked even if only for a few hours either side of the high tide.[20]

In 1736, a lease refers for the first time to the house built by Barnes on the New Quay as being the *New Inn*, later to be known as the *Castle Inn*.[21] It was now owned by John Summers, mariner, who appointed various landlords to run it. Summers was the captain of a ship, the *Marcella*, which was left to him by Arthur Holdsworth in his will of 1753, so he clearly was one of their circle. It soon became the leading inn in the town, because of its convenient position. Its fine first-floor room overlooking the water was often used for court hearings in preference to the old Guildhall, which was becoming run down. When a jury was called to consider John Seale's Coombe Mud case in 1741 it met at the *New Inn*. When prize ships were brought into the harbour, an Admiralty Court would meet in the same room to establish if it was a lawful prize and to whom it should be awarded. Auctions of ships were often held there, by the curious method of 'Sale by the Candle'. This involved lighting a candle of a certain length at the beginning of the proceedings, and the highest bidder before it went out was the winner.[22]

The *New Inn* passed by marriage to John Browne, Summers' son-in-law, who later also inherited Cubitt's house to the south and by 1782 had combined the two houses into a larger inn which was already being referred to as the *Castle*.[23] It had its own brewhouse at the back, fed by a stream of fresh water, and by 1774 a magnificent new stable block had been built across the lane at the back.[24] It hired out horses but, even though turnpikes were being built, the roads into Dartmouth were still too steep for wheeled vehicles such as coaches. During Browne's ownership were added the fine bow windows which still form the elegant front of the building (*see* plate 42). They were remarked upon by B. Maton, in his tour of Devon in 1794.

Some time in the later part of the century a Playhouse stood in Duke Street, just opposite the Butterwalk, on the site of Messrs. Hawkes and the two shops to the west. It was demolished, probably by fire, by 1789, when the materials belonging to it were sold.[25] The Great Conduit had stood in the middle of what is now Duke Street ever since the early 17th century, but as part of a rebuilding scheme several houses near it were taken down, and the conduit moved next to the bridge to the New Ground in 1799.[26]

At the eastern end of the Butterwalk was Mrs. Hatton's Coffee House, where sales by the candle were also held (*see* plate 48). Coffee houses had become the fashionable places for merchants to meet to discuss business deals. Robert Cranford, whose family came from Dittisham, had already established in the town a business as 'dealers in coffee and tea' by the 1770s.[27]

A poorhouse for the parish of Townstal was set up in 1775 on the site of St Clare's chapel, in the middle of a triangle of land between what is now Browns Hill Steps, Clarence Hill and steps on the east. A building adjoining the actual poorhouse, on the same site, was opened in 1820 as a Bell's (monitorial) school. When these buildings were sold and taken down in 1850, St Clair's Terrace was built on the site. There was another poorhouse in St Saviour's parish, at the top of Modbury Lane, on the south side, now converted to houses. For the poor of St Petrox there was one in Southtown opposite the junction with Swannaton.[28]

During the 18th century, a number of lime kilns were built in creeks along the edge of the river Dart, one being at Warfleet (*see* plate 23). They burnt a mixture of culm from South Wales and local limestone, both brought in by small ships, to make powdered lime. Farmers collected it in carts to fertilise their fields, while builders used it both as mortar and as a wash to paint the outside of houses. As the lime was highly inflammable, it was produced as near as possible to where it was needed.

At the close of the 18th century, the French wars made travel to Italy and France impossible for the rich, and the completion of turnpikes encouraged travel to Devon instead. Writers such as Swete and Maton sang the praises of the beauties of the Dart, and this encouraged the development of the tourist industry.

Chapter Fourteen

The Early Nineteenth Century

Wars with France, 1793-1815

Wars with France lasting over 20 years, when the newly independent American colonies sided with the French, hit the Newfoundland trade hard. The Americans sank 80 ships fishing for cod there in 1795.[1] Vancouver, writing in 1808, said that while 120 ships annually had been involved in this trade before the war they were now reduced to only thirty. He reports that there were 230 ships registered in the port, which included Brixham, Torbay and Salcombe, providing work for 1,144 men. Shipbuilding provided the main employment for men, while the women and children made much money in gathering cockles and mussels at low water.[2]

83.   The frigate *Dartmouth* built at Sandquay in 1813.

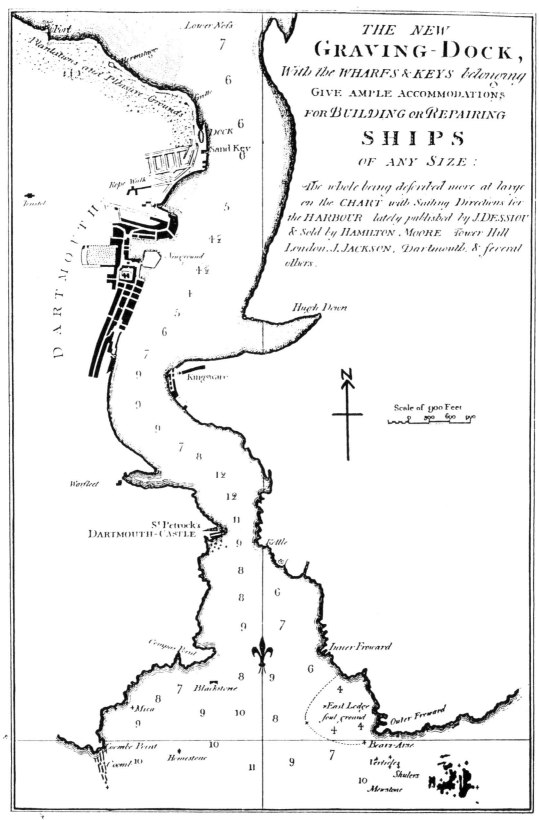

84. The Seale Shipyards at Sandquay in 1812, when the lease was put up for sale. The graving-dock, building sheds and rope walk are shown, as is the layout of Dartmouth streets and the New Ground before the New Road or other 19th-century improvements were carried out.

Despite losses to French privateers, the Newmans did maintain some shipments of English goods to Newfoundland during the war, helped by naval vessels which escorted convoys across the Atlantic. However, by the end of the war the colonists had learned to be more self-sufficient. They built their own ships and began to buy cheaper manufactured goods made in the factory towns of northern England. A further blow to the trade was the development of gas lighting, which cut the demand for trayne oil previously used for lamps.

The decline in shipbuilding for the Newfoundland trade was somewhat offset by contracts for ships for the Navy — 16 ships were built in Dartmouth between 1800 and 1813. The main shipbuilders were Tanner, Newman and Avery. However, Newman went bankrupt between 1803-6, and Tanner between 1807-10, so these were uncertain times for the shipyard workers.[3] Seale's docks at Sandquay were expanded and used for some of these ships. A map and sale particulars of 1812 show they included a wet dock 255 feet long. They were taken over by Gibbs who built schooners there after the war. Other shipbuilders like the Nichols family worked from Hardness, building ships for coastal and Atlantic voyages.

The war appeared to be over in 1814, when Napoleon had been defeated and exiled to Elba. A note in St Saviour's baptism register for that year by the vicar, Robert Holdsworth, tells how they celebrated the peace at a feast paid for by the inhabitants and M.P.s:

> In June 1814, 2,300 of the poor inhabitants of Dartmouth were feasted on hot roast beef and plum pudding and ale with the greatest order at nine tables each containing about 250 persons. There was also a grand procession of all the trades with their respective banners and implements . . . extending from Bearscove to the New Quay . . . attended by a military band.
>
>   In the evening a grand display of fireworks, and the trees on the New Ground the two following days were illuminated with a variety of coloured lamps.

The following year, however, Napoleon was back, and had to be defeated again at Waterloo. The *Bellerophon*, carrying the Emperor on his way to his final exile in St Helena, anchored in Torbay, and the local people had the chance to go out by boat to see him pacing the deck.

Charities under Scrutiny: The Charity Commission

Despite the peace, the number of poor seemed to be increasing. This led reformers nationally to enquire what had happened to the money given over the centuries for charity in many boroughs. In 1821 a government commission toured the country to find out, and wrote a detailed report.

Gifts to the poor by donors from the 16th century onwards are still recorded on boards in the parish churches, their purposes varying widely. Audian endowed a water conduit and an annual sermon. Ley gave money which was used to build and maintain an almshouse in Southtown. Richard Kelly endowed the Widows' Houses, for widows of seamen, which lay between Higher and Lower Street. A third almshouse was founded by Lovering in Ford Lane, for poor seamen or their widows. Shapleigh left £100, the interest on which was for loans to 'decayed owners of shipping'. Ann and Mary Ford gave £600, partly to maintaining a Latin schoolmaster, and an English schoolmaster who would teach English, arithmetic and navigation, provided the Corporation continued to pay £10 as before to the Latin master. Prestwood left £50, the interest to be spent on food for the poor on election day. Dyers' Gift left money to provide clothes for the poor, and there were many more for one parish or another.

More from lethargy than villainy, little charity had been distributed for years and, where it had been, few accounts had been kept. The overseers of St Petrox had complained back in 1814 to the mayor Arthur Hunt that the Corporation had not given them Audian's gift to distribute for 22 years. A few days before the commissioners arrived, he hastily handed over five years' arrears for the poor! The commissioners found the funds of all the charities mismanaged, if not actually absorbed into the Corporation's income. No loans to decayed seamen had ever been made. Lovering's almshouse had been burnt down in 1794 and the site left derelict. The other two almshouses still existed, and the Southtown one had been rebuilt on a new site, but little of the money had been given to the residents. The Corporation had not appointed another English schoolmaster since the last one died in 1805, and had ceased to pay the £10 to the Latin schoolmaster who therefore had no free scholars. Meat and bread were given out on election days, and £8 every Christmas for 'shifts' for the poor, but little else.[4]

The Commissioners made a critical report and ordered that proper accounts be kept, property repaired and let at economic rents, and money distributed to the poor as the donors had requested. The trustees had to be appointed regularly and to make annual reports to the Commissioners. There was at least a government watchdog, who though usually sleepy had the power to bark and bite if it wished.

After the War: Peace and Hope of Progress

Both the Holdsworths and the Newmans realised that the best days of the Newfoundland trade were over for them and made plans accordingly. The Holdsworths sold their lands in Newfoundland, while keeping those in Portugal. The main branch of the Newmans no longer lived in the town, but at Mamhead, and had an office in London.

Arthur Howe Holdsworth, however, did not desert the town, and set out to improve it. The family grip during these last years was total. One brother Robert, as has been seen, was vicar of Townstal and acted as treasurer for the borough. Another, Henry Joseph, had a bank in the town, in partnership with his cousin Henry Holdsworth and John Hine. A third, Charles, became vicar of Stokenham but helped in the town's affairs. Even his mother, a redoubtable widow who had brought up her family alone after her husband's early death, kept the church accounts for 43 years.

The contribution of the family was summed up in an inscription by Robert in the baptism register of 1814-16:

> The new galleries of St. Saviour's in the transepts and near the south side of the nave were begun in the mayoralty of Robert Holdsworth, the writer of this, and ended in the mayoralty of his brother Henry Joseph Holdsworth. The Alderman's seats were planned by Arthur Howe Holdsworth, M.P. for the borough, and executed by Mr. Lidstone, carpenter, 1815-1816.

Reuben Lidstone, the carpenter, slipped inside the seats a note which was not discovered until 1887 when they were repaired. It is a cry from a working man, whose voice is rarely heard:

> When this you see remember me that I am not quite forgotten . . . that the times are very bad . . . for working men get 14 shillings a week, and flour 5 pence a pound, potatoes 1 shilling a stone . . . and one half the men can get no work. You may depend their pride is come to grief, for instead of ducks and geese they are forced to eat sheep's head.[5]

The beautiful carving of these Corporation seats illustrates the artistic gifts of Arthur Howe. He could be generous, too: he and Archdeacon Froude of Totnes paid for the education of William Brockedon, whose large painting of 'The Widow's Son', now in the church, won a £100 prize. Holdsdworth was equally interested in scientific developments. He had by this time bought Warfleet grain mill and in 1819 converted it to make fine quality paper. It was driven by the largest water wheel west of Bristol. However, it cannot have been a financial success, as he sold it in 1825. He also patented an improved rudder for ships, water-tight bulkheads, a fireproof magazine and many other ingenious devices.

85. St Saviour's showing the new galleries, built 1814-16.

86. A. H. Holdsworth designed these Corporation seats in St Saviour's, which were made by Mr. Lidstone in 1816. The fine 15th-century screen and painted stone pulpit can also be seen.

The New Road and the Market, 1823-8
In a determined effort to restore the flagging economy of Dartmouth, Arthur Howe
Holdsworth obtained from parliament an Improvement Act in 1815, giving powers to build
a market, widen, pave and light streets, and pull down buildings if need be. In 1823 the
engineer James Rendell designed a new road up to Townstal, at a gradient which for the
first time enabled horse-drawn carriages to come in and out of the town, and which joined
the existing turnpikes to Kingsbridge and Modbury. At the bottom of the hill it ran alongside
the old mill pool, and was linked to the Butterwalk by knocking down some houses in Foss
Street. Completed in 1825, it was known simply as the New Road until its name was
changed to Victoria Road in honour of Queen Victoria's jubilee.

Next, on land reclaimed from the west end of the mill pool, a new market was built by
1828. The work was supervised by the Rev. Charles Holdsworth, and financed with £1,300
loaned at 5 per cent interest by his mother and sisters. The interest was paid out of the
borough income so that no extra rates fell on the town.[6] The family entertained the Duke
of Clarence — later William IV — at Mount Galpin in 1828, and the lanes up which he
passed were from that time called Clarence Street and Clarence Hill.

87. Pound note issued by the Dartmouth bank, signed by H. J. Holdsworth and J. Hine.

However, many in the town did not consider the family benefactors, especially those who
lost their money when the Holdsworth bank failed in the general banking crash of 1825.
Their old opponent from Mount Boone, John Henry Seale (1781-1844), led a group who
opposed a Harbour Bill proposed by the Corporation in 1829, which aimed to place warping
buoys in the harbour and charge merchants dues for this and other improvements for the
benefit of shipping. As a result of a petition against it, the Bill was rejected.

Reform of Parliament

In 1829, reform of Parliament was very much in the air nationally and was being proposed by the Whigs. When one of the sitting members for Dartmouth died, Arthur Howe Holdsworth, who had not himself served as M.P. for 10 years, was elected in a bye-election by the usual small group of mayor, aldermen and freemen. Holdsworth, a Tory, opposed measures then being passed to give votes to Catholics and Dissenters, long excluded from political life.

Seale's group, calling itself the Party of Civil Liberty, and led by Dr. Puddicombe, issued a writ of *quo warranto* in the Court of King's Bench, challenging the legality of the election of the mayor, Whitney, on the ground that it was by the aldermen alone, and not the whole body of freemen. The same objection applied to the previous five mayors, and so to any freemen chosen by them, which called into question the legality of elections of M.P.s. The court upheld this view, and Whitney was forced to resign. On 28 June a writ of *mandamus* was issued ordering that a new mayor be elected. The matter was urgent, as a general election was to be held on 19 July for which the mayor would be Returning Officer. On 10 July, when the writ was delivered, a 'tumultuous assembly of the corporate body and inhabitants took place at the Guildhall', demanding to be made freemen. The aldermen ignored them and elected Henry Holdsworth as Mayor.[7]

When election day came, Seale and Willoughby stood as candidates. The votes of 122 householders who supported them were declared illegal by the mayor because they were not freemen. A. H. Holdsworth and his friend John Bastard were declared elected by 21 votes each. Seale petitioned against the result, in a 38-page attack on the whole system. He pointed out that, by the decision in the *quo warranto* case, all the freemen for the last 130 years had been chosen by illegally elected mayors, and those entitled to become freemen had been refused their rights in order to keep a small ruling clique in power. 'How far shall this admitted and convicted rotten piece of corporation be allowed to maintain the benefits of their usurpation?', he demanded.[8]

In 1832, public opinion against such cases, and many worse, forced Parliament to pass the Reform Act, which gave the vote in towns to the Ten Pound Householder, one who owned or rented a house worth £10 a year. But there was a sting in the tail for Dartmouth: it was one of the small or 'rotten' boroughs which lost one of its members in order to give seats to the many growing towns in the North and Midlands. In the election which followed in 1833, the 267 newly enfranchised householders voted almost unanimously for John Henry Seale as their new Whig member of Parliament.

The Floating Bridge and the Horse Ferry

At the same time as all this upheaval about parliamentary elections, Seale was pressing ahead with a scheme to improve the crossing of the river for vehicles. Until then there had been two rowing ferries across the Dart, both owned by the Fownes-Luttrell family, one running from beside the *Plume of Feathers* in Kingswear to the end of Bearscove, and the other from Hoo Down to the New Ground. Neither could take a wheeled vehicle.

As a result of Seale's efforts, an Act of Parliament was obtained to build a floating bridge, attached to two chains, crossing the river from Sandquay. It was designed by Rendel, who had built the New Road. It opened in August 1831, together with a new road to link it to Hillhead, and was at first driven by a steam engine. On the opening day over 60 carriages and their horses were transported, four at a time, over to Dartmouth, along with many more saddle horses and pedestrians. The roads on the Dartmouth side left much to be desired: Coombe Road and the narrow Clarence Street and Foss Street were still the only routes to the New Road out of the town on the west.

88.   The floating bridge in about 1840, from the east bank of the Dart.

In fact, despite its obvious advantages as the first vehicular crossing of the mouth of the river, the floating bridge company lost money from the start. The charges, laid down in the Act, did not cover the cost of the steam engine, or the expense of building the approach roads and other works, yet the owners were obliged by the Act to run it even at a loss. By 1835 they were losing so much money that they were forced to give up the steam engine as too costly. Instead, two blind horses were installed to work a treadmill, which pulled the ferry across on two chains. Seale bought out the other shareholders and his family became the sole owners.[9]

In 1855 the bridge broke its moorings and sank, and was out of action for two years. Some local tradesmen obtained a writ of *mandamus* ordering the company to rebuild or repair it. In 1856 a new, but also horse-driven ferry, was built by Kelly's of Dartmouth which lasted until 1867. In that year a steam ferry was finally built be Philip & Sons.

From Kingswear, meanwhile, the Luttrells by 1840 had started the horse ferry, rowed by two men with very long oars, which could carry one horse-drawn vehicle and on the route used by the present lower car ferry, moving the landing slip from the south to the north side of the Castle Dairy block on the Dartmouth side to provide wider access.[10]

New Brooms and Law Suits

The Reform Act of 1832 brought to power a Whig government which dealt with corruption inside the boroughs. A commission investigated the affairs of municipal corporations, and its report on Dartmouth was heavily critical of the nepotism and other shortcomings of the ruling group.[11] While a new law to amend matters was being prepared, the magistrates — who still numbered four Holdsworths among them — gave a bond under the town seal to

89. The horse ferry, on the route of the present lower ferry, about 1840, rowed by two men with very long oars. This was owned by the Luttrell family of Nethway.

90. A later view of the horse ferry.

91. Arthur Howe Holdsworth, the last Governor of Dartmouth Castle, and last member of the family to be involved in the borough's affairs. He was M.P. from 1802-20, and 1829-33.

Arthur Howe for over £1,240 at 4½ per cent interest being 'costs paid by him in defending the rights of the Corporation', in an unsuccessful attempt to preserve the corrupt old system.[12] Ironically, this debt had to be paid by the new Council which replaced the Corporation in 1836 under the Municipal Corporations Act. After 1832, no Holdsworth or any of that group was mayor, and when the new rules of 1836 gave the vote to householders no more Holdsworths were elected to the Council.

Arthur Howe left the town and lived at Brookhill, Kingswear, from where he later moved to the Beacon, built in 1848. Other members of the family soon vacated Mount Galpin. John Henry Seale seemed to have triumphed: he was made a baronet in 1838 and continued to represent the town in Parliament until his death in 1844.

The newly elected Council of 1836 was inexperienced in government, and Holdsworth watched with some enjoyment as they grappled with problems which he did not hesitate to increase if he could. Many were non-conformists, with no love of the Church of England which had for so long excluded them from political rights. By the new Act, councils were not allowed to hold advowsons, and clergy could not be Councillors. Robert Holdsworth therefore resigned from the Council, and the advowson was put up for sale. However, before it was sold, Holdsworth also resigned as vicar of Townstal and became vicar of Brixham. The Bishop of Exeter, as was his right, appointed as vicar a young man of 26, thus cutting the value of the advowson as no new owner could appoint until he died. In the absence of other bidders, Seale bought it for £377, whereas the Council had hoped it was worth £800.[13]

Legal opinions were now sought as to the liability of the Council to pay for the salary of the vicar and the upkeep of St Saviour's. Documents were consulted back to 1372, and learned counsel advised that the Council need only pay the vicar £13 6s. 8d. for Townstal and £5 for St Saviour annually, and that they were not liable for repairs, these being the responsibility of the 'parishioners'.[14] The division between 'parishioners', those who actually used the churches, and the whole population was now brought into the open. There was great ill-feeling on both sides.

In view of what was to happen later, it is worth looking at the main items of Corporation income just before 1836. These included:

1834	£.	s.	d.
Church money (pew rents)	160.	8.	0.
Market rents	180.	0.	0.
High rents (of property)	196.	0.	0.
Renewals (entry fines for leases)	342.	0.	0.
Tithes	375.	19.	4.
Petty Customs	195.	1.	3.

The whole came to nearly £1,800 and covered all the town's expenses, so that it was never necessary to charge rates.

One by one these were to go, many lost in lengthy legal disputes. Two successive town clerks were dismissed, and successfully claimed compensation. Arthur Howe Holdsworth now demanded payment of his bond for £1,249. When the case was heard in Chancery, the town lost, with costs awarded to Holdsworth. Counsel for the Corporation advised them to appeal, so they mortgaged their tithes to pay for the next round. By 1844 they had lost again: with the original bond and costs for both sides in both actions they were out of pocket by nearly £7,000. To pay for this they had to mortgage their market rents as well as their tithes. One after another of the Corporation's assets passed into the pockets of lawyers.

Everyday life in mid-century Dartmouth, 1830-1860

The 1830s opened with an epidemic of cholera, from which 46 people died in the Hardness area where so many of the shipyards were. The disease, which had spread from Asia, hit all ports and its effects were worse because of overcrowding and the almost total lack of main sewerage. The population was growing, from 3,412 in 1801 to 4,115 in the 1841 census, but for the poorer classes there were no more houses, nor any room to build them. Existing houses were divided up into tenements with families in each room, a practice which continued until the beginning of the 20th century.

The decline in the Newfoundland trade hit shipbuilding, which was now confined to coastal vessels — schooners, sloops and brigs. The main firms involved were the Folletts, Nichols and Gibbs, each of whom built ships not only in Dartmouth but also in Kingswear and Galmpton. Alfords were building in Dartmouth, too, and later moved to Kingswear.[15] Some shipbuilders, like the Folletts and Gibbs, became shipowners as well, often several members of the family being partners. A few men like Robert Harris the banker owned as many as 15 ships, but the majority simply owned one ship. A large number of people of all occupations took shares in ships as a way of investing their savings.

The trade done by these ships was almost entirely coastal, bringing coal and other basic supplies in and taking cattle, sheep or pigs out.[16] The few foreign ships came in mostly for repairs. The petty customs for the period averaged £200 to £300, but on close examination more than half came from Torquay, Brixham and Salcombe which were expanding while Dartmouth stagnated.[17]

For the really poor, emigration was a possible alternative to the poor law and the soup kitchens. The *Exeter Flying Post* of the 1840s carried advertisements for free passages on ships leaving from Plymouth for those wishing to go to Australia where there were plenty of jobs for labourers, shepherds, miners, blacksmiths and other craftsmen, and female domestic servants. Letters were printed from those who had gone there, reporting good wages and living conditions.

In 1837 Arthur Holdsworth, as principal shareholder of the Dart Steam Navigation

92. The harbour about 1841 showing Dartmouth and Kingswear. Steamships are using the river, and some villas such as Gunfield House have been built.

93. Dartmouth Harbour in 1841, by W. Thomas, drawn to support the borough's unsuccessful attempt to secure the contract for the mail packet steamers.

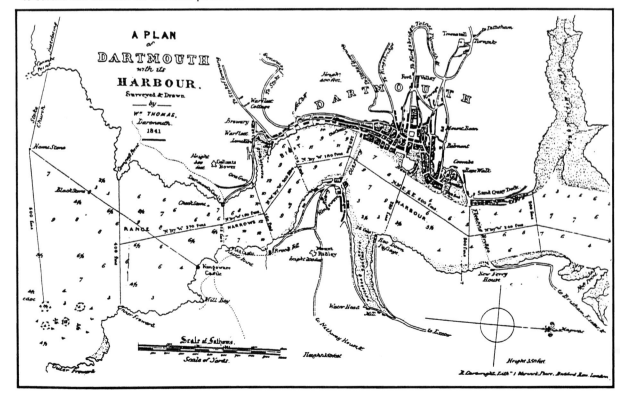

Company, introduced a steam paddle ship for the run to Totnes. This three-masted lugger had been built at North Shields — a sad indication that the Dart shipyards had not moved into the age of steam.

In 1840 an Admiralty Commission was considering Dartmouth amongst other ports as the station for packet steamers for mail to the West Indies. Sir John and the Council made every effort to secure the contract for Dartmouth when they visited the town. Even Governor Holdsworth wrote a powerful plea setting out the merits of the harbour. The whole matter was tied up with the rapid development of the railway just then, which was already being built to Exeter, and was projected to Totnes and Plymouth. Sir John wrote offering his shipyards at Sandquay for a mail steamer terminus, linked to a railway carried over the river by a bridge at Greenway to join the main line near Totnes, as well as having facilities for steamers at any state of the tide. Mail could have reached London in four to six hours. The Commission recommended Dartmouth as the best port, but the government none the less awarded the contract to Southampton.[18]

This was a big blow for Dartmouth. Anticipating a great increase in trade, the *Castle Inn* had closed for six months for major rebuilding, during which the roof was raised and the castellations built around the top to make it look more like a castle. It now became known as the *Castle Hotel*, and began to provide accommodation for the growing number of wealthy people who were coming on holiday to Devon because of its natural beauty.[19]

Royal Visitors

Among the visitors was Queen Victoria herself in August 1846. She had already been to the town in 1833 before she became queen. On this occasion she was on the royal yacht *Victoria and Albert* on a summer cruise with Prince Albert and their children when it took shelter in Dartmouth on the way to Plymouth. She recorded in her Journal for 20 August:

> Put into that beautiful Dartmouth . . . in pouring rain, the deck swimming with water, and all of us with umbrellas; the children most anxious to see everything. Notwithstanding the rain, this place is lovely, with its wooded rocks and church and castle at the entrance. It puts me much in mind of the beautiful Rhine with its fine ruined castles and the Lurlei.[20]

She came again in August 1856, once more on a cruise on the royal yacht with Prince Albert and the children. It was the day before the Regatta opened — an annual event since 1834, and a time of great festivity then as now. Prince Albert took a trip up the river in the new steam paddleboat *Dartmouth*. Later the whole family went in coaches to admire the view from Swannaton turnpike and visited the Seales at Mount Boone. That evening every house on the quay and the waterside put a candle in each window in the queen's honour. The royal party slipped away at dawn, but the queen had sent the Regatta committee a cheque for £25 to be given as a prize in the races. It was after this visit that the title 'Royal' was added to the Dartmouth Regatta.[21]

The growing popularity of the river for visiting yachtsmen helped to encourage the building of villas which took full advantage of the best views. Among those built at this time were the Wilderness and Derwent House (*c.*1825), the Gunfield (1840), Warfleet House (before 1841), The Keep (1850), and Ravensbury (1855), as was Holdsworth's Beacon (1848) on the Kingswear side.

Public Buildings and Institutions

Some public facilities were provided during these years. A library was built on the New Road, near the market, in 1833, and a Gas Company was formed in 1836 which soon provided gas lighting for the town from the gas works on the eastern end of Hardness. What is now Anzac Street (then Hanover Street) was straightened by the removal of two houses north of the churchyard, and in the square west of the church an island block of houses was built, on one end of which was a new gaol.[22]

The people of Dartmouth raised the money to build the Subscription Rooms in the New Road in 1849. Part of it was used as a school for 130 children run by the British and Foreign Schools Society, for non-conformists. In Southtown was the National School, for 100 Anglican children, which was built in 1823.[23]

In 1854 the town's first newspaper, the *Dartmouth Chronicle*, started publication, founded by young Robert Cranford, whose family were involved with it until 1938. Robert was a reforming Liberal in politics, whose father had supported John Henry Seale, but the paper gave fair coverage to opinions on both sides. Cranford was on the Council for many years, and mayor once. The *Chronicle* reports of what was actually said at Council meetings make a refreshing contrast to the official minutes, which seem designed to conceal the truth. There is also much information about life in the town and it makes fascinating reading.[24]

Elections, 1844-60

It would be pleasing to report that elections became less corrupt after the Reform Act of 1832 but, without a secret ballot, bribery and intimidation were common. In 1844, following the death of Sir John Henry Seale, a contested election was held between a Conservative, Joseph Somes, said to be one of the largest shipowners in the country, and a Liberal George Moffat, a general merchant in London. Somes won by seven votes. John Teage, a retired merchant who was mayor in 1837, wrote to a friend in Newfoundland with news from Dartmouth about this election:

> The town was in a sad uproar for a fortnight . . . Moffat is endeavouring to unseat Somes, charge laid against him for being a contractor under government, bribery and false votes, it being before a committee of the House of Commons . . . many have been paid handsomely, say £5, 10, 15, 20, 25, and £50. A good day's catch of fish!

The Commons Committee upheld Somes' election: he was not a government contractor at the time he stood for Parliament, and they dismissed the bribery accusations. He took over part of Sandquay shipyard, and was proposing to build a 500- to 600-ton ship there when he suddenly died. There was then a bye-election in which Moffat defeated the new Conservative candidate by 14 votes. Teage wrote soon afterwards that Moffat, too, had ordered a ship to be built at Follett's yard. Voters could be bribed, not merely by direct handouts of fivers, but by prospective employers from afar who promised to bring work to the town. After Sir John Henry Seale, no more local men were elected to represent Dartmouth.[25]

Sir Henry Paul Seale, who had succeeded to his father's estates, continued to support the Liberals until 1852, when he decided to change to the Conservatives. He never stood for Parliament, but was mayor 16 times. His nephew, Charles Seale-Hayne — whose father had added Hayne to his name on inheriting the Hayne fortunes — was an energetic Liberal, a barrister by profession and involved in many business ventures to boost the town's economy.

This led to a split in the family and town, with considerable bitterness. In the 1852 election Sir Henry supported the Conservative Herbert, who defeated his Liberal opponent, backed by Seale-Hayne, by 11 votes. The Liberals successfully sued Sir Henry, who was mayor at the time, for denying votes on a technicality to 42 Townstal householders to ensure the Conservative victory.[26] In a parliamentary election the following year, Seale-Hayne himself stood as a Liberal, against the Conservative Caird backed by his uncle Sir Henry. Lindsay, a wealthy shipowner whose ships called at Dartmouth, threatened that unless Caird was elected he would stop his ships using the port, and 'You would not see another ship in the harbour'. It was hardly surprising that Caird won by 30 votes.

Seale-Hayne had become chairman and driving force behind the Dartmouth and Torbay Railway, which planned to extend the line, already completed from Exeter to Newton Abbot, with a branch to Torre, as far as Kingswear. In another parliamentary election in 1859, Herbert stood as Conservative, while Seale-Hayne withdrew in favour of Schenley, after the latter promised to invest £3,000 in the railway company if elected. When Schenley won by seven votes, Herbert's side appealed, alleging bribery. A Commons enquiry found that Schenley had sent down £1,400 to his Dartmouth agent to distribute among the voters — known locally as 'passing money through the conduits'! Seale-Hayne was exonerated of involvement in this, but a new election was ordered. The Conservative James Dunn won, the Liberal having withdrawn because he said no one could win for either party unless they were bribed. The affair confirmed the town's reputation for corruption. 'Put money in your purse' was the advice sarcastically given by the *Illustrated Times* to prospective candidates.[27]

When Dunn died, a bye-election was held in which Seale-Hayne stood against the Conservative Hardy, who had Sir Henry's support. Hardy won by two votes. Seale-Hayne bitterly attacked the whole system. Bribery was not the only way to secure votes: landlords like his uncle — who owned many of the houses in the borough — could force tenants to vote their way by threat of eviction, or shop keepers by threat of withdrawing custom. Seale-Hayne campaigned for the secret ballot, and for larger constituencies which would make such practices impossible, both achieved by 1871. Before then, in 1868, Dartmouth had lost its separate representation for ever, absorbed into the newly-created Torquay constituency. Not even the name remained of a parliamentary borough going back nearly 600 years.

Chapter Fifteen

Sixty Years of Expansion, 1860-1914

In 1858 an editorial in the *Dartmouth Chronicle* deplored the lack of progress in the town, where almost nothing had changed since 1831. So much of the Council's former income had been lost that they had to charge rates, and even then could not pay their debts. However, during the next 20 years all was to change: old property was knocked down, roads built, the railway arrived, *Britannia* came to the river and a new Harbour Commission began to improve the port.

The Waterbaileywick

Up to 1860 the Council still held the lease of the waterbaileywick, when Governor Holdsworth, the last of the 'lives', died. Relations with the Duchy of Cornwall for the past 10 years had been increasingly acrimonious as the Council seemed unable to supply them with proper accounts of the dues collected. After endless delays in extracting replies to their letters, Duchy officials decided the Council was corrupt, incompetent, or both, and refused to renew the lease.[1] Suddenly the Council lost the income from the Duchy dues (as petty customs were now called), then worth £300 a year, as well as from quayage, anchorage and other payments which they had claimed as waterbailiffs.

Worse, the Duchy was demanding from all landowners compensation for past encroachments onto the river by buildings on land reclaimed from between high and low water. From the Council, the Duchy demanded compensation of £100 for all the building on land reclaimed from the river, such as the New Ground and New Quay, while disclaiming any responsibility for repairs to the quays which had formerly been paid for out of the dues. When the Duchy finally threatened to sue them, Council had to agree to their terms. To add insult to injury, in 1864 they were forced to return the silver oar, symbol of their office of waterbailiff, which had been given them in 1721 by Prince George.

The new collector of the Duchy dues, John Brooking the town clerk, increased the rates to try to recoup the money he had paid to buy the lease. A group of merchants and interested landowners formed the Duchy Defence Committee and, as a test case, Hunt, of Henley & Hunt who traded to Newfoundland, refused to pay. The Duchy sued them: the case was finally settled in 1868 by a compromise to save the expense of a longer suit but it confirmed their right to the dues.[2] After this Torquay, Brixham and Salcombe were set up as separate ports, not under Dartmouth, and the Duchy agreed in 1870 to sell most of their rights to the newly-formed Harbour Commission.

The *Britannia* and the *Hindustan*

In 1863 the Admiralty decided to station H.M.S. *Britannia* in the Dart as a training ship for naval cadets. Anchored just above the floating bridge, she soon had 230 cadets on board, and was joined in 1865 by H.M.S. *Hindustan*. In 1869 the *Prince of Wales*, which had been launched in 1860 but never fully rigged, replaced the first *Britannia* and took over her name. The town was delighted, as this boosted its economy in many ways: in supplying the cadets' needs as well as attracting visits from their parents. From the start it was hoped that a permanent college on land would be built one day. In 1877 the Prince of Wales sent his two sons to be trained there — Princes Albert Victor and George, the latter to become

156

94. The two most important events of the mid-1860s are shown in this print: the broad guage locomotive is seen steaming out of Kingswear station, while *Britannia* and *Hindustan* are ready to train cadets for the Royal Navy on the Dart. The floating bridge can be seen in mid-stream.

95. A view of Kingswear station in the 1870s showing the railway embankment across Waterhead Creek, with the jetty built out into the river, and the *Dolphin* double-ended ferry waiting at the original covered pontoon from the station for passengers. The old *Plume of Feathers* has been rebuilt to make the *Royal Dart Hotel*.

George V in 1910. This started a tradition to be followed by princes of the royal family ever since.

The Railway reaches Kingswear, August 1864

The railway finally reached Kingswear after numerous delays and at vast expense: the Dartmouth and Torbay Railway Company had spent more than three times its estimates.

On 10 August 1864, with ships in the harbour decked for Regatta, the official opening took place when a train carrying dignitaries arrived at Kingswear. The line was opened to the public on 16 August. By the following year, the Kingswear station had been built, along with a floating jetty to the passenger ferry. On the Dartmouth side a floating pontoon with a booking office was fixed in deep water, with long floating jetties to connect it to Spithead. A proper station in Dartmouth had to wait until after the building of the embankment, and was not finished until 1889.

In 1869 the railway company bought the specially-built steam ferry *Dolphin*, a paddle steamer which was pointed at both ends to enable her to go in either direction, to take passengers across the river. She remained in service for nearly 40 years until replaced in 1908 by the twin-screw steamer the *Mew*. She in her turn lasted 46 years until 1954, having been converted to take cars in the 1930s.[3]

Seale was already thinking about hotels for the passengers expected on the railway. He bought and rebuilt the old *Plume of Feathers*, transforming it into what is now the *Royal Dart Hotel*. Those wishing to join or leave the passenger ships soon to call at Kingswear could save themselves two days sailing in the Channel by taking the train.[4]

From 1871-91 the most regular of these passenger ships were Donald Currie's Cape & Natal Steamers, which arrived about twice monthly at Kingswear before leaving for Cape Town. These 'Castle' liners were the last word in luxury: the *Walmer Castle* could carry 80 first-class passengers in two-berth cabins with portholes, and its kitchen could cater for 1,000 people. The journey to the Cape took 24-28 days. Another shipping line called at the port en route from London to Barbados and Demerara.[5]

Dart Harbour Commission, 1863

However, much more money was needed to provide the necessary wharves, piers and facilities for bigger ships, if they were to be attracted to the port.

Seale-Hayne, whose energies in this cause were prodigious, took advantage of the end of the Council's lease of the waterbaileywick and a new Act of 1861 to set up the Dart Harbour Commission which held its first meeting on 28 August 1863. Its first members were himself, as chairman, and four other directors of the railway, two representatives chosen by Dartmouth Council and one by Kingswear parish. They were empowered to build or maintain quays, provide buoys, lights or beacons, or do anything else to encourage shipping, with powers to borrow money for these purposes. The first works to be authorised were all to do with the railway: to make wharves and a pier, a road alongside Waterhead Creek to the *Plume of Feathers Inn*, and to dredge the harbour to enable ships to moor alongside the railway.

The D.H.C. soon went on to build a new light near Beacon House, Kingswear, a Day Beacon on the hill above the village to help ships find the harbour, and they blasted away the Pin Rock, a hazard to the large steamers they hoped to attract. A fish quay was provided at Kingswear alongside the new pier, a gridiron at Hoodown where vessels could be cleaned, and a large steam crane. To pay for all this Hayne and two other directors lent money at 6 per cent, and a further £14,000 was borrowed from the Public Works Loan Board. After the Duchy had established their right to their dues in the test case against Hunt, they agreed in 1870 to sell them for £2,000 to the Harbour Commission, the sum to be recovered by a tax on coal. Once this had been paid, the D.H.C. inherited most of the former rights of the waterbaileywick over the river. The Duchy, however, still owns the 'fundus' or bed of the river, by which it claims to this day to charge for mooring in it.[6]

The Bunkering Trade

Seale-Hayne's business interests included the River Dart Steam Packet Company which he set up with other partners in 1859. The company's steamers *Louisa* and *Mary* competed for the run to Totnes and it started a service to the Channel Islands on the *Éclair*.[7]

It was the steam packets which first needed regular supplies of coal, which had for more than a century been imported on sailing colliers from Wales for domestic fires and, more recently, to make gas. As the number of steamships increased, so did the need for a place with deep enough water and calm conditions where they could refill their coal bunkers — the origin of the name of the trade so important to the workers of Dartmouth for a century.

Hulks began to be moored in mid-river, where even large ships could lie alongside, such as that put there by Powell-Duffryn for their Welsh coal in 1876. Advertising by this firm's

96.   The *Agamemnon* called at Dartmouth to bunker on her way back from Penang, an early customer for the new bunkering trade. The growth of new houses in Kingswear can be seen, following the sale of the Luttrell lands in 1874.

agent G. H. Collins, who sent circulars describing the port's advantages to all the leading steamship owners, led to a vast increase in ships bunkering in the port.[8] The *Dartmouth Chronicle* reported that 160 ships visited the port to coal in 1879, with 45 from Norway — the early days of a trade which was to last until the Second World War as their ships called to bunker on their way to and from the Mediterranean. With the opening of the Suez Canal in 1880, ships called in at Dartmouth on their way back from the Far East.

Another side of bunkering was the supply of gas coal, which was brought to Kingswear by sea from the north-east coalfield, and sent on by rail to the Torquay Gas works. This had started in the 1870s and went on until 1963.

There were several companies in the bunkering business, all competing for trade, the chief ones being the Channel Coal Company, Renwick-Wilton, G. H. Collins and Forwoods.[9] The volume of the work can be seen from the customs returns of ships which show that in the peak year of 1890, 747 ships bunkered in the port. Numbers varied from year to year, falling to 404 in 1896, and rising to 600 in 1901 according to the figures given in the *Chronicle*. These are in addition to ships such as the passenger liners, coastal cargo ships, fishing or sailing vessels or, of course, naval ships.

Town Improvements

Newcomen Road and the end of the Pool
Meanwhile, the Council was spurred on to draw up an ambitious improvement scheme for the town, having set themselves up as a Local Board of Health. A new pure water supply was urgently needed, the connection between cholera and sewage-polluted water having recently been proved. The old conduits, patched up from time to time, still served most of the inhabitants, but now a reservoir was built in the 1860s on land on the Seale estate at Norton, at Guttery Meadow, soon supplemented by extra reservoirs at Ford Meadow. For many years the water ran short every summer, and even in the early 20th century people were still fetching it in buckets from some of the conduits. The Great Conduit, long a landmark at the end of the Butterwalk, was pulled down in 1868.

The state of the old Guildhall, between Higher Street and Lower Street, had been described in 1853 in a report by Dr. Lewis, who had been sent to inspect the Watch House on its ground floor which served as an occasional prison. It was directly over the common sewer, and the stench was such that on his visit the constable could not stand it even for five minutes and 'left the room retching'. The Council chamber was on the second floor, entered from Higher Street, and even there 'on hot days . . . the smell and atmosphere is intolerable'. He said the whole Guildhall was unsuitable for use, and a new one should be built elsewhere.[10]

Bell's Plan
William Bell won a competition to solve the town's problems with a proposal for a new road and sewerage scheme which was carried out between 1864-7. A road suitable for carriage traffic linking Southtown with the Quay was formed by demolishing a swathe of old houses between Higher and Lower Streets, knocking down the old Guildhall and the house of Thomas Newcomen along with many others. Thomas Lidstone, a local architect, later built into his new house on Ridge Hill, Newcomen Cottage, plasterwork and windows from Newcomen's house and others demolished at the same time. The Newcomen Road, named after the inventor, was built in a series of arches like a bridge, and is quite a feat of engineering for its time.

In Southtown houses above Bearscove Castle were demolished, and huge retaining walls built to widen the road south as far as the old Southcote Manor House, which finally came down in 1905, leaving only its name in the Manor Gardens to show where it once stood. From that point the narrowness of the road shows what the rest was once like.

Meanwhile, in 1868 Call and Pethick, engineers, started work on the new drainage scheme: every part of the town was dug up and new sewers laid. When in 1986-7 Dartmouth was next re-sewered, their work was revealed, and very impressive it was. The recent upheaval suffered by the present-day population gives some idea of what it must have been like in 1868 when all digging was without benefit of bulldozer, and in addition over 50 houses had already been demolished for Newcomen Road. Lower Street was widened to improve access from the Lower Ferry, and by 1880 the houses in Fairfax Place had been set back and rebuilt with splendid decorative frontages.

The Guildhall

Bell's plan had suggested that since the old Guildhall would come down, a new one should be built on the land reclaimed from the Pool. Sadly, this was not done. As what was supposedly a temporary measure, a room was rented in the Assembly Rooms for Council meetings in 1865 (*see* plate 48). In 1875 the Council, led by the mayor Dr. Puddicombe, proposed trying to raise £3,000 by public subscription to build a new Guildhall. £400 was collected, and then public

97. The China Shop, Fairfax Place. This was part of a block rebuilt in 1880 when the road was widened, replacing houses from the 16th century. Robert Cranford, owner of the *Dartmouth Chronicle*, was responsible for these houses with their flamboyant imitation of the old Dartmouth style.

generosity dried up. Sites were considered, the Market place and the Pool (when filled in) being the most favoured. However, this was at the height of ill-feeling between the Council and the vicar Foster who, angry at their refusal to take responsibility for repairing St Saviour's church, organised a petition against the scheme as it would increase the rates. Meanwhile the Assembly Rooms were becoming positively unsafe. In 1877 the mayor Sir Henry Seale had to ask the public attending a meeting there not to stamp, as vibration might be dangerous! They considered using the Subscription Rooms, but these were let out on a long lease to trustees who were unwilling to release them.

In 1878 the Council bought from the Bible Christians for £733 their chapel in the New (Victoria) Road, built in 1867, and spent another £100 on converting it into a Guildhall. The Assembly Rooms were sold and demolished in 1880. The Council went on meeting in their converted chapel until 1901, when the Subscription Rooms became available, the lease having ended. They then sold the chapel to the Primitive Methodists, and moved into one end of the Subscription Rooms, converted to serve as a Guildhall by 1902. However, they were not too happy with this arrangement, and in 1903 they held a competition for a new municipal building, to include a market, town hall, offices, and library, estimated to cost £7,500. The competition was won by Mr. Luke, but there was soon a dispute with the Council with the result that the whole plan was abandoned. The Council stayed in the Subscription Rooms, but in 1909 they built an extension onto the east end, put up by R. T. Pillar at a cost of £318. This solution saved the rates, but Dartmouth deserved a better Guildhall than this one, which is still in use.[11]

Public Health and Hospitals

In 1871 a report on epidemics and the sanitary state of the town was written by Dr. Buchanan, a government inspector sent down because of fears for the health of the cadets

98. The Pool at low tide, an eyesore and a health hazard. It was filled in, 1876-7, and soon afterwards Mayors Avenue was built on the reclaimed ground to link it to the Embankment.

on *Britannia*. Buchanan reported that the cases of infection which had occurred among the cadets had not, in fact, originated in Dartmouth. He was, however, scathing about the state of the Pool — 'the general cesspool and filth place of the town . . . pervaded by an abominable stink' — and of the fact that the majority of houses were not connected with the recently built sewer. The fact was that many landlords refused to provide W.C.s for their tenants or to connect them with the main sewer. They continued as of old to use cess pits, to throw their sewage into the harbour if they lived beside it, or into the street if they did not. Dr. Buchanan recommended that the borough should be provided with an isolation hospital.[12]

The danger that they might lose *Britannia*, and the business it brought to the town, was one of the few things which stirred the reluctant authorities to act. Over the next few years, the Pool was finally filled in with the rubble from all the demolished buildings. By 1883 the present Mayor's Avenue was built on the reclaimed land, to join up with the new Embankment, cutting off the old shipyards from the water (*see* plate 101).

The Cottage Hospital

The town progressed gradually towards a public hospital, thanks first to Dr. Puddicombe, who in 1873 built a small cottage hospital in his garden in Southtown. He lost money over it as the Council refused to make any contribution to it so that poorer people could be treated. In 1887, in honour of Queen Victoria's jubilee, money was raised to set up a hospital in a house on Bearscove. This was not a suitable building and, after a campaign by the mayor F.C. Simpson, a purpose-built hospital was opened on the new South Embankment in 1894, paid for by public subscription. This hospital charged fees, unless one obtained a 'recommend' from one of the subscribers who had the right to put forward so many 'deserving' cases a year for free treatment. A child might be sent round to the back door of the house of a subscriber — perhaps his father's employer — to explain that father had had an accident, and wait while it was decided whether he would be given one of the free places.

The hospital was enlarged in 1925 and after the Second World War became part of the National Health Service, when all treatment became free. A new wing was added in 1974, with the aid of money raised by the League of Friends. It remains an indispensable provision for the area west of the river.

For a short time there was also a town isolation hospital for patients suffering from infectious diseases who could not be put in the cottage hospital. This was provided in 1914 in a corrugated iron shed at Jawbones, in very primitive conditions, and was used until 1922, after which most cases were taken to Paignton. It was closed in the 1930s.

The Floating Hospital

Meanwhile, in response to a government order to all ports to provide an isolation hospital for cases of infectious diseases brought in on ships, Dartmouth's Port Sanitary Authority bought an old ship, the *Mayfly*, and set it up as a floating hospital in 1893. It survived until 1923, becoming gradually more and more unfit for use, and was finally replaced by the *Kingswear Castle* paddle steamer. By this time the Ministry of Health decreed that such ships were out of date, and she was re-sold to her original owners, the steam packet company, in 1927. Over more than 30 years, the ships had treated an estimated 33 cases, but their existence could have saved an epidemic in the town.[13]

Schools

There were many small private fee-paying schools in Dartmouth, often run by the clergy, and before 1870 there had been three schools for the poor: one for Anglicans, the St Petrox

99.   The Cottage Hospital and Mission to Seamen, Bearscove, in 1887.

National school in Southtown, a Catholic school in the recently built St John's church, and one for non-conformists in the Subscription Rooms. The one set up in the former Townstal workhouse building on the St Clare's site had closed by 1850. In 1872 the St Petrox school was closed after a Government Inspector condemned it as so unsatisfactory that the grant was withdrawn. To comply with the Education Act of 1870, a Board School for girls was built in Higher Street, which opened in 1874. The Subscription Rooms were used as a school for boys, and St Saviour's Sunday School building in South Ford Road for infants. Attendance was not compulsory, and fees were charged, so not surprisingly, attendance figures were low. Only 336 children attended out of an estimated 800 who should have been there. In 1880 the School Board bought the property next door to the Higher Street school, and enlarged it so that all the children could be in the one building. Parents were now obliged by law to send children.[14]

Non-Conformist Churches

Non-Anglican churches were expanding fast during this time. In 1856, a group of Plymouth Brethren is first recorded as having a small chapel in Clarence Street, from where it had moved to a room in Back Lane by 1873.[15] The Roman Catholics had had some supporters in the town since refugees had arrived at the time of the French Revolution, and they had met in a house in Clarence Street. In 1868 they bought land in Newcomen Road and built the St John the Baptist church, with a schoolroom and house for the priest adjoining. The first priest was Father John Laborie-Rey.

The Baptist chapel was still in its building in Chapel Lane, off Higher Street, which had been built in 1824. *Kelly's Directory* of 1878 records that it was being renovated in that year at a cost of £340, which suggests a growing membership. After the Second World War, by which time new houses were being built at Townstal, the Baptists sold the old chapel there and built a new one in the middle of the housing estate to which many of their members had moved.[15]

The old Independent church started by Flavel had continued at the back of Foss Street where in 1811 an energetic new minister, the Rev. Thomas Stenner, started the Sunday School, which taught the children to read, write and sew. There was soon such a demand that they started a session on Saturday afternoons, as well as three on Sundays before the evening service. The main object was to enable the children, who in those days would be working every weekday, to be able to read the Bible and so follow religious teaching. The church kept records of the births of their members, who included the Nicholls, shipbuilders, and some of the Lidstones.[17]

In 1895 a new Flavel church was built on land recently reclaimed from the Pool, at a cost of £1,200, and the old one was used as a Sunday School. In 1943 this was demolished by a German bomb, which luckily missed the main church, and it was rebuilt after the war as the Flavel Hall.

The Wesleyans had set up a group in a house in Brown's Hill Steps as early as 1782, but by 1816 had collected enough money to build their first church on the present site which then faced the Mill Pool, now the market. Among its first members were the elder Robert Cranford and his wife, and later George Philip of the shipbuilding firm. By 1827 there were Wesleyan groups in most of the surrounding villages, including Kingswear, Cornworthy, Dittisham and Capton, often meeting in members' homes at first. In 1874 the Dartmouth church was extended, at a cost of £2,300, to include the house on the east, and could seat 640 people, with another floor above for the Sunday school.[18]

Two other groups of Methodists had churches with large congregations. The Bible Christians built a chapel next to the Subscription Rooms, costing £600 in 1867, which they sold to the Council for a Guildhall. They built a new chapel, with a house for the minister beside it, in Newcomen Road in 1885. The Primitive Methodists met first in Clarence Street, and later at a 'little iron church' in Crowthers Hill. They then bought the former Bible Christians' chapel from the Council in 1901. In 1932, the three branches were united by a national agreement and all used the Methodist church in the Market Square, the other two chapels being sold. The one in Newcomen Road became the Library, while that in Victoria Road was pulled down and is now Tozers printing works. In 1938 the facade of the Methodist church was extensively altered, the centre front windows being renewed to form three long windows. It remained in use until 1982, when it held its last service. Its future use is a matter of some controversy.

It must be remembered that the congregations of all these churches, usually among the least wealthy in the town, had to pay out of their own pockets to build and maintain their chapels, and support their ministers. They were against extravagance by the local Council, and had no sympathy with claims by the vicar that the rates should be used to repair St Saviour's church.

Controversy and Lawsuits

The Embankment Scheme

As early as 1871 there was talk in Dartmouth of building an 'esplanade', to encourage yachts and tourists to visit the town. In 1879 Samuel Lake proposed that the Council should ask the Harbour Commission to dredge the harbour and build a sea wall, using the mud to put behind it. A glance at a photograph of the waterfront before 1880 makes clear the need for it, with ships only able to reach the warehouses built for the Newfoundland trade at high tide. By 1881 the D.H.C. had drawn up a scheme for an Embankment 600 yards long, starting at the end of the Lower Ferry slip and extending north to where the gas works then stood, the site of the present Boatel. The advantages of the scheme were that, like other neighbouring towns such as Torquay, Teignmouth and Dawlish, Dartmouth would have a beautiful promenade which would attract tourists. Also, the dredging involved would enable larger steamers to use the port, which would provide employment.

The whole scheme was estimated to cost £30,000, of which it was hoped that Dartmouth Council would pay £13,000 from the rates for the part from the gas works to the railway pontoon, while the D.H.C. would finance the southern section by a tax on coal imported into the town (excluding bunkering coal), and on yachts. Harbour dues could not be raised, otherwise the steamer traffic would go elsewhere.[19] However, close examination reveals that the Dartmouth people would pay the bill for both sections — by rates in one, and through the tax on domestic coal in the other. The most vocal and well-organised objectors were the yacht owners, led by Francis C. Simpson, who was rear-commodore of the new Royal Dart Yacht Club. He had arrived in the town in 1873 and started to build steam yachts in a yard at Silver Street, which would be cut off from the river by the embankment. He began to organise the poor people to object because their coal would be dearer, in an unlikely alliance with wealthy yacht owners and those who would lose their river frontage.

Simpson had been on the Council earlier, when he had opposed the new Guildhall and supported the vicar, Foster, in his disputes with the borough over their liabilities towards St Saviour's, in both of which he had come into conflict with Hockin the town clerk. He had since then resigned, but now he stood again in 1881. To stop him being elected the existing Council blatantly rigged the election, with the connivance of Hockin. All four anti-embankment candidates' nomination papers were declared illegal on a technicality. Sir Henry Seale was elected mayor, while his nephew Seale-Hayne was chairman of the Harbour Commission: in this case the Seale family was united in support of the scheme.

Simpson appealed against the election result to the courts, which ordered fresh elections. He and his three supporters thereby joined the Council by mid-1882, but his opponents were in a majority there. A petition signed by 400 voters against the scheme was organised by him and sent to parliament as it was debating the Harbour Commission's bill, resulting in a clause being inserted that the Council could contribute money to the scheme only if they had a two-thirds majority in favour. The proposed tax on yachts was dropped, leaving the whole sum to be paid by the coal tax — in other words by the poor rather than the rich. Simpson demanded that the decision by the Council on whether to contribute should be deferred until after the November election, when he was confident of winning more seats for the anti-embankment group. For the same reason, in October 1882 the old Council

100. The need for an Embankment can be seen from this photograph of the 1870s showing the waterfront before building. Ships could only reach the warehouses on a high tide, and lay beached on the mud until the next one.

101. The completed Embankment, photographed during Regatta week, 1887. The large steam/sailing yachts in the harbour were of the type built by Messrs. Simpson and Strickland at Sandquay at the time.

carried through by a nine to five majority a resolution to pay between £10,000 and £13,000 towards the scheme for the northern end of the Embankment.[20]

Fortified by this, the D.H.C. signed the contract with the contractor, Messrs. Thomas, for £24,000 and work started straight away. It took three years, and was completed in 1885. However, in the November elections, in the largest poll ever recorded, four more anti-embankment councillors were elected replacing those in favour of the scheme. Simpson was elected mayor, and the town clerk Hockin dismissed. The new Council declared the decision of the previous Council to finance the scheme illegal and tried to get an injunction to stop the work. A series of law suits followed to establish whether the Council was liable to pay its contribution, and costs mounted on both sides. The first two rounds confirmed that the old Council had been within its rights to vote the money. However, the new Council, led by Simpson as mayor for the next 10 years, refused to pay and the Harbour Commission was forced to sue them. By 1891 they had lost their case in both the Lower and Appeal Court, and had to abandon the idea of appealing to the House of Lords as they were on the verge of bankruptcy.

The Commission had had a series of misfortunes, the worst of which was an award against them of over £4,000 plus costs because a steamer had gone aground in the harbour owing to a misplaced buoy. Two insurance companies which had loaned them money demanded repayment when they failed to pay the interest. When the Embankment — which was being built while all the law suits rumbled on — was completed in 1885 they were unable to pay the contractor the balance he was owed. Even their London solicitors, with the somewhat apt names of Messrs. Batten and Proffitt, were suing them for their fees. They thus had to agree to a compromise whereby the Council would pay only £2,600 as their full contribution towards the work, and received in return the whole of the Embankment, the reclaimed land, and the Boat Float. The anti-embankment committee now disbanded after 10 years, congratulating themselves on what a fine bargain they had made.

The Harbour Commission had to pay the bill. In 1895 they were discharged from bankruptcy with the aid of a loan of £35,000 from the Naval Bank, on the security of the harbour dues. With this they settled their debts, though the unfortunate contractors who had built the Embankment were paid only 10 shillings in the pound 10 years late. Yet the increased volume of trade which came to the town fully justified the Embankment scheme. Harbour dues in the 1870s averaged £650. By 1885 they had doubled to £1,379. Their peak in 1890 topped £2,500, after which the average was around £2,000, falling to £1,800 just before the First World War. The fall was partly due to the increasing size of steamers, the largest of which now could not use Dartmouth harbour. The Council might argue that shipping ought to bear the whole cost of what was done mainly for their benefit: but shipping was the main employer in the town. In any case, the Embankment soon proved a boon for all the people: a site for a hospital, hotels, houses and a station, a convenient landing place for colliers and pleasure boats, and a promenade for all, especially appreciated at Regatta time.

The Vicar and the Charity Commission

During the same years as the Council was fighting the battle over the Embankment, in the end successfully, they had another legal suit on their hands which they were to lose. This concerned their liability to maintain the fabric of St Saviour's, and pay towards the vicar's stipend, both of which they thought had been settled in their favour in 1846.

A new vicar, the Rev. Priestley Foster, came to the town in 1871. Foster had previously been a curate in Torquay, and his promotion was bought for him by two ladies who paid £700 to Sir Henry Seale, owner of the advowson, to secure it for him. He brought with him from Torquay and appointed as one churchwarden, traditionally chosen by the vicar, a friend Shuttlewood , but was soon at odds with the other churchwarden chosen by the parishioners, Percy Hockin the town clerk. He regularly attacked in the pulpit the mayor, then Robert Cranford the owner of the *Dartmouth Chronicle*, and other councillors, most of whom were parishioners, and had public rows with his own curate, organist and verger.[21]

Foster had a financial problem in that pew rents, used for many years to pay church expenses, had been declared illegal, and people did not like contributing money to replace them. The roof of the tower was leaking so much that the organ, then in the west gallery, was being damaged. However, his scheme to remove the organ to the chancel, and have the choir there too, aroused great opposition from those who suspected him of 'Romish practices'. In the course of his disputes with his parishioners he reduced the services to only one on Sundays, unless they would pay for another, and refused to ring the bells or have the organ played on the grounds that the tower and gallery were unsafe. Foster was demanding that the Council pay for the repairs, which they refused to do.

Foster founded a rival newspaper, the *Dartmouth Advertiser*, setting up as editor his friend Shuttlewood, a tobacconist by trade. He used the paper to print attacks on the leading councillors which he had written but were never signed by him. Before long, libel writs were flying back and forth. Shuttlewood got into financial trouble, and Foster did not hesitate to make him bankrupt, replacing him with another editor Leyman, equally ignorant of the trade. In 1876, after local papers had been full of Foster's doings, the Plymouth-based *Western Daily Mercury* carried a satirical article about Foster and his newspaper which led Foster and Leyman to sue them for libel. The particular phrases to which they objected were the claims that one editor of the *Advertiser* was a bankrupt, and the other a 'convicted felon'. The law suits ran for two years, in the course of which it was revealed that Leyman had indeed been convicted for felony — for stealing feathers which he and his wife used to take from featherbeds in hotels after unpicking the stitches in the cover! He had served a year in prison for this crime. The plaintiffs argued that since he had served his sentence, he was no longer a felon, and it was unfair to blacken his character by revealing it. After two trials and an appeal the jury failed to agree, and the case was discharged, it being up to the plaintiff to apply for a new trial. The *Mercury* felt it had achieved a moral victory, at a cost of £1,000 in legal fees.[22]

The divisions in the church disputes overlapped with those of the town at large. Francis Simpson was a high churchman who supported Foster both in his desired changes to the services and in his belief that the Council held property which rightfully belonged to St Saviour's. He was chosen by the vicar as 'his' churchwarden to replace Shuttlewood, while Hockin remained the parishioners' warden. Hockin, as town clerk, controlled all the town records and was the leading spokesman for the view that the Borough did *not* have any responsibility for St Saviour's. When the Council was trying to raise money to build a new Guildhall, a scheme supported by Hockin, Foster and Simpson started a petition against it which led to its being dropped. When, as has been related, Hockin supported the Embankment scheme and tried to prevent Simpson's group being elected to oppose it, Simpson started legal proceedings against the Council. As soon as he was elected and became mayor, Hockin was dismissed as town clerk.

By this time Foster had resigned his living and left the town in 1878. However, his parting shot was to refer the whole question of the origins of the town property to the Charity Commission, which already supervised the much smaller group of properties given for parochial charities. They demanded to see all the original deeds back to the 14th-century charter of St Saviour's, including all the town leases of property. The horrified Council employed Stuart Moore to go through and translate their records — he produced the first calendar of their archives as a result — but his researches only supported the view that much of the early property had been given for religious purposes. The town faced the fact that its last remaining source of steady income, outside the rates, was under threat.

The Charity Commission sued the Council in the Court of Chancery, which ruled in 1883 that lands originally given for charitable purposes had been combined with those legitimately owned by the borough. As by this time it was almost imposible to identify which was which, they ordered that 93 properties out of the 213 then owned should be handed over to the Charity Commission, and a scheme drawn up whereby the income from them should be used for their original purposes, in which the upkeep of St Saviour's was included. In 1890 the Dartmouth Charities was set up, with a group of trustees to manage the property: collect rents, arrange for repairs, decide on investments or sales. Any profits made were to be distributed between St Saviour's church, repairs to conduits, and gifts to the 'deserving' poor. The income, small at first, has grown over the years, and the proportions going to various purposes has changed. It is, for instance, no longer used to maintain conduits or provide schooling. Since 1950, one third has gone to St Saviour's, one sixth to Dartmouth Council to maintain ancient buildings, and one half to people in need. In 1909 the trustees of all the small charities were combined into a body called the Dartmouth United Charities, which is responsible for the spending of this half of the income.[23]

Chapter Sixteen

Rich and Poor, 1860-1914

The Last of the Seale Family

The Seale family gradually lost their pre-eminent position as lords of the manor over the last 30 years of the century. Sir Henry Seale disposed of some of his Dartmouth lands: Southtown was sold in 1864, and by 1873 Mount Boone, Coombe and the Floating Bridge were bought by the Raleigh Estates. The family kept Norton Park, and Sir Henry served

102. Seale mourning hatchment, St Saviour's.

103. Norton House, always owned by the Seale family, became the main home of Sir Henry Seale after he sold Mount Boone in 1871. It was considerably rebuilt by him.

five times as mayor of Dartmouth between 1877-1882 at the height of the Embankment controversy, but was the last of his family to do so. He was chairman of the Harbour Commission until his 90th year, and died in 1897 aged 91. Charles Seale-Hayne resigned from the Harbour Commission because of the acrimony aroused by the Embankment, and took his talents elsewhere. He served as Liberal M.P. for Ashburton from 1885 until his death in 1903, and was Paymaster General under Gladstone from 1892-5. When he died, a bachelor, he left £150,000 to found the agricultural college near Newton Abbot which bears his name. Dartmouth could ill afford to lose his abilities or his wealth.

George Parker Bidder — The Calculating Boy
This period saw the emergence in the town of a new class of entrepreneur, often self-made men, whose wealth and expertise were acquired elsewhere but who were prepared to invest

in projects to stimulate the economy. George Bidder was one of these, who first came to the river by yacht in 1858 and decided he would like a house there. He had started life as the fifth son of a blacksmith in Moretonhampstead, but became known as The Calculating Boy after it was found he could do amazing calculations in his head without ever having been to school. His father made money by taking him round to display his genius at fairs. Some wealthy gentlemen paid for him to go to school and then to Edinburgh University, where he studied civil engineering. He was a friend and partner of Robert Stephenson, building railways and docks not only in England but in Europe, and became a rich man. In 1861 he bought Paradisé, built six years before, and changed its name to 'Ravensbury', after his house in Surrey.[1] He was among the first members of the Harbour Commission. He became a friend of Samuel Lake, then experimenting with the idea of steam trawlers. Bidder designed a new type of steam trawler which was built by Philip in 1872, called *Edyth* after his daughter. Mrs. Bidder re-opened the St Petrox school for poor girls. With Lake and others he was involved in promoting the Torbay paintworks, and re-opening a slate quarry at Buckland.[2] He was on the Council in 1868 and was a keen supporter of the Embankment scheme, the original plans for which were drawn up by his office. His son George P. Bidder II, a barrister, gave evidence in favour of the Embankment scheme when the Harbour Commission's bill was before Parliament in 1882. Before this, the elder Bidder had bought

104. Ravensbury, *c.*1860, home of George Parker Bidder from 1861-78.

Stoke House, in Stoke Fleming, and was about to move there when he died in 1878. His wife and unmarried daughters lived there for many years afterwards. The bitterness in the town may have made them decide to leave — another casualty of the feud with Simpson.[3]

Samuel Lake

Samuel Lake was a self-made man who was Dartmouth-born. He had gone to sea at the age of ten, and spent many years in India where he was given the Albert Medal for bravery in helping to rescue 420 pilgrims from a shipwreck. He returned to his birthplace in 1866 a rich man, and financed a scheme to build twelve steam trawlers, the orders being spread among the local shipyards in 1867-8. He also bought a screw-tug, to tow trawlers in or out of the harbour in light winds. These were not a great financial success, and Dartmouth did not take off as a fishing port. Meanwhile Lake built a row of concrete cottages along Coombe Road, a new material at that time but one which has stood the test of time since they are all still standing. He also built Redwalls, a fine villa in Townstal. With a partner Armesson, he bought an orchard from Sir Henry Seale at Coombe where there was a good seam of clay, and set up a brickworks, turning out 20,000 bricks a week. As this was at a time of building boom, they must have had a ready market and were even exported to London. Lake later withdrew, leaving the firm to be run by Armesson. He founded the Torbay paintworks, and the Buckland slate quarry, with Bidder and others. It was Lake who first persuaded the Council to promote the Embankment scheme, and he was no doubt angered by the opposition to it. In the 1880s he left Dartmouth to construct the docks at Milford Haven, and another good man was lost to the town.[4]

William Henley

William Henley was another Dartmouth-born man who is a good example of the Victorian philosophy of self-help. He never became rich or famous but the Henley Museum in Anzac Street reflects his life and varied intellectual interests.

   Like his father before him, he was an ironmonger and tinsmith, with a shop in Foss Street. Henley was born over the shop, in 1860, one of a large family. His schooling consisted of a brief period at a 'dame school', after which he was taught by the Baptist minister until he left at 12 to work in his father's shop. His first scientific experience was working with tin and other metals, for in those days such shops did not just sell goods but made and mended them, too. After a 12-hour day in the shop, he educated himself in a surprising range of subjects by buying second-hand books. He also taught himself to draw, paint, and make architectural drawings. Always interested in the history of his town, he drew many of its old buildings which were at that time being demolished (*see* plates 28 and 65). He learnt photography, and left a large collection of glass slides. He made himself a microscope, and hundreds of microscopic slides, some mounted on glass ringed with enamel, which are of real beauty besides their scientific interest. Letters preserved in the Museum show that Henley corresponded with some of the leading scientific figures of his day about his many interests — all this in his limited leisure time after his working day. The rooms which now form the Museum were once his workshop, his shop being at 'Henley's Corner' between Foss Street and Duke Street, and have been restored to suggest Henley at work with his microscope, surrounded by his pictures and cherished possessions. Photographs show what Dartmouth was like during his lifetime. All these were preserved after his death in 1919 by his devoted sister Ellen Pamela Henley, who opened the Museum in his memory.

Shipbuilders

Shipbuilding remained as always one of the major employers in the town, and the yards were busy from 1860-1914. Henry Nichols was head of the last of the old firms, building clippers and trawlers at King's Quay up to 1879, when he died at a great age. The most active yards were at Sandquay, where Redway's were building a series of trawlers, many for the North Sea fishery but also some of the steam trawlers for Lake. After a serious fire in 1878 they went bankrupt, and Redway later joined Lake at Milford Haven. Moores at Higher Sandquay built schooners and trawlers, the latter for the North Sea fisheries.[5]

The Philip Family
Newcomers included George Philip, who had come to the port from Scotland in 1854 as foreman to Kelly at Sandquay, and in 1858 took over the yard when his employer retired. Philip also worked with Couch at the Coombe yard in the mid-1860s. He was joined by his son Alexander, who had trained in iron and steel shipbuilding at Lairds of Birkenhead. Philip & Son built both timber and composite ships at their yards at Sandquay, which in the 1870s were sandwiched between Redway's. During those years they built brigs, schooners

105. The *Retriever*, built by Philip in 1876 for the Newman Company, and used on the Newfoundland run.

and trawlers mainly for the North Sea fisheries, but also steam trawlers such as the *Edyth* for Bidder and for London owners. Their first all-steel vessel was the *Totnes Castle*, built in 1896 for the River Dart steam packet service. In 1891 Philips acquired all the yards at Sandquay, and in 1918 bought Noss works after Simpson Strickland went bankrupt. This made them the leading employers in the town, and the family continued to own and manage the firm through five generations until the 1960s.[6]

Francis C. Simpson

An even more recent arrival was Francis Simpson, who came to Dartmouth by 1873 when he lived at Derwent Lodge, Southtown, but in 1875 bought a house on Ridge Hill which he renamed Combecote. He was a marine engineer, who went into partnership first with Denison. Samuel Kingdon and William Froude of Chelston had recently patented a compound steam engine which was smaller, more efficient and less expensive, thus suitable for smaller vessels such as steam yachts. Simpson and Denison became agents for building these engines in 1880, and set up an engine house to build them at the bottom of the garden at Combecote. They began building steam launches and later steam yachts at King's Quay in Nichol's old yard.[7] Simpson was a keen yachtsman, and soon became a leading member of the Royal Dart Yacht Club, which must have been good for business. He opposed the Embankment scheme partly because it cut off his shipyard from the main river, and partly because he feared the effect of a tax on yachts on his business. In the end, the tax on yachts was dropped, but the building of the Embankment forced him to move to Sandquay in 1883, to Redway's old yards. In 1890 the Denisons retired and he formed a partnership with Strickland, a wealthy relative of his wife. His money financed the move to Noss Point, which took place in 1891. The railway at that time ran right through the site, carried across the creeks either side on wooden viaducts.[8]

The new complex there was the most modern that money could buy, including offices, design rooms, and workshops of all descriptions. There were engineering and boiler shops, carpenters' and coppersmiths' sheds, and a steel boatbuilding shed. A tramline ran round the yard between the fitting and boiler shops. With the aid of a huge overhead travelling crane, boilers could be moved to any part of the works (*see* plate 110). There was even a device producing hot water for the men's tea, enabling a shorter lunch break and earlier finish to the day. Boats brought workers across the river to the site. The range of work done was now greatly expanded. It included private launches --in 1893 one for a Russian Count — and pinnaces for the Admiralty. In 1897 there were 230 men working there, some on a 77-foot boat built in 10 sections for river work in New Zealand, and a steel boat built in five sections for transport to an African lake.[9] An early catalogue illustrated a steam yacht of 192 feet, designed as a 'state yacht for river work', and a 'fast light draught boat as built for a Colonial river', 91 feet long. Another drawing showed 'Police patrol launches as built for South America'.[10] Dartmouth-built ships were being used all over the world in this last great age of Empire.

Up to the First World War both Simpson's and Philip's kept going: Simpson launched 32 vessels in 1912, and 29 in 1913, while Philip launched 11 and 8 in the same years.[11] However, the war hit Simpson's badly. Simpson was now old, and his younger partner Strickland went off to fight. One son was killed in the war, another was by now vicar of St Saviour's and the third son was not interested in the business. In 1916 the firm went bankrupt and in the end was bought in July 1918 by Philip and Son.

The End of the Broad Gauge Railway, 1892

The railway to Kingswear, which was losing money, was taken over by the Great Western Railway in 1876. The broad gauge used on the line was uneconomic, as most of Britain's lines had been built to the standard gauge. In 1892 the G.W.R. decided that the whole line from Paddington to Penzance, including the branch to Kingswear, must be changed to the standard gauge of 4ft. 8½in. Over one weekend hundreds of men worked in teams round the clock to move one set of rails inwards. All the engines and rolling stock had also to be scrapped and replaced. The G.W.R. was to own the railway until the coming of British Rail in 1947.[12]

The Building of the Naval College, 1902-5

As early as 1875 the government began looking for a site for a land-based college to replace *Britannia*, and after stiff competition from other ports, Dartmouth was chosen as the most suitable, over £620,000 being voted to pay for it. Nothing happened for over 20 years, and with every change of government the rival ports, especially Portsmouth, tried to reverse the original decision and gain the college for themselves. By 1896 the site earmarked for the

106.   View of the newly completed Britannia Royal Naval College in Regatta week, probably in 1908.

building belonged to the Raleigh Estates, who refused to sell. The use of compulsory purchase powers was rare in those days, and the National Defence Act of 1842 was used, which gave powers to buy for reasons of defence even against the owners' wishes. The final decision whether to act was taken by two deputy lieutenants specially appointed for the purpose, who met and listened to military and naval experts' opinions on the issue. One,

Kelly, was 'strongly against taking any man's land against his will'. The other, Watson, argued that the benefits to the West Country of having the college outweighed this, and Kelly gave way. The very next day a marine was sent to erect a pole in the centre of the site, as a challenge, forcing Raleigh Estates to take an action for trespass in the High Court which they lost. The building of the college then started.[13]

Sir Aston Webb was the architect, and work began on the terraces for the main building in 1898. However, when two cadets died of 'flu on *Britannia*, the sick quarters were built before the rest of the college. In 1902 King Edward VII came to lay the foundation stone, crossing the river in the *Dolphin* amid scenes of great excitement. The new college was completed by 1905, and has ever since been the most striking building in the harbour. The age of entry had by now been raised to about 15 years. The young Prince of Wales (later Edward VIII) and his brother (George VI) followed their father as cadets from 1909-11. On leaving, the Prince of Wales pleased the town by returning to it the Silver Oar of the waterbaileywick which had been taken away amidst such ill feeling in 1864. In 1905 the old *Hindustan* was towed away to Plymouth, where she continued to be used until 1921 as an artificers' training ship.

Soon after 1914 the Naval College needed more accommodation, to train double the number of naval officers, and the building of a new block began behind the main building. The *Britannia* stayed in Dartmouth until 1916 when, in the midst of the First World War, she was towed away for scrap to the sounds of 'Rule Britannia'. Everyone in the town turned out to see her passing: it marked the end of an era.

Everyday Life at the Turn of the Century

The population of Dartmouth grew rapidly at this time, reaching over 7,000 by 1910. The only new land which had come on to the market was when Mount Boone and its garden were sold in 1905, soon snapped up for plots on which middle-class villas were built. In Southtown, too, new houses for the well-to-do were built, often used as holiday homes by families who arrived complete with servants for the social events of the Regatta period. The same was true on the Kingswear side, where the population had more than doubled as a result of the railway, and the sale of the Luttrell lands in 1874 led to the building of many beautiful houses overlooking the river. A few rows of terraced houses were built for the better-paid workers who had steady jobs, but not nearly enough for the poorer section of the community.

The Coal Lumpers

Those who loaded coal were known as 'lumpers', and were casual labourers paid only for the hours they were employed, as were dockers in those days. They worked in small gangs of six or eight men, in competition with each other, each gang earning, between 1890 and 1910, 2d. a ton between them for loading up a ship with coal, sometimes with steam winches, otherwise by hand. Loading 200 tons took about four hours, which worked out at one shilling an hour. That was not a bad rate at the time if the work had been continuous, but it was not. First, you had to 'rush for the job'. Runners were placed at Compass Point and other high ground to spot steamers on their way. They knew which shipping lines normally bunkered in Dartmouth, and read in the *Lloyds Shipping Gazette* when a ship had left its last bunkering port. As soon as a likely ship was sighted, the runners raced to tip off their gang, who waited on the Embankment or Bearscove where there was a bench for them (*see* plate 99). The first man to put his leg over the iron ladder on the wall of the cove won for his gang the job of mooring the ship, at 10d. a man, in addition to the bunkering. Then there was a race to the coal hulks in their gigs (rowing boats). The winners won the job of bunkering the ship: the losers had no work, and no pay.[14]

The men could be called out, night or day, at the same rate and never knew what their weekly wage could be. A good week might bring £1 7s. 0d. (£1.35) but at other times they might earn nothing at all. Many became crippled by arthritis by standing around in all weathers. By 1913 the men were still being paid 2d. a ton, while the cost of living and other wages had risen. There was a world recession in shipping, and keen competition for the shrinking traffic. After a visit in 1914 by Ernest Bevin — later Foreign Secretary in 1945 — the lumpers joined the Dock and General Workers Union.[15] Bevin urged them to try to get the best wage for their labour, and the advantage of unity with workers in other docks, so that they could not be used to break each others' strikes. When the men demanded 3d. an hour, the coaling companies, who hated unions, stationed a tug outside the harbour and directed steamers to Portland — the equivalent of a lock-out. The union persuaded the Portland men not to handle the diverted ships, but the strike ended without the men having gained their wage rise because they could not afford to hold out any longer. However, the need for a national union was accepted, and from then on every gang insisted that its men joined the union.

The Mission to Seamen opened in Bearscove in the 1880s (*see* plate 99), providing shelter and recreation for the men in a warm room with newspapers, such as the *Shipping Gazette*, and books. No intoxicants, gambling or bad language were allowed, and it was hoped to discourage the men from drinking away their wages in the public houses. Later, during the First World War, it was moved to what is now the Tall Ships restaurant on the South Embankment.

A Coal Lumper's Family Described
Because they had to be near the waterfront, ready day and night to dash out to coal a steamer, most of the lumpers and their families lived in Higher and Lower Street, Bearscove and Southtown. They crowded into tenements in old houses once built for wealthy merchants but where now there were sometimes 15 families in one house, each in one room, sharing one water

107. Higher Street, about 1900, looking north. The houses on the left were let as tenements, one family to a room, with as many as 15 families in one house. Many coal lumpers lived here, to be near to the river.

tap and water closet in a yard outside. The dangers of the overcrowding were seen in 1912 when a fire at a house next to the school in which 32 people were living caused the death of a mother and three of her children. Such houses were quite profitable to landlords, who could collect over £40 a year in rents.

Children in such families had to learn early to supplement the family wage by doing jobs out of school hours: fetching water from the conduits, chopping sticks, or running errands. Many of the wives took in washing, all to be done in the wash-house in the yard, with the one communal tap and copper to boil the water. They produced meals from the cheapest ingredients: hog's pudding, chitterlings, sheep's head. All had to be cooked on the coal fire in the one living room. On Sundays those with no ovens would take their joints in a tin, surrounded by vegetables, to the baker who would cook it for them for two pence. In the market twice a week the soup kitchen went on right up to 1939 providing a bowl of nourishing stew with vegetables and a hunk of bread for $\frac{1}{2}$d., and people used to queue up with their own bowls for it. It was financed by charity, the ingredients provided by local butchers and vegetable shops.[16]

Though money was tight, people still living remember those days with affection, even pride: as everyone else lived much the same way there was no sense of grievance. One lady described how she lived with her parents, who had nine sons and three daughters, in Hardy Cottages, now pulled down, behind the Embankment. They had three rooms: a kitchen/living room on the ground floor, with a coal fire which heated the oven and hot water boiler. On the first floor was a bedroom for the parents and the three girls, while above that was the boys' bedroom. The only lighting was by oil lamps or candles. Some of the older boys had left home before the youngest of the 12 was born, so not all were there at once. With four other cottages they opened on to a small yard, in which was a communal tap, a wash house and two water closets, which they all took turns to keep clean. In the cottage they used chamber pots, which had to be emptied in the W.C.s. Father always had a bath after he had coaled a ship, and for this water was carried by bucket from the tap, heated in the boiler behind the fire, and then poured into a tin bath in front of the fire. Meanwhile, all the children were turned out! They all had their bath on a Saturday night. The wives had to take turns to use the wash house. They never had new clothes, only 'pass ons', and mother was kept busy repairing or altering clothes to fit. The girls would only have one dress and two pinafores, which her mother would always have spotlessly clean every day for school. Though they had a few blankets, there were not enough for the winter, so they hired some for one shilling each from a little shop in St Saviour's Square. All the babies were born in the cottage, with the help of a midwife who was a relative. No doctor was ever called.

To help with food, her father had a small garden out by the castle where they grew all the vegetables they ate, and kept chickens. Mother went out every day to feed these, and they never bought eggs. The boys caught mackerel when they were shoaling and these could be dried for future use. If meat was short, it was kept for father. Fish could often be bought cheaply: three pennyworth of dabs would feed the family, and the fishermen often gave away spider crabs as no one else would eat them. They never bought fruit, but picked wild berries and occasionally scrumped apples. Every morning one of the children would go round to the bakers who sold off yesterday's stale bread cheaply. Their entertainments had to be what was provided free. They all learnt to swim at Sugary Cove, though sometimes they had to take turns to wear the one costume. They were always first out to watch the Regatta, and could earn money by looking after people's boats. In spite of all these hardships, they seemed very happy.[17]

On the Eve of the First World War
For the 25 years after the completion of the Embankment the Council did not undertake any great changes, but they then considered buying Coombe Mud in order to continue the

road north to Sandquay. However the outbreak of war in 1914 meant that the scheme had to be postponed.

The town Council tended to be complacent about the state of slum housing, since many of them were themselves landlords, and undertenants did not then have the vote. Charles Peek, mayor 1911-12, expressed the opinion that 'the people themselves were responsible for the state of their houses. There were some who, if you put them in a new house, would soon convert it into a slum'. This variation on the belief that 'they'll only put coals in the bath' was not uncommon. The infant mortality rate was then 105 per 1,000 — as compared with 9 per 1,000 in 1987, and reflected the low living standards of the poor. All the same, the population was rising, since births exceeded deaths.

In 1914 the Local Government Board sent down Dr. Mivart to inspect the sanitary administration of the town, and his report was highly critical. He described the tenement houses, many built back to the cliff, with shared and often broken closets, and the layers of filthy wallpaper harbouring bugs. He singled out for special condemnation Collaford Lane, St Saviour's Court, and Silver Street. He recommended that the town should appoint a properly-qualified inspector to deal with the problems and see that the new laws under the Town Planning Act of 1909 were carried out. The report was dated April 1914: any plans the Council might have had were shelved until after the First World War and the bugs living behind the wallpaper were reprieved.

Chapter Seventeen

Between Two World Wars

Soon after the First World War broke out, Thomas Wilton, of the coaling firm Renwick-Wilton, was elected mayor. He served for five successive years and was knighted afterwards. The Cottage Hospital was used for wounded soldiers, and most of Dartmouth's young men disappeared into the army or navy. In 1916 a large group of coal lumpers went off together to France. The Naval College went on training cadets all through the war, but the staff were called up and replaced by retired officers.

As in every town in Britain, families waited in fear for the arrival of the telegram announcing the death of their men. The Battle of Jutland left many bereaved families in the town. In 1916 Corporal Veale was awarded the V.C. for having rescued a wounded lieutenant from in front of the German lines. Lieutenant Eric Shiner, son of the headmaster of the newly opened Boys' School in Victoria Road, won the M.C. A letter in the *Dartmouth Chronicle* of 1917 from Private Gaston related how he was recovering in hospital after being partially buried for six hours in mud 'like quicksand' in a trench during the Battle of the Somme. His Captain led a party who placed rifle slings under his armpits and dragged him out — in the dark, otherwise the German snipers would have got them. Many local men were in the 2nd Devon Regiment when in June 1918 they were told to hold a position north of Aisne, and fought until every officer and soldier was killed, wounded or taken prisoner. On the other side, over 600 German prisoners were reported to be working on Devon farms, replacing Devonians called up to fight. Not only men were called up, but horses, too: the horses used to drag the guns and wagons through the mud of the western front were commandeered from the farms.[1]

The danger to shipping using the Channel was from submarines, which took a terrible toll. Among their victims buried in the local cemetery were Swedes, Japanese and Arabs. John Pillar, skipper of the motor pilot boat *Mellrose*, reported sighting four U-boats off the harbour in 1916, for which he was mentioned in dispatches. Four U-boats were destroyed in this area in the four years of war.[2] Stationed in Dartmouth during the war was the Royal Fleet Auxiliary vessel *Racer* with divers aboard, a salvage vessel ready to go to the aid of ships damaged in the Channel and bring them in for repairs.[3]

Philip & Son Between the Wars

The shipyards went on working during the war, although badly hit by the loss of foreign orders which had formerly provided much of their work. Philip's turned out over 80 vessels during the war years, including whalers, launches, tugs and steam pinnaces for the Admiralty and War Office. By the end of the war they had taken over Simpson's yard at Noss and were now the main shipbuilders in the port. They also bought the Floating Bridge, now a vital link between their two yards. Until 1921 the railway ran across Noss Point alongside the shipyards. After the wooden railway bridges across the creeks either side were found to be unsafe, the line was diverted round the edge of the creek. A private siding enabled materials to be delivered direct to the works.

Philip's remained the town's major employers, but fluctuations in orders during the inter-war years meant that jobs were never secure. In 1923, the last good year, they built 32 vessels of all sizes including the river steamer *Kingswear Castle*. In 1924-5 they built two chain car ferries for Torpoint and one for Tynemouth, and another passenger boat for the

108. The Motor Pilot boat *Mellrose* in 1915, under pilot John Pillar. It reported four enemy submarines in 1916. Between February 1916 and January 1918 four enemy submarines were destroyed. John Pillar was mentioned in dispatches, and awarded a sum of money in thanks by the Admiralty.

River Dart Company, the *Clifton Castle*. However, the numbers fell to half by 1927. There was a revival from 1928-30 during which time the *Hercules* tug was built for the Crown Agents. She was one of the biggest tugs in the world, 158 feet long, and was used in Colombo harbour, where she was reported as still active as recently as 1983.

In 1931 only five vessels were produced, three of them 16 feet or under, as the Wall Street crash hit the rest of the world. From then until the end of 1936, ship production never reached double figures. In 1935 Philip's built two light ships for Trinity House, which proved to be the first of many. The threat of war in 1937 brought new orders from the Admiralty and Air Ministry, and the yards were busy again building mine-laying lighters, landing craft, and scows. Once again, about 500 people were employed at Noss and Sandquay, most from Dartmouth but some came to Noss from Dittisham by boat and from Torbay by train.[4]

Just before the war, Philip's built for the Admiralty the *Research*, a non-magnetic vessel with its own laboratories for oceanographic research. Its hull was of Burma teak, and brass was used for all the metalwork. It was launched in April 1939 by Mrs. H. Spencer Jones,

109. The Floating Dock at Sandquay alongside Philip's shipyards in the 1930s. Coombe Mud is being filled in at the time of this photograph. It was completed and grassed by 1937.

110. Noss Works in the 1930s, with the *Tongue* lightship, one of many built by Philip's both before and after the Second World War. The works were originally built by Simpson Strickland in 1891, when they were the most modern of their kind, and bought by Philip's in 1918.

wife of the Astronomer Royal, and was a project which won great prestige for the yard. Sadly, on the outbreak of war, her work was stopped, and after the war she was scrapped.[5]

Philip's main drawing office where ships were designed and costed was at Sandquay, along with the pattern shop which made accurate templates of every metal plate which were then passed to the boiler makers to make the real thing. Also at Sandquay were shops for electricians, painters, joiners, plumbers and coppersmiths, sail riggers, and a foundry and smiths' shop. Between 1921 and 1961 there was also a floating dock and two patent slips. At Noss there were building berths from which larger ships could be built, fitted out, repaired and launched. There were large cranes including two travelling cranes, and a sheerlegs, as well as shops for electricians, plumbers, platers, painters, joiners, shipwrights and a saw mill.

An apprenticeship at Philip's was something for which local parents were willing to pay to secure a good training in a craft for their sons. They had to serve five years, earning only five shillings a week, but they learnt the job under one of the skilled men in their chosen trade. When they had served their apprenticeship, skilled men could earn £3 a week in the 1930s, and had a trade which could be used elsewhere, both in and out of shipbuilding. Joiners, for instance, made cabin furniture in high-quality wood, and were much valued in the building industry. Painters, plumbers, electricians and metal-workers likewise had marketable skills. The men had, and still have, an enormous pride in the ships produced by the yard, which are still to be found all over the world, a tribute to the good workmanship which went into them.[6]

Shipping in the Harbour 1919-39

The number of ships using the port in 1919-21, as shown by the shipping dues, equalled the best pre-war years. Then it fell to a half, and the following year to a third of those figures. The slump led shipowners in 1923 to lay up in the Dart 29 large merchant ships, most over 3,000 tons. It became a familiar sight between the wars to see these vessels, three abreast, moored between Noss and Ditisham, waiting for an upturn in trade for which they could again be used. By 1931-2 the number rose to 37, but was gradually reduced as things grew better after 1936. Among those often in the port were three Bibby line ships, the *Dorsetshire*, *Somersetshire* and *Lancashire*, which were used as government troopships but moored in the Dart when not required. All these increased the income of the Harbour Commission but did little to provide work for the town.

By the later 1930s the number of ships visiting the port rose to over 400, though the harbour dues were still not much over one third of the pre-1914 level. There had been a gradual change-over from steam to diesel in shipping after 1918, which hit the bunkering trade, but even in the 1930s half the visiting ships came to coal. In 1938, the last full pre-Second World War year, 100 Swedish ships called to coal, with 18 more from Norway and Denmark, which kept up the long-standing Baltic connection. There were 34 ,ships from Holland, and 13 each from Finland and Italy. Little of this trade was to survive the coming war.[7]

The Coal Lumpers

The coal lumpers were badly hit by the slump of the 1920s and· early '30s. Many were unemployed. Since forming their union they had negotiated a system of working known as the 'Pool', whereby, instead of 'rushing for the job', each gang in turn was given the work on a rota, and the money at the end of the week was shared. Shop stewards saw that there was fair play, and strict rules were enforced. By tradition, only sons of coal lumpers were admitted to the labour force, and all had to be union members. However, none of this helped if there were no ships to coal. In 1922-3, the worst year, there was a strike leading

111.   Loading coal for Torquay gasworks from colliers into railway trucks, at Kingswear in the 1930s.
This gave work to coal lumpers up to 1963 even after steamships disappeared. In the background are
large Bibby liners, used by the government in the 1930s as troop carriers, and laid up in between jobs.

to a lock-out lasting nine months. The men, who had earned high wages during the war,
had already accepted a 10 per cent cut in pay, followed by another of 35 per cent forced on
them by the collapse of world coal prices. The employers now refused to take them on
unless they took a further 15 per cent reduction and ended both the Pool and the rota. To
force the men to comply, they closed the port to all bunkering ships. After nine months,
and the intervention of the union nationally, a compromise was reached. The lumpers were
allowed to keep the Pool and rota, but had to accept the pay cut, with no overtime pay on
work up to midnight. Work continued to be scarce until the mid-1930s, as laid-up ships did
not need coaling.[8]

Town Improvements Between the Wars

Houses
Aided by government grants, the Council in the 1920s began an attack on the most
overcrowded houses which had been condemned in pre-war sanitary reports and often known

as 'little Gorbals'. The population of Dartmouth in 1929 was nearly 7,500, the highest ever, and the problems for the poor were acute. The old former merchants' houses in Higher Street were the first to go in 1925, to be replaced by the Higherside flats. It was cheaper to pull them down than restore: but older residents agree that those pulled down were as good as the few, such as the 'Cherub' (*see* plate 30), which miraculously escaped and are now among the most valuable and frequently photographed in the town.

Progress was slow because of the shortage of land near the waterfront, since the worst-housed people like the lumpers had to live in that area. Thus the decline in numbers in the bunkering trade made easier the solution ultimately adopted: to build up at Townstal, where land was bought from the Raleigh Estates. St Saviour's Court, west of the church, and Hardy's Cottages behind the Embankment both came down. By 1937 the first 80 houses were being built at Britannia Avenue, with three bedrooms, kitchen and bathroom as well

112. St Saviour's Court was pulled down in 1935 and the people rehoused on the new Townstal estate.

as a garden, all for 10 shillings a week — the same rent as had been paid for the squalid accommodation in St Saviour's Court.[9]

Schools
In 1916, during the First World War, a new school was built in Victoria Road to relieve overcrowding in the Higher Street school. This became the Boys' School, for all ages from 7 to 14, then the leaving age, the infants still going to Higher Street along with the girls. In 1919 a 'secondary' school was set up in Fairview Road, to provide what we would call 'grammar' school education for those who had passed a scholarship examination. Fairview was a Victorian house with a garden on a steeply-sloping hill, on which some laboratories were built for science. This school had a struggle from the first to reach sufficient numbers to make it economic. Matters were not helped by the great fall in the birth-rate during the 1920s and '30s, and its future was still uncertain when the Second World War broke out.

The North Embankment
Meanwhile, the Council and the Harbour Commission had completed the Embankment scheme by carrying the riverside road north across Coombe Mud to the Floating Bridge and Sandquay. In the enquiry into the scheme in 1926, it was revealed that the Ministry of Transport and Devon County Council had agreed to contribute to the scheme because of 'the large increase in the number of vehicles on the road and the increasing popularity of this part of England, together with the new form of holiday making'. Figures showed that the number of vehicles crossing the floating bridge had doubled between 1924 and 1925 to 18,000 and had reached 33,000 in 1926.[10] It can be seen that present traffic problems go back a long way, and already by the 1920s Dartmouth was on the way to becoming a major holiday resort for those with cars. The scheme was passed with no opposition, and was finally completed in 1937. Coombe Mud was filled in (*see* plate 109). It had become in the 1920s a graveyard for abandoned vessels, including an English submarine brought in for scrap and used as an adventure playground by local children. All this was covered over and by 1937 replaced by Coronation Park, a fine recreation area for the town. Boatyards which had fronted the mud, such as Lavers, were paid to move elsewhere or closed. For the first time in 700 years, no shipyards were left either side of Hardness shore.

Visitors to the Area
In July 1939 there was a royal visit of more than usual importance, when King George VI and the Queen arrived on the Royal Yacht *Victoria and Albert* with their daughters Princesses Elizabeth and Margaret, and Lord Louis Mountbatten. On their visit to the Naval College Prince Philip, then a cadet there, was first introduced to Princess Elizabeth whom he was to marry in 1947.

As more visitors took holidays in the area, hotels and boarding house were opened. Some large houses were still kept for holidays by richer people who came with their servants, especially for the Regatta. Sailing was still mainly a rich man's sport, especially with the 'J' class yachts. However, in the 1930s there was a great increase in dinghy-racing, which widened its appeal. Philip's workers were given the time off — though not, in those days, with pay — and there were entertainments for all, on land and water. In one year flying boats visited the Dart — forerunners of today's Red Arrows. There was often a circus, always a fair, with a fireworks display making a spectacular end to it all. In 1939 the centenary Regatta was held with an extended programme of events, overshadowed by the imminence of war. The Regatta flagship slipped away quietly in the middle of the events, called to active service, and war broke out on 1 September. The *Dorsetshire* was converted into a hospital ship, and she too went off to war.

The Second World War

Dartmouth was much more directly involved in the Second World War than the First. As in the first war, the same mayor, William Row, remained at his post throughout, as did the Harbour Master Bob Griffiths who had first come to the town as master of a ship being laid up in the early 1930s. He was to witness the greatest build-up of shipping that the port had ever known. In the early days, several hundred children arrived as evacuees from London, followed later by many of their mothers. When the Dunkirk evacuation took place in May 1940 the ferryboat *Mew* responded to the government's call and went off under full steam to help. However, she drew too much water for the shallow beaches there and was not used. As the Germans in that year overran all the French Channel coast and the Channel Islands, they were only 60 miles from Devon, well within range for air attack.

Early in the war the Admiralty had decided to move the cadets to a safer place, Eaton Hall in Cheshire. The college became a communications centre for the armed forces. Instead of cadets were the W.R.N.S., whose numbers built up to 700 by 1944. They lived in 'Wreneries' in large houses on both sides of the river, including Newcomen House, Broadstones, the Manor House, Woodford, Devonia, Warfleet and Derwent Lodge in Dartmouth, and the Mount, the Beacon and Inverdart in Kingswear. The *Royal Dart Hotel* in Kingswear became H.M.S. *Cicala* the Coastal Forces H.Q. and mess while Kittery Court became the C.F. Officers' Quarters. The W.R.N.S. also had launches for river work.[11]

Between July 1940 and November 1944 there were 667 air raid alerts in the area, mostly caused by small fighter planes which carried a few bombs and a machine gun, but which could do serious damage if they hit their target. They flew so fast that warnings were usually heard too late for people to take shelter. Bombs fell on isolated farms and villages of no military significance. A boy recalls leaping into the hedge from his bicycle to escape being machine-gunned by a casual German fighter plane. A single plane flying up the river to Dittisham machine-gunned a navy barge, whose naval occupants jumped into the river and were killed.

Philip's became busy as soon as war started, and during the war produced 230 steel and wooden vessels ranging from corvettes to wooden mine-sweepers and mine-layers. They also made air-sea rescue launches for the Air Ministry. In September 1942 two German M.E. 109s coming from the Dittisham direction dropped cannon shells on the boat loft at Noss and machine-gunned the yard, causing 23 deaths and many injuries. Lethal pieces of machinery and galvanised metal were flying everywhere. Among the dead were two women, and eight men from Dittisham, who used to row there every day. The same planes hit the Naval College, where a Wren was killed. As the telephone lines at Noss were destroyed by the attack, they could not send for help to Dartmouth. Fortunately a W.R.N.S. picket was nearby and came to take the injured across to the Hospital. The Manager of Philip's later received the M.B.E. for the speed with which he re-started production after this attack.

In May 1940, 77 small Belgian fishing boats arrived in the Dart, carrying fishermen and their families who had fled as their country fell to the Germans. They settled in Brixham, where they had much in common with the fishermen there, and many of the men joined up to fight. Soon there was also a contingent of Free French men in Kingswear, who joined General de Gaulle's forces, and were provided with a number of Motor Launches (MLs) by the British which became the independent 20th ML flotilla. They did convoy and rescue duties in the Channel, later using Motor Torpedo Boats. President Mitterand was among those in this fighting force, and to revive old memories of his time here in he came back in 1984 when he was taken on a river trip to see Brookhill, which was their headquarters, and Longford, the French officers' Quarters. Their knowledge of the geography of the French coast played a vital part in many daring raids, when they slipped out at night to carry agents on special missions to link up with the Resistance or to attack German-held targets.

113. The Corvette *Nigella*, K 19, Flower Class, built by Philip's in 1940. Her sister ship *Penstemon*, built in 1941, sank a German U-boat west of Madeira on 17 December 1941.

A convoy system was soon introduced for the coastal shipping. now threatened not only by mines and German U-boats but by attacks from the air and by E-boats based in Brest. A group of eight to ten merchant ships would reach the port in the late afternoon. A man who worked for the Dartmouth Coaling Company recalls how he was sent out to board them as they were entering harbour, to find out if they needed any supplies, such as provisions or chandlery, which he would obtain from local suppliers before nightfall.[12] Each ship carried its own barrage balloon, as a protection against low-flying aircraft. They stayed overnight, protected by a boom placed across the mouth of the harbour. This updated version of the old chain between the castles of medieval times consisted of a steel mesh reaching to the bottom of the river which could be raised to keep out U-boats or lowered to allow in friendly shipping. When the merchant ships left the next day to do the next leg of their journey up or down channel, they were escorted by R.N. destroyers, including some supplied by the U.S. under lease-lend and a Polish destroyer the *Krakowiak*.[13] Also used were MLs, some of which were built at Galmpton shipyards. These, though small compared with the usual R.N. vessels, were fast enough to deal with E-boats, their German equivalent, and could attack aircraft or submarines. Some of these vessels, such as the *Western Lady*, are still being used today for passengers on day trips.

Despite all this, casualties were heavy. In 1937 Philip's built the Motor Yacht *Campeador* for Vernon MacAndrew. He was a wealthy Scot who lived at Ravensbury. A keen yachtsman himself, he had encouraged dinghy sailing by providing boats for youngsters who did not own them. When war broke out, though over military age, he offered himself and his yacht to the Navy for patrol duties. He and two fellow members of the Royal Dart Yacht Club were appointed sub-lieutenants in the R.N.V.R. and on the *Campeador* joined a flotilla of ships which patrolled the seas in the Channel during the severe winter of 1939-40. In June 1940 the *Campeador* struck a mine and was blown up, MacAndrew and his two friends being among the 20 who were lost with her.[14]

Among the casualties brought into Dartmouth were the bodies of Swedish seamen whose ship had been sunk nearby. A Dutch oil tanker spent several days outside the harbour, being too large to enter it, and the skipper said he knew the Germans had him marked down for attack. He was right: he was torpedoed before he reached Torbay, with the loss of all on board, and the ship with its full cargo of oil burned for days just off Kingswear. The Dartmouth Coaling Company had one of their lighters bombed just opposite their offices, with the loss of several lumpers who were coaling a visiting ship.

The worst bomb attack on the town came on a Saturday morning, 13 February 1943, when one German aircraft swooped low over the town without any warning. Its first bomb hit Higher Street, demolishing the *Town Arms* and a shop, and killing two people. The second hit the Midland Bank, and brought down the whole corner of Duke Street and Foss Street, including the old Tudor House and the Flavel church hall. There had been a bad raid on Plymouth the night before and many rescue workers had gone over there to help, but the A.R.P, Home Guard, soldiers, W.R.N.S, and Civil Defence forces worked for two days to try to rescue those trapped. Fourteen people were killed, including women and children. One baby in his pram survived, but his mother was killed. Every property in Foss Street was damaged, and the Butterwalk so badly shaken that it was feared it would fall down.

Some parts of the town were out of bounds to ordinary people, including Gallants Bower and the castle area. Here were the coastal defence batteries, and the training ground for a group of Commandos who had their H.Q. in the old Warfleet Brewery and had exercises in the woods and coves by the castle. Opposite the brewery, in the Old Coach House, was the terminus of the Atlantic Cable which used to receive all the most secret information about progress of the war. The Home Guard also trained on Gallants Bower.[15]

In November 1943 the inhabitants of the area, from Strete to Torcross, and inland as far as Blackawton and East Allington, were told they would have to leave their homes and farms, which were to be taken over by the United States forces for 'exercises'. This was because Slapton Sands bore a striking resemblance to the part of the French coast which was to be the target for the largest amphibious operation of the war: the Normandy landings. Just before Christmas, U.S. forces began to occupy the area, while officers took over the Naval College to prepare their training programme. For the next five months, the most realistic exercises took place using live ammunition, when troops covered by bombardment from naval ships disembarked from landing craft onto beaches on which barbed wire, mines, and gun emplacements imitated German defences along the coast of 'Fortress Europe'. U.S. troops were in camps all over the evacuated area, from which everyone else was banned.

The River Dart gradually filled up with landing craft and shipping for the invasion, some like the Seebees brought from the U.S., others British built. Coronation Park, so recently finished, had been turned over to Nissen huts for building and repairs, and slipways were built from the Embankment so that vehicles could be driven on or off vessels. All the way up to Dittisham ramps and hards were built on the edge of the river where these craft could be beached for underwater repairs and cleaning.

Between 22 and 29 April 1944, the very realistic 'Exercise Tiger' took place, in which landing craft full of soldiers and all tanks and equipment set off, joined up with others from other ports along the Channel coast, and simulated the time it would take to cross to

114.   American soldiers in a tank beside Coronation Park, during training for D-Day.

115.   The U.S. Landing Ship Tank, no. 289, was brought back into Dartmouth for repair after damage during Exercise Tiger.

France. Unfortunately, in the dark, some German 'E' boats slipped in among them and sank two L.S.T.s and seriously damaged a third. Over 700 Americans were drowned, and the damaged L.S.T. was brought back to Philip's for repair. The rest of the exercise involving landing on Slapton beach went ahead, with more casualties because the supporting naval vessels fired too low and killed their own men. The damage which would be caused to morale, if this became known, led to threats of court-martial to anyone who revealed anything of this tragedy. Controversy has raged ever since as to what happened to the bodies of the almost 1,000 killed, after rumours that some of them were buried in a field in the area.[16]

The date of 'D' Day was a closely guarded secret, but on Sunday 4 June hundreds of tanks came streaming into the town, and more troops converged down all the roads towards the harbour. People were ordered to stay indoors. Up river the same was going on at Dittisham and Greenway, and in Torbay, too. A Wren officer recorded these last hectic days in her diary as she delivered the top secret Admiralty orders. Among the hundreds of American vessels was 'G' squadron, a British group of three flotillas totalling 39 Landing Craft Tanks, and a flotilla of six Landing Craft Assault vessels. Each could carry four Sherman tanks, or an equivalent cargo of lorries or similar vehicles. The ships' company on each vessel consisted of 12 men, all technicians, to deal with engines, generating sets, radio, electrics or to man the guns.[17] On Monday 5 June 485 ships set off, taking the whole day to clear the harbour. At dawn on the following day they attacked the beach code-named 'Utah', on the eastern side of the Cotentin peninsula, Normandy. That morning, 6 June, the news bulletins announced that the invasion of France had begun. The training on Slapton had been worthwhile: fewer people were killed in the actual landings than in Exercise Tiger.

Chapter Eighteen

Dartmouth Since 1945

As peace came in 1945, to the old problems of the '30s were added those caused by wartime bombing and post-war shortages of all materials for building. The Butterwalk plasterwork had been carefully removed, in pieces, after the bombing, but the rest of the building was in such a state that the Council at one time considered pulling it down. The outcry at this threat to the town's finest building prompted a search for funds to help restore it. This was instigated by Percy Russell, and a grant was finally obtained, aided by a gift from the American Pilgrim Trust. The building was then restored with great care, every piece of plaster returned to its place, and the exterior drainpipes which were so conspicuous a feature of early drawings were removed. Once again it became the pride of the town. In the 1970s the Council undertook a major restoration of the old market, while retaining its attractive 19th-century appearance and cobbled courtyard.

Over the next 15 years there was a perceptible improvement in the living conditions of the town. The Townstal estate was continued, making use of some 'Cornish' prefabricated units at first, and gradually people were moved from the most unsatisfactory houses such as those in Silver Street, which was renamed Undercliff. The houses in Higher Street destroyed by bombing were rebuilt, and the Flavel Hall replaced the demolished Independent church hall.

An industrial estate with sites for factories was provided near to the new houses at Townstal, in an attempt to provide more varied employment for the town. This had a certain success, but Dartmouth is not well served by trunk roads from the Totnes side, on which there are still many places where two large lorries cannot pass each other, and at the height of the tourist season roads can become jammed. Transport costs for raw materials coming in and finished goods going out are therefore higher than in competing areas. The building of College Way in 1974 was a welcome relief for the overburdened Victoria Road but, without a widening of the roads to Totnes and Kingsbridge, the problem remains.

Schools

At the end of the war, there were three 'elementary' schools: the old Girls' school in Higher Street, a Catholic school attached to St John's church, and the Boys' school in Victoria Road, at all of which the school leaving age was 14 though soon to be raised to 15. There was also the Grammar school in Fairview, where the numbers had always remained small. In 1953 when a new Grammar School was built at Churston, all the Dartmouth children who passed the '11+' were transferred there. They crossed the river by ferry and took the train. The Higher Street school then became a primary school for boys and girls up to 11, while all those over 11 who did not go to Churston went to the Secondary School in Victoria Road which also took over the Fairview buildings vacated by the Grammar School for extra classrooms and laboratories.

This went on until 1971, when one morning it was discovered that a laboratory in the garden of Fairview had slid down the hill in a landslide, and the main building was declared unsafe. It proved to be a blessing in disguise, as the County Council was obliged to bring forward a plan to build a new school at Milton Lane, Townstal, to replace the buildings lost at Fairview. The first instalment of this school was now built, with laboratories and practical rooms, and the school had to endure the inconvenience of being split between

116. The Council restored the early 19th-century market, with its attractive cobbled courtyard. It attracts crowds every Tuesday and Friday.

two sites. The new school was built as a Community College, so that its premises could be used by the adult population for further education. It was not until 1987 that classrooms were built there to replace the Victoria Road school, so that the whole school was again on one site. It takes children only up to the age of 16, after which they can go to Churston, Totnes, or Torquay Technical College.

Meanwhile, the old primary school in Higher Street was closed, and a new one opened in 1974 on a site beside the Community College at Milton Lane. A Catholic primary school was built next door. All the town's schools are therefore on one site, with ample playing fields around them, and near to the Townstal houses. The old primary school was then converted by the South Hams District Council into self-contained flats for old people who needed sheltered accommodation with a resident warden.

Shipbuilding at Philip & Son
Philip's returned to peacetime production, and for 15 years after the war kept busy, employing about 400 or 500 men at Noss and Sandquay. Trinity House ordered five new

light ships in 1945, a welcome return to their pre-war work, and more were to follow. One did not have to pay for apprenticeships now and, as before, good craftsmen with high standards of workmanship were trained in all the shipbuilding trades. However, as Britain's colonies became independent after the war, the firm lost most of the former Crown Agents' orders. They did get some government contracts, such as for a series of inshore minesweepers which were built at Sandquay in 1951-4.

Their long experience in building river passenger boats and ferries led to a series of orders for these, such as the new *Dartmouth Castle* launched in 1946, with more 'Castle' boats later. For the lower car ferry they built a float in 1957, and two tugs, *Hawley IV* and *V* in 1966. A new higher ferry in 1960 replaced one which had been in use since 1921 using an engine built in 1896 for the previous ferry. Orders, however, came from much farther afield: two passenger ferries for Wallasey harbour in 1950 were followed by another two for Birkenhead in 1957, these last capable of carrying 1,250 passengers. In 1960 Philip's completed two double-ended ferries for service from Portsmouth to the Isle of Wight, the *Fishbourne* and the *Camber Queen*. The last of this type was the *Shannon Heather* car ferry, built at Noss in 1968, which would carry 36 cars and up to 250 passengers across the two-mile-wide Shannon river in Eire. One hundred men worked on her, and completed her in five months.

From 1956 the yard was busy with a series of 'Sun' diesel tugs for use on the Thames, but by the early 1960s orders were down to single figures. The firm had to lay off 150 workers, and the floating dock was towed away. In 1965 Philip sold the yards to Reeves the timber merchants of Totnes, who imported much of their timber up the Dart.

Reeves decided to set up a yachting marina at Sandquay, and to transfer all the shipbuilding work from there to Noss. The former offices were transformed into the *Marina Hotel* and restaurant, while facilities for yachts were provided where once ships had been built.

At Noss, where new offices were built for the displaced Sandquay staff, Reeves continued with some of the traditional work done by Philip's, such as the *Shannon Heather* car ferry. They also experimented with a hydrofoil, but after the first one no further orders came. The work force was by then down to 120. They built several large steel pontoons, and a passenger boat for the Manchester Ship Canal. Despite all their efforts, in 1969 Reeves announced that they had made continuous losses, and put the firm, including the higher ferry, up for sale. It was bought by Philip Pensabene, owner of a Bridgwater firm which made pumps and heating systems. He announced that he hoped to build ships at Noss if it was economically viable.

The first new job for the yard was the construction of *British Steel*, a 50-foot ketch in which Chay Blyth was soon to sail round the world from east to west, against all the prevailing winds. This, it was hoped, would be the first of many steel yachts. She was launched in August 1970. By the time Blyth had completed his epic voyage of 292 days, over 80 men, including many those who had built *British Steel*, had been laid off. No more steel orders had come in, and it was decided to concentrate on fibreglass yachts, coupled with an expansion of the ship repair service. For this a patent slipway capable of taking longer ships was built.

Two types of fibreglass yacht were produced, the 27-foot 'Philippa', and the 36-foot 'Atlantic Clipper', of which nearly 50 were built over four years. A marina was set up at Noss, where large yachts can be berthed, with all facilities for service and repairs. Since then, with the British merchant fleet reduced to a fraction of its pre-war size, the fact had to be faced that shipbuilding was no longer an economic proposition. The yard has therefore concentrated on ship repairs and refits, which provide few jobs compared with the pre-war years. It is sad to reflect that, since the mid-1970s, for the first time in 700 years, no more ships have been built beside the Dart.[1]

117. Repair of *Stewart Venture* at Noss.

118. Kingswear and the marina, giving
access by pontoon to yachts.

Shipping and the Bunkering Trade

The coal lumpers, too, found their jobs disappearing along with the steamships, as the merchant fleets of the world turned to oil. For a few years there were jobs unloading ships carrying gas coal for the Torquay gas works, but only 28 men were employed instead of up to 300 before the war. In 1962 that contract ended, and the coal ships came no more. The huge cranes which had for so long been a feature of the Kingswear waterfront were removed, leaving unused the port's capacity to take a 2,000-ton ship alongside the quay and railway network.[2] The loss of the coal trade was the final blow for the railway, which was sold in 1972 to the Dart Valley Railway Company, which now only operates a summer service for tourists.

Shipping using the Dart has shown a similar decline. In 1967 there were 58 visiting ships — compared with over 400 in the later 1930s. By 1987, the number had fallen to 13. The most regular ships calling at the Dart since the 1960s have been the Danish-owned 'Bres' liners whose bright red ships brought timber from the Baltic up to Reeves' timberyard at Totnes. They too seem to be vanishing, with only one so far in 1989.[3]

Instead there are three marinas, at Kingswear, Noss and Sandquay, with about two

119. Crabbers at Kingswear have become the main commercial users of the port in the past 20 years. New technology enables them to fish far out in the Channel on beds hitherto unexploited. Live crabs are sold to the French, and crabmeat produced for sale in England.

thousand small yachts. There are also the pleasure boats who are kept busy with visitors all the summer. However, none of these provide jobs in the winter apart from some repair work.

Fishing
One success has been crabbing: there are now 33 crab boats registered in the port — the largest fleet in the country. This has become not only a local but an export trade, with ships arriving to carry live crabs back in special tanks to sell in France and Spain. Lorries arrive daily to take the bulk of the catch to factories where they are transformed into crabmeat, and deep frozen.

Fishing generally has declined. Mackerel which used to shoal in thousands in and outside the river only 20 years ago have been so overfished by large ships in the Channel that they are now almost a rare sight. Visitor who want to fish are taken out in boats to the Skerries and there are well supported fishing festivals on certain week-ends during the year. None of this is commercially viable except as part of the holiday industry.

Most Recent Changes 1974 – 2007
In 1974 after nearly 700 years Dartmouth ceased to be an independent borough and became part of the South Hams District Council (SHDC) whose powers extended from the Dart to Kingsbridge with its headquarters in Totnes. While the town still has its Mayor and Councillors, it no longer has its petty sessions court, its planning powers or, apart from the Butterwalk and Market, control of most of its corporate property, all now transferred to SHDC. The river since 1975 is managed from Totnes to the mouth of the Dart by one body, the Dart Harbour and Navigation Authority (DHNA) while SHDC runs the Lower Ferry.

A major improvement of the Embankment was carried out after 1985 when the century old crumbling foundations were replaced by a paved walkway six metres wider, and raised to prevent flooding in the town centre. The riverside walk provides a unique advantage to Dartmouth, greatly enjoyed by locals and visitors. The town was completely re-sewered during the same period. In 2002 South West Water (SWW) opened a new sewage works in Old Mill Creek, to serve not

The Flavel (2005): this fine piece of modern architecture provides a large new library, a cinema and place for live performances of all sorts.

only Dartmouth and Kingswear but also new houses in Townstal. In addition a major SWW project for the river called *Clean Sweep* has replaced all the sewers which once flowed straight into the Dart. By the Boatfloat, the old covered ways became ramps to the new pontoons, now extended for use by the ferries and pleasure boats. More pontoons have helped to meet the ever increasing demand for moorings.

The greatest change in the appearance of Dartmouth in the past twenty years has been the building of large numbers of houses in Townstal, where now more people live than down by the river. Many former Council tenants took advantage of the right to buy their houses at low prices, after this became legal in 1980. Over the years these have been resold at much higher prices, thus reducing the stock of low-cost accommodation. Housing Associations such as Tor Homes took over the responsibility of building new homes both to rent and for sale. Their choice of tenants is made from people from the whole SHDC area on the basis of need: having a job in the town is not a plus point. Dartmouth Town Council has no say in who gets the houses. They complain that young locals whose wages are the lowest in the district are priced out of their home town. Whereas before only 13% were on state benefits, recently this has risen to nearly 50%, since most are unemployed, drawing sickness or other benefits. As many newcomers are single rather than families there has not been an increase in the total population. The Community College is struggling to maintain its numbers when parents can choose to send their children to other schools in Totnes, Kingsbridge or Torbay. To foster healthy activities for the young a new Sports and Leisure Centre was built in 2004, and a Community Centre followed in 2005, providing facilities for all ages. Still lacking is an indoor swimming pool at the Sports Centre, a park which could serve as a social centre for mothers and babies, a medical and dental centre, but planned for 2008 are two new supermarkets.

In the lower part of Dartmouth a major improvement has been the opening of the Flavel Centre in 2005. This fine piece of modern architecture provides a large new library, cinema and place for live performances of all sorts. It may however be used more by those in lower Dartmouth than Townstal, while the old Guildhall loses income from the activities it once provided.

In the same year Britannia Royal Naval College, always an important feature of the life of the town and providing jobs, celebrated the centenary of its shore-based establishment. It has set up its own museum and provides tours of the building to visitors brought up to the college by coach.

With no new land available for building in lower Dartmouth some existing sites have been redeveloped. Upstream from the Higher Ferry and adjoining the Marina hotel new riverside houses have been built where once Philip's shipyard designed and built boats. At Warfleet the Pottery finally closed in July 2002, ending the last productive jobs on a site where once there had been a mill and brewery. The mill building now forms holiday apartments, with a row of newly built terraced houses in the yard outside. Many larger houses in the town have been split up into flats, which provide good jobs for carpenters and building workers. However all these houses are aimed at people buying holiday homes, which in 2005 formed nearly 20% of the old town but a higher proportion of those down by the river. They do not provide children for the local schools, or support for local societies, only more cars.

In Dartmouth today most shops are aimed at tourists, selling gifts or casual clothes, with few individual food shops. Hotels, bed and breakfasts, pubs and restaurants depend on visitors and provide many of the jobs available even though they are highly seasonal. While no ships are built by the Dart, more and more sailors want moorings for their boats: but each boat owner requires a car space from which to unload. DHNA welcomes an increasing number of cruise liners visiting the port, where the natural beauty of its estuary still remains its greatest asset. The saying by an old Dartmothian still holds true:

**The river is the mother of Dartmouth: when the river is full,
our bellies is full; when the river is empty, our bellies is empty.**

Notes

Key to Abbreviations used in Notes

C.C.C.	Calendar of Compositions, Commonwealth
C.S.P.Col.	Calendar of State Papers, America and West Indies
C.S.P.D.	Calendar of State Papers Domestic
D.M. Chron.	*Dartmouth Chronicle*
D.A.S.	Devon Archaeological Society
D.C.R.S.	Devon and Cornwall Record Society
D.H.C.	Dart Harbour Commission
D.H.N.A.	Dart Harbour Navigation Authority
D.R.S.	Devon Record Office
D.C.O., W.D.	Duchy of Cornwall Office, Water of Dart
E.F.P.	*Exeter Flying Post*
Opp.	Oppenheim, *Maritime History of Devon*
S.H.D.C.	South Hams District Council
T.D.A.	Transactions of the Devonshire Association
W.	Watkin, *Dartmouth Pre-Reformation*
W.C.S.L.	West Country Studies Library

Chapter One: 1. Alexander, 'The Anglo Saxon Conquest of Devon', *T.D.A.* (1919-24). 2. Grinsell, *Barrows of South and East Devon*, D.A.S. Proceedings (1983). 3. Pearce, *The Kingdom of Dumnonia*. 4. Rose-Troup, 'The New Edgar Charter and the South Hams', *T.D.A.* (1920). 5. Reichel, 'Origin and Upgrowth of the English Parish', *T.D.A.* (1920). 6. Royal Albert Museum, Exeter. 7. Sites and Monuments Register, Exeter. 8. Taylor, *Village and Farmstead*. 9. Todd, *The South West to A.D. 1000*. 10. Watkin & Rogers, excavation report (D.A.S.). 11. Wood, *Domesday — A Search for the Roots of England*.

Chapter Two: 1. Thorn (Ed.), *Domesday Book: Devon*, two volumes (Phillimore, 1985). 2. W., p. 3 onwards. 3. Opp. p. 5. 4. W., p. 353. 5. Reichel, 'The Hundred of Coleridge', *T.D.A.* (1911). 6. Ibid. 7. Stoke Fleming Parish History, p. 5. 8. W., p. 2. 9. W., p. 4. 10. Stoke Gabriel Parish History. 11. *Domesday Book: Devon*, Ed. Thorn, Vol II, 1-71. 12. Reichel, 'The Hundred of Haytor', *T.D.A.* (1908). 13. Reichel, 'The Hundred of Coleridge', *T.D.A.* (1911). 14. Knowles and Hadcock, *Medieval Religious Houses in England and Wales*. 15. W., p. 278. 16. Seymour, *Torre Abbey*, pp. 204-5. 17. Ibid., pp. 213-16. 18. Ibid., pp. 217-18. 19. Ibid., pp. 219-29.

Chapter Three: 1. W., pp. 5-7. 2. W., p. 6. 3. W., p. 16. 4. W., p. 44. 5. W., pp. 6-8. 6. W., p. 8. 7. W., p. 11. 8. W., p. 9. 9. W., p. 280. 10. W., p.280. 11. W., p. 14. 12. D.R.O., DD 67897. 13. W., p. 414. 14. W., p. 23. 15. W., p. 28. 16. D.R.O., DD 67989. 17. W., p. 32. 18. W., p. 355. 19. W., p. 35. 20. W., p. 33. 21. W., p. 38. 22. W., pp. 38-41. 23. W., pp. 42-3. 24. Stanes, 'Sir Guy de Bryan', *T.D.A.* (1960). 25. D.R.O., DD 61470. 26. W., p. 155. 27. W., p. 45. 28. W., p. 7. 29. W., p. 14. 30. W., p. 2. 31. W., p. 280. 32. W., pp. 281-2. 33. W., p. 282. 34. W., pp. 282-5. 35. W., p. 53. 36. W., pp. 55-6. 37. W., pp. 285-6. 38. W., p. 289. 39. W., p. 98. 40. W., pp. 328-31. 41. W., pp. 291, 144. 42. W., pp. 162-3. 43. W., pp. 299-300. 44. C.S.P.D., 1545, 496, 54. 45. Watkin, 'The Lost Chapel of St Clare', *T.D.A.* (1929).

Chapter Four: 1. W., p. 59. 2. W., p. 359. 3. W., p. 361. 4. Gardiner, Intro., xii-xiv. 5. W., p. 44. 6. D.R.O., DD 68217, 68219. 7. W., p. 365. 8. W., pp. 366-8. 9. Gardiner, pp. 177-8. 10. W., pp. 368-9. 11. Opp., p.17. 12. Russell, p. 40. 13. W., p. 370. 14. W., p. 88. 15. Gardiner, p. 191. 16. W., pp. 71-2, 374. 17. Gardiner, p. 196. 18. Pistono, pp. 151-2. 19. W., pp. 375-6. 20. W., pp. 376-8. 21. Russell, pp. 42-5. 22. D.R.O., S.M., p. 471. 23. Russell, p. 47. 24. Gardiner, pp. 201-2. 25. W., pp. 381-2. 26. W., pp. 414-6, 116. 27. W., p. 310. 28. W., pp. 116, 123. 29. W., p. 398. 30. Clifford, 'Robert Wenyngton', *T.D.A.* (1916). 31. W., pp. 185, 273. 32. Clifford, *T.D.A.* (1916). 33. Ibid. 34. Alexander, 'Parliamentary Representation in Devon, 1439-1509', *T.D.A.* (1937). 35. W., pp. 400-1. 36. W., p. 402.

Chapter Five: 1. W., p. 7. 2. W., p. 44. 3. D.M. Chron., 1/1/1859. 4. W., p. 54. 5. W., p. 20. 6. W., p. 19. 7. W., p. 44. 8. W., p. 201. 9. Hayne family papers. 10. W., p. 124. 11. W., p. 206. 12. Summerson, *Crown Pleas of the Devon Eyre, 1238* (D.C.R.S.). 13. W., p. 74. 14. Devon Fleet of Fines, no. 860. 15. Devon Lay Subsidy, ed. M. Cash. 16. W., pp. 247-53. 17. W., pp. 193-246. 18. W., p. 222. 19. W., p. 213. 20. W., p. 49. 21. W., p. 99. 22. W., p. 294n.

Chapter Six: 1. W., pp. 401-2. 2. W., pp. 405-6. 3. W., p. 409. 4. D.R.O., DD 61199A. 5. W., p. 409. 6. D.R.O., DD 61249A. 7. C.S.P.D., 25/12/1583, 139 (57). 8. Dartmouth Castle Guide, pp. 16-18. 9. C.P.S.D., 30/6/1522, 2355. 10. C.P.S.D., 1539 (I) 655. 11. D.R.O., DD 61375, 61391A. 12. D.R.O., DD 61397. 13. D.R.O., DD

61355. **14.** D.R.O., DD 61263B. **15.** W., p.412. **16.** D.R.O., DD 61429. **17.** D.R.O., DD 61376. **18.** D.R.O., DD 61413. **19.** D.R.O., DD 61412A, 61554, 61461 (1588). **20.** C.P.S.D., 1540, 613 (34). **21.** D.R.O., DD 61499A. **22.** C.P.S.D., 1545, 95, 54 and Youings, *Devon Monastic Lands*. **23.** D.R.O., DD 61445. **24.** W., p. 328. **25.** D.R.O., DD 61391, 61397. **26.** Back, p. 208. **27.** D.R.O., DD 61352. **28.** Cresswell, *T.D.A.* (1911). **29.** D.R.O., DD 61501. **30.** D.R.O., DD 61352. **31.** D.R.O., DD 61360. **32.** D.R.O., DD 61370. **33.** D.R.O., DD 67951. **34.** D.R.O., DD 61499A. **35.** D.R.O., DD 61391, 61397, 61409. **36.** C.S.P.D., 1554, 58, 66, 75. **37.** D.R.O., DD 61447, 61455. **38.** D.R.O., DD 61461 (1586), DD 61543-4, 61559D, E. **39.** D.R.O., DD 61461 (1586). **40.** D.R.O., DD 61461 (1593).

Chapter Seven: 1. Compton Castle Guide, Gilbert family tree. **2.** Parish Register, Stoke Gabriel. **3.** Devon Lay Subsidy, 1543, ed. Stoate. **4.** D.R.O., DD 61409. **5.** Champernowne, *The Champernownes*. **6.** C.S.P.D., 12/1/1569. **7.** Champernowne, *The Champernownes*. **8.** C.S.P.D., 1569, Vol. II, p. 72. **9.** C.S.P.D., 1570, Vol. II, p. 244. **10.** Champernowne. **11.** Prince, *Worthies of Devon*. **12.** C.S.P.D., 11/7/1578, p. 22 (66). **13.** C.S.P.D., 23/9/1578, p. 600 (70). **14.** Hakluyt, *Voyages*, pp. 236-82. **15.** Barlowe, *The First Voyage to Roanoke, 1584* (Old South Leaflets, no. 92). **16.** Letter from Ralph Lane, 3/9/1585, quoted in above. **17.** Hakluyt, *Fourth Voyage to Virginia*. **18.** C.S.P.D., 10/10/1585, p. 273 (13). **19.** Roberts, 'Sir John Gilbert', *T.D.A.* (1959), p. 99. **20.** Markham, *John Davis*. **21.** Hakluyt, *Second and Third Voyages of John Davis*. **22.** C.S.P.D., 3/3/1594, p. 452. **23.** C.S.P.D., 11/2/1593, pp. 313-4, 332-3.

Chapter Eight: 1. C.S.P.D., 27/8/1585, p. 262. **2.** C.S.P.D., 10/12/1585, p. 291. **3.** C.S.P.D., Sept./1587, p. 427. **4.** C.S.P.D., 21/12/1587. **5.** Devon Muster Rolls, 1588, Ed. Stoate. **6.** C.S.P.D., 5/7/1588, p. 499. **7.** Windeatt, *T.D.A.*, pp. 312-321 (original lost). **8.** D.R.O., DD 67841. **9.** C.S.P.D., Sept. 1588, p. 548. **10.** C.S.P.D., Aug. 1588, p. 539. **11.** C.S.P.D., Sept. 1588, p. 549. **12.** Russell, 'Firebeacons in Devon', *T.D.A.* (1955), p. 269. **13.** Chart, R. Adams, no. 2. **14.** Martin and Parker, *The Spanish Armada*, p. 58. **15.** Ibid., pp. 61-5. 44-5. **16.** Hakluyt, *Spanish Armada*, p. 375. **17.** Martin & Parker, *The Spanish Armada*, pp. 170, 286. **18.** C.S.P.D., 8/8/1599, p. 537. **19.** C.S.P.D., 27/7/1588, p.513; C.S.P.D., 29/8/1588, pp. 538, 68. **20.** C.S.P.D., 29/8/1588, p. 538, 57. **21.** C.S.P.D., 14/10/1588, p. 551. **22.** C.S.P.D., 8/9/1588, pp. 542, 545. **23.** C.S.P.D., 5/11/1588, p. 557. **24.** D.R.O., DD 67841, 67905. **25.** C.S.P.D., 13/12/1591, p. 143. **26.** C.S.P.D., 14/2/1595, pp. 10; 3/5/1596, pp. 213-4. **27.** Opp., p. 50. **28.** C.S.P.D., 3/11/1596. **29.** C.S.P.D., 27/7/1599, p. 263. **30.** C.S.P.D., 8/8/1599, p. 279 (17). **31.** C.S.P.D., 10/4/1599, p. 178. **32.** Opp., p. 51. **33.** C.S.P.D., 16, 19, & 21/9/1582. **34.** Opp., p. 50, n. 3. **35.** D.C.O., W.B.F.'s Accounts, 1592-1600. **36.** D.R.O., DD 61461. **37.** D.R.O., DD 61508-61529. **38.** D.R.O., DD 61953. **39.** D.R.O., DD 63248, 63193, 62687. **40.** D.R.O., DD 62322, 62417. **41.** D.R.O., Luttrell Papers, 12138. **42.** D.R.O., DD 63558. **43.** D.R.O., S.M. 2005, 1799. **44.** D.R.O., DD 62404, 62604, 62560.

Chapter Nine: 1. Compton Castle Guide, p. 33. **2.** Ibid., p. 35. **3.** Rosier, *True Relation of the Voyage of George Waymouth* (1905). **4.** Compton Castle Guide, p. 34-5. **5.** Horden, *The New World*, pp. 263-4. **6.** Compton Castle Guide, p. 35. **7.** King, *The Mayflower Miracle*, pp. 50-3. **8.** *The Champernowne Family*, p. 246. **9.** Ibid., pp. 257-8. **10.** Russell and Yorke, 'Kingswear and its Neighbourhood', *T.D.A.* (1953), pp. 68-9. **11.** D.R.O., DD 61927. **12.** Opp., pp. 55-7. **13.** D.R.O., DD 61927. **14.** D.R.O., DD 61981. **15.** D.R.O., DD 61978. **16.** D.R.O., DD 62067. **17.** D.R.O., DD 61621. **18.** D.R.O., DD 62257. **19.** D.R.O., DD 62203. **20.** D.R.O., DD 63038b. **21.** C.S.P.D., 1625-9, Addenda, p. 217. 261. **22.** D.R.O., DD 62275, 62038b. **23.** D.R.O., DD 62205, 62447, 62468. **24.** Bourhis, Table XXXIX. **25.** Windeatt, 'A Merchant Company in Totnes', *T.D.A.* (1908). **26.** Andriette, *Devon and Exeter in the Civil War*, p. 180. **27.** D.R.O., DD 62075. **28.** St Saviour's Parish Register. **29.** D.R.O., DD 62718. **30.** I. Smart's recent researches suggest this was on the site of the coastguard's station in Southtown. **31.** D.R.O., DD 62701. **32.** D.R.O., 1392 M/L 1643-5. PO **33.** D.R.O., 1392 M/L 1643/1. **34.** D.R.O., 1392 M/L 1645/19. **35.** Quoted by Windeatt, 'Dartmouth Mayors and Moralities', *T.D.A.* (1912), pp. 663-7. **36.** D.R.O., DD 68465. **37.** C.C.C., pp. 1131-2. **38.** Opp., p. 67. **39.** Quoted from H. of C. Journal in Seale papers. **40.** Windeatt, 'John Flavel', *T.D.A.* (1911). **41.** Seale papers.

Chapter Ten: 1. Seale papers, Torquay library. **2.** Stoke Fleming Parish History. **3.** C.C.C., 1646. **4.** Ashprington Church Guide and B. Cresswell. **5.** Youings, *Devon Monastic Lands* (D.C.R.S.). **6.** Cresswell, Ashprington. **7.** D.R.O., 2927A, Ashprington PO1. **8.** Cresswell, Ashprington. **9.** Sam Cox, *Memories*. **10.** Cresswell, Cornworthy. **11.** Cresswell, Stoke Gabriel. **12.** Parish registers. **13.** Russell and Yorke, 'Kingswear and its Neighbourhood', *T.D.A.* (1953), p. 66. **14.** D.R.O., DD 61461. **15.** D.C.O., waterbailiff's A/Cs, 1592-1600. **16.** D.R.O., DD 67841-4. **17.** Russell and Yorke, *T.D.A.* (1953), and Teage papers; Vivian, *Visitations of the County of Devon*. **18.** Dittisham Church Guide. **19.** D.R.O., DD 61376. **20.** D.R.O., DD 61569a. **21.** D.R.O., 1392 M/L 1643/1. **22.** Rev. Ault's notes, Dittisham church. **23.** Hutchings, *A Village Boy's Story*.

Chapter Eleven: 1. D.R.O., S.M. 3086. **2.** D.R.O., DD 63122. **3.** Windeatt, *T.D.A.* (1911). **4.** D.C.S.R. *Guide to Non-Conformist Registers, 1538-1837*. **5.** Copy of deed of Baptist church, courtesy of Paster Paul. **6.** Grant and Gwyn, 'The Huguenots of Devon', *T.D.A.* (1979). **7.** Allen, *The Newcomen Memorial Engine*. **8.** Rolt, *Life of Thomas Newcomen*. **9.** I. Smart believes Lidstone mistook Newcomen's house for the more elaborate house of Staplehill next door. **10.** D.R.O., DD 62558. **11.** Russell and Yorke, 'Kingswear and its Neighbourhood', *T.D.A.* (1953). **12.** D.R.O., DD 63520. **13.** D.R.O., S.M. 2003. **14.** C.S.P.D., 1679. **15.** C.S.P.D., 1682. **16.** C.S.P.D., 1685. **17.** D.R.O., DD

63410, 63616. **18.** C.S.P.D., 1685. **19.** Windeatt, 'The Dismissal of Sir Edward Seymour', *T.D.A.* (1870). **20.** Letter in possession of Arthur H. Holdsworth, quoted by him 1857. **21.** C.S P.D., 11/6/1690, 28/7/1691. **22.** Prince, *Worthies of Devon.* **23.** Alexander, 'Dartmouth as a Parliamentary Borough', *T.D.A.* (1911). **24.** Hayne family papers.

Chapter Twelve: 1. D.R.O., DD 63999, 65161. **2.** D.M. Chron., June 1869. **3.** Naimer and Brooke, *History of Parliament 1754-90.* **4.** D.R.O., DD 63895. **5.** D.R.O., DD 63778 & Seale papers. **6.** D.R.O., DD 63295. **7.** D.R.O., DD 64405-64436. **8.** D.R.O., DD 64470-2, 64915, 64237 & Seale papers. **9.** D.R.O., DD 65061. **10.** D.C.O., W/D correspondence. **11.** D.R.O., DD 65503. **12.** D.R.O., DD 65657. **13.** Alexander, 'Dartmouth as a Parliamentary Borough', *T.D.A.* (1911). **14.** Seale papers. **15.** D.R.O., S.M. 2005 5/8/1793.

Chapter Thirteen: 1. C.S.P.D., America and West Indies, 1668, no. 1666. **2.** D.C.O., W/D correspondence, 1673. **3.** Thomas, *Newfoundland Journal, 1794.* **4.** C.S.P.D., America and West Indies, 1718, 1765, p. 647. **5.** Stoate, *Devon Hearth Tax, 1674.* **6.** From Dalley's tables, Musgrave collection, B.M.; additional Mss. 11255, courtesy H. E. S. Fisher. **7.** M. de Martins, *Essay on Privateering* (1801). **8.** Figures from D. Starkey, University of Exeter. **9.** Hayne family papers. **10.** Seale family papers. **11.** P.R.O. H.C.A., 26/4. **12.** D.R.O., 1032 F/Z 7, and *Gentleman's Magazine,* June 1745. **13.** P.R.O. H.C.A., 32, 118 (2). **14.** P.R.O. H.C.A., 32, figures from D. Starkey. **15.** E.F.P., Apl. 1781. **16.** Seale papers, copies in Torquay library. **17.** D.R.O., DD 63651. **18.** D.R.O., DD 648084. **19.** Leases courtesy of F. Bennett. **20.** D.R.O., DD 63105. **21.** D.R.O., DD 64066. **22.** E.F.P., various dates. **23.** D.R.O., DD 65423. **24.** D.R.O., DD 65194. **25.** D.R.O., S.M. 2005, 1789. **26.** D.R.O., S.M. 2005, 1799. **27.** D.R.O., DD 65180. **28.** D.R.O., DD 65979.

Chapter Fourteen: 1. Newman papers. **2.** Vancouver, *Agriculture of Devon* (1808). **3.** E.F.P., 1803-10. **4.** Charity Commission Report, 1821. **5.** Quoted by E. H. Back. **6.** D.R.O., S.M. 2005, 1827-9. **7.** E.F.P., 29/10/1829, 22/7/1830, *Times* (courtsey I. Smart), 22/6/1860, *Western Times,* 6/3/1830. **8.** Seale papers. **9.** K. S. Perkins, *Rendell's News,* Aug. 1981. **10.** I. Smart. **11.** *Dartmouth Papers II,* ed. T. Jayne. **12.** D.R.O., Corporation Minute Book, 1833. **13.** D.R.O., Corporation Minute Book, 1836-7. **14.** D.R.O., Corporation Minute Book, 1836-7 & DD 66886. **15.** D.R.O., Shipping registers, Port of Dartmouth. **16.** D.R.O., DD 66272/3. **17.** D.R.O., council accounts, 1830-40. **18.** *Dartmouth Papers II,* ed. T. Jayne. **19.** E.F.P., 11/1868. **20.** D.M. Chron., 1/5/1868. **21.** D.M. Chron., Aug. 1856. **22.** D.R.O., council minutes. **23.** *White's Directory, 1850.* **24.** D.M. Chron. **25.** Teage family papers. **26.** E.F.P., 1852, and council minutes. **27.** D.M. Chron, 1856.

Chapter Fifteen: 1. D.C.O., W/D papers. **2.** Seale papers, Duchy dues, copy in Torquay library. **3.** I. Smart in C. R. Potts, *Newton Abbot to Kingswear Railway.* **4.** D.M. Chron., 1864. **5.** D.M. Chron., 1871, weekly. **6.** D.H.C. minutes, 1863 onwards, and D.M. Chron., 1867-70. **7.** Clammer and Kittridge, *Paddle Steamers on the Dart* and D.M. Chron. **8.** D.M. Chron., 3/3/1876, 1897, 1901. **9.** I. Smart, as above. **10.** Courtesy I. Smart, P.R.O., MH12/60. **11.** D.M. Chron. & council minutes, 1877. **12.** D.M. Chron., Mar. 1871. **13.** Dr. Giles Keane, D.M. hospitals. **14.** D.M. Chron., 1872, 1874, 1880, and schools files D.R.O., 2380C/151. **15.** *Kelly's Directory.* **16.** Pastor Paul. **17.** D.M. Chron., 6/8/80; L. W. Lawson-Edwards, Devon Non-Conformist Registers. **18.** D.M. Chron., 21/8/1874, Mrs. Plowright. **19.** D.H.C. minutes. **20.** D.M. Chron., 1881-5. **21.** D.M. Chron., 1872-7. **22.** *Western Daily Mercury,* 1878. **23.** D.M. Chron., 1883, Charity Commission Reports, 1890 & 1909.

Chapter Sixteen: 1. Clarke, *The Calculating Boy.* **2.** D.M. Chron., 5/6/1874 & 21/1/1876. **3.** D.M. Chron., 1860s and 1870s. **4.** Info. from D. Collinson and D.M. Chron., 1870s. **5.** D.M. Chron, 1860s and 1870s. **6.** Philip's Centenary Booklet, 1858-1958. List of ships launched lent by P. Pensabene. **7.** D.M. Chron., 8/10/1880. **8.** D.M. Chron., 1882, D.H.C. improvement scheme, 1882. **9.** D.M. Chron., 28/4/1893. **10.** Simpson Strickland catalogue No. 7. **11.** D.M. Chron., 1914. **12.** Potts, *Newton Abbot to Kingswear Railway.* **13.** Papers lent by Dr. T. N. P. Wilton. **14.** T. Blamey's and M. Pillar's memories. **15.** D.M. Chron., 1914. **16.** S. Bell's and Mrs. Lidstone's memories. **17.** Mrs. M. Williams' memories.

Chapter Seventeen: 1. D.M. Chron., 1914-18. **2.** Info. from H. Hutchins. **3.** Miss Harrison's memories. **4.** Philip, list of ships built. **5.** Roy Skinner's memories. **6.** R. Jones' memories. **7.** D.H.C. records. Lloyd's Shipping Registers from E. Bovey. **8.** M. Pillar's memories. D.M. Chron., 1923. **9.** I. Scawn, H. White, memories. **10.** D.M. Chron., 1/19/1926. **11.** Macleod, *A Wren's Diary.* **12.** P. Clare, memories. **13.** D. Griffiths, *Century on the River Dart II.* **14.** Russell, *Dartmouth.* **15.** J. White's memories. **16.** Small, *The Forgotten Dead.* **17.** M. Gilbert.

Chapter Eighteen: 1. Info. from scrap-book cuttings, F. and D. Hannaford. Philip's list of ships. **2.** D.M. Chron., 1962. **3.** D.H.C. records. **4.** S.H.D.C. figures.

Bibliography

Primary Sources (Manuscript) (Abbreviations in notes in brackets)

A. In Devon Record Office:

Dartmouth Borough Archives (D.R.O.): Ref. DD 60,000-68,000 and calendar; Stuart Moore's Calendar; Borough Constitution Books, SM 2003-2009; Borough Minute Books, R 9/1 onward; Local Board of Health and Urban Sanitary Board minutes, R 9/8 onward; Port Health Authority Minutes, R 9/95.

Other papers: Parish Registers; Tithe maps and apportionments; Documents re. tithes & advowson, R 9/1/ Z, 1-28; Land Tax returns, 1747-1831; Poor Law papers, all parishes; Port of Dartmouth Shipping Registers, 1824 onward; Piracy Petitions, Q/S 128 41-3 & 42, 33; St Petrox churchwardens' accounts, 2537/A PW 2, 3, 9; Chanter: Replies to Diocesan Queries, B 225, 228; Miles: Parochial History Collection, 1774-7; Seymour papers, 1392 M/L/1643-6; Hayne family papers, 1032 F/Z; Luttrell papers, 12188.

B. West Country Studies Library (W.C.S.L.): Census returns.

C. Public Record Office (P.R.O.): MPH 233 S BP/660, MPH 1210 L BP 690 (Map Dept.); HCA 26/22, 23, 24, 25, Letters of Marque; HCA 32, prize cases; E 190/937/10-E 190/951/8, 17th-century Port Books; E 190/976/9-E 190/1002/7, 18th-century Port Books; C 12/5/7, Chancery Masters exhibits; SP 12/181, 185, 212, 213, 215, 216, Armada.

D. Duchy of Cornwall Archives: The Water of Dart (D.C.O., W.D.).

E. Dart Harbour Navigation Authority (D.H.N.A.): Minute books, Dart Harbour Commission (D.H.C.), 1863 onward; Day Book, 1974-89; Records of ships laid up, 1920-40.

F. Seale family papers: lent by Sir John Seale.

G. Newman family papers: lent by Lady Ann Newman.

H. Teage family papers: lent by Rev. A. Teage.

I. Hayne family papers: 4 vols., held by author.

J. Dittisham Manor Court Book, and other records: in church.

K. Records of ships built by Philip & Son.

L. Lloyd's Shipping Registers, 1936-74.

Printed Sources (including books or articles being wholly or largely transcripts of documents)
Back, E. H., manuscript transcript of documents, *c.*1900-10, St Saviours, held by Mrs. Parr Ferris.
Barlowe, Arthur, *The First Voyage to Roanoke, 1584* (Old South Leaflet n. 92).
Burke's Peerage and Baronetage.
Burke's Landed Gentry.
Calendar of State Papers: Domestic, 16th and 17th centuries (C.S.P.D.).
Calendar of Compositions: Commonwealth (C.C.C.).
Calendar of State Papers: America and West Indies, 1660-1765 (C.S.P.Col.).
Cash, M., *Devon Inventories*, 16th and 17th centuries (D.C.R.S.).
Charity Commission Reports, Dartmouth and other parishes, 1821, 1890, 1909 (T. Besley, Exeter, 1826).
Dartmouth Chronicle (D.M. Chron.) from 1854 (copies with Torquay library, I. Smart, and *South Hams Gazette*).
Dartmouth Papers, Ed. Tom Jaine:
    I. Mivart, 'Report on Public Health and Housing', 1914.
    II. Holdsworth, Arthur Howe, 'The Advantages of Dartmouth's harbour as a station for foreign mail packets', 1841.
    III. 'Report of the Royal Commission on Municipal Corporations on Dartmouth', 1835.
    IV. Holborrow, W, 'Building Development in Dartmouth, 1580-1660'.

Devon Feet of Fines, 1272-1369 (D.C.R.S.).

Directories: Pigot, Kelly, White, 19th century.

Domesday Book: Devon, Ed. C. and F. Thorn (Phillimore, 1985).

Early Tours of Devon and Cornwall, ed. Chope, R. P. (Exeter, 1918) for J. Leland, 1553-4; Daniel Defoe, 1724; Dr. R. Pococke, 1750; W. Maton, 1794-5.

Exeter Flying Post (E.F.P.), Truman, microfilm, West Country Studies Library (W.C.S.L.), Exeter.

Gardiner, G., *West Country Shipping, 1388-1493* (D.C.R.S.).

Gentleman's Magazine, 1740 onwards (Exeter City Reference Library).

Hakluyt, R., *Voyages and Documents* (O.U.P., 1958).

Howard, A. J., *Devon Protestation Returns, 1641* (privately printed, 1973).

Hutchings, Ewart, *A Village [Dittisham] Boy's Story* (unpublished, *c*.1985).

Knowles, D. and Hadcock, R. N., *Medieval Religious Houses in England and Wales* (Cambridge, 1940).

Lysons, S. and D., *Magna Britannia: Devonshire* (Thomas Cadell, 1822).

Macleod, Moyra, *A Wren's Diary* (1943).

Peskett, Hugh (Ed.), *Nonconformist Registers Guide, 1538-1837* (D.C.R.S., 1979).

Prince, J., *Worthies of Devon* (Yeo and Bishop, Exeter, 1701).

Risdon, T., *Survey of Devon, 1630* (1811).

Rose-Troup, F., 'The New Edgar Charter and the South Hams' (*T.D.A.*, 1929).

Stoate, T. L., *Devon Subsidy Rolls*, 1524-7 (1979), 1543-5, 1581, 1647 (1986), privately published.

Stoate, T. L., *Devon Muster Rolls*, 1569, 1588 (1977), Hearth Tax, 1674 (1982), privately published.

Stoke Fleming Parish Documents (1953).

Summerson, Henry, *Crown Pleas of the Devon Eyre of 1238* (D.C.R.S.).

Thomas, Aaron, *Newfoundland Journal, 1794* (Longman [Canada], 1968).

Vancouver, C., *General View of the Agriculture of Devon* (London, 1808).

Vivian, J. L., *Visitations of the County of Devon* (1620).

Watkin, Hugh, *Dartmouth: Pre-Reformation* (Devonshire Association, 1935).

Western Daily Mercury, Plymouth library.

Windeatt, E., 'Fitting out of two vessels against the Armada' (*T.D.A.* 1880).

Windeatt, E., 'Dartmouth Mayors and Mayoralties' (*T.D.A.*, 1911, 1912).

Youings, J., *Devon Monastic Lands* (D.C.R.S.).

Allen, J. S., *The Newcomen Memorial Engine* (Newcomen Society pamphlet, 1981).

Andriette, E. A., *Devon and Cornwall in the Civil War* (David & Charles, 1971).

Boland, Michael (Ed.), *John Flavel: The Mystery of Providence* (Puritan Paperbacks, 1963).

Bourhis, J. J., *Traffic du Port de Dartmouth 1599-1641* (University of Bretagne).

Champernowne, C., *The Champernowne Family* (unpublished, 1954).

Clammer & Kitteridge, *Paddle Steamers on the Dart* (Twelve Heads Press, 1987).

Clamp, A. L., *American Assault Exercises at Slapton, 1944* (1984).

Clark, E. F., *George Bidder: The Calculating Boy* (K.S.L.,1983).

Compton Castle Guide (1971).

Cresswell, Beatrice, *Notes on Devon Churches* (W.C.S.L.).

Darby, H. C., and Welldon Finn, R. (Eds.), *Domesday Geography of S.W. England* (1967).

Davies, H. C. and Grove, R. W., *The Royal Naval College at Dartmouth* (Gieves & Hawkes, 1980).

Davis, R., *Rise of the English Shipping Industry in the 18th century* (1962).

Ellis, *A History of Torquay* (1930).

Finberg, H. P. R., *Early Charters of Devon and Cornwall* (1963).

Fisher, H. E. S. (Ed.), *Exeter Papers in Economic History*:
    (1) 'The South-West and the Sea' (1968).
    (17) 'Studies in British Privateering' (1987).

Fisher, H. E. S., *The Portugal Trade* (1971).

Galbraith, V. H., *The Making of Domesday Book* (Oxford, 1974).

Grinsell, L. V., 'Barrows of South and East Devon' (*D.A.S. Proceedings*, 1983).

Henley, E. P., *William C. Henley: His Days and Ways* (1927).

Higham, R., 'Security and Defence in South-West England before 1800' (*Exeter Studies in History*, 19, 1987).

Horden, N., *The New World* (Aldous, 1973).

Hoskins, W. G., *Devon* (Collins, 1954).

Hoskins, W. G., *The Westward Expansion of Wessex* (1970).

Hoskins, W. G. and Finberg, H. P. R., *Devonshire Studies* (Cape, 1952).

King, J., *The Mayflower Miracle* (David & Charles, 1987).

Markham, C. R., *John Davis* (Philip, 1889).

Martin, C. and Parker, G., *The Spanish Armada* (Guild Publishing, London, 1988).

McConaghey, R. M. S., *Medical Records of Dartmouth, 1425-1887* (1960).

Oppenheim, M. M., *Maritime History of Devon* (University of Exeter, 1968).

Pearce, Susan, *The Kingdom of Dumnonia* (1978).

Philip and Son, *The Dartmouth Shipbuilding Industry, 1853-1953* (1953).

Potts, C. R., *The Newton Abbot to Kingswear Railway* (Oakwood Press, 1989).

Ralegh-Radford, C. A., 'The Pre-Conquest Church and Old Minsters in Devon', *Devon Historian* (1975).

Rolt, L. T. C., *Thomas Newcomen* (MacDonald, 1963).

Russell, P., *Dartmouth* (1950; reprinted by Dartmouth Museum).

Russell, P., *History of the Congregational Church in Dartmouth* (1956).

Saunders, A. D., *Dartmouth Castle Guide* (1983).

Small, K., *The Forgotten Dead* (1988).

Seymour, Deryck, *Torre Abbey* (1977).

Stanes, R., *A History of Devon* (Phillimore, 1986).

Starkey, D., *English Privateering* (Exeter, 1985).

Taylor, C., *Village and Farmstead* (Philip & Son, 1983).

Thorn, F., *Understanding and Interpreting Domesday Book* (D.A.S., 1988).

Todd, M., *The South West to A.D. 1000* (Longman, 1987).

White, *History of Torquay* (1878).

Wood, M., *Domesday: A Search for the Roots of England* (Guild Publishing, London, 1986).

Articles in the Transactions of the Devonshire Association (T.D.A.)

Karkeek, P.,'Shipping in 14th Century Dartmouth' (1880, 1881).

Pearson, J. B.,'Church Houses in Devon' (1900).

Reichel, O. J.,'The Hundred of Haytor' (1908).

Reichel, O. J., 'The Hundred of Coleridge (1911).

Reichel, O. J., 'Origin and Upgrowth of the English Parish' (1920).

Windeatt, E., 'John Flavel' (1911).

Windeatt, E., 'Dartmouth Mayors' (1914).

Cresswell, B., 'Church Goods Commissioners in Devon' (1911).

Watkin, H., 'Foundation of Dartmouth and Kingswear churches' (1911).

Watkin, H., 'Greenway House' (1918).

Watkin, H., 'The Lost Chapel of St Clare' (1929).

Alexander, J. J., 'Dartmouth as a Parliamentary Borough' (1911).

Alexander, J. J., 'The Anglo-Saxon Conquest of Devon' (1919-24).

Alexander, J. J., 'Parliamentary Representation in Devon' (1937).

Clifford, E. T., 'Robert Wenyngton' (1916).

Morgan, F. W., 'The Domesday Geography of Devon' (1940).

Shorter, A. H., 'The Paper Making Industry in Devon' (1950).

Russell, P. and O'Neill, 'No.5 Higher Street' (1951).

Russell, P. and Yorke, G., 'Kingswear and Its Neighbourhood' (1953).

Russell, P. and Everett, 'No.13 Higher Street' (1959).

Stephens, W. B., 'West Country Ports and the Struggle for the Newfoundland Fisheries' (1956).

French, K. and C., 'Devonshire Plasterwork' (1957).

Roberts, J., 'Sir John Gilbert' (1959).

Stanes, R., 'Sir Guy de Brian' (1960).

Gardiner, D., 'John Hawley of Dartmouth' (1966).

Pistono, S., 'Henry IV and John Hawley' (1979).

Grant, A. and Gwyn, R., 'The Huguenots of Devon' (1985).

Index

Numbers in bold refer to pages on which illustrations of the subject appear.

Useful website: **www.dartmouth-history.org.uk**
This site is designed to assist those interested in researching the history of Dartmouth and its
environs. The Dartmouth History Research Group is a non-profit making voluntary organisation
dedicated to the research and recording of the history of Dartmouth and surrounding villages,
and to making this reasearch available to the general public. Membership is open to all.